Maybe It'll Rain Tomorrow

Volume Two
of

From the Gulf to God Knows Where

~o~

Living in Australia's Outback

Maybe It'll Rain Tomorrow

Marion Houldsworth

First published in 2007 by Central Queensland University Press

Second published in 2012 by Boolarong Press, Salisbury, Brisbane, Australia.

National Library of Australia Cataloguing-in-Publication entry

Author:	Houldsworth, Marion.
Title:	Maybe it'll rain tomorrow : living in Australia's outback /Marion Houldsworth.
ISBN:	9781921920851 (pbk.)
Subjects:	Country life--Australia.
	Australia--Social conditions.
	Australia--Description and travel.
Dewey Number:	994

Disclaimer
Some expressions and terminology which formerly were in common usage, may seem offensive to some readers. They are included in the interests of historical accuracy, and no hurt or offence is intended by the author.

Typeset by John James

Front Cover photo: Hugh Brown; Living Colours Photography — www.savethekimberley.com

Back Cover photo: Hugh Brown; Living Colours Photography — www.savethekimberley.com

Cover Design by John James

Printed and bound by Watson Ferguson and Company, Salisbury, Brisbane, Australia.

ABOUT THE AUTHOR

Marion Houldsworth was born in Mount Morgan, Central Queensland, and grew up in Western Queensland and Townsville. She was educated at Blackheath College, Charters Towers, Rockhampton Girls' Grammar School and the University of Queensland. Together with her husband she taught for many years in the Northern Territory and New Guinea.

Her previous published works include;

Hearts Bright with Hope; *A Grammar School Diary*

The Morning Side of the Hill; *Growing Up in Townsville in World War Two*
(James Cook University Press)

The Immigrant Boy; *A Townsville Boyhood, 1912 - 1918*
(James Cook University Press)

Barefoot through the Bindies; *Growing Up in North Queensland in the Early 1900s*
(Central Queensland University Press)

Red Dust Rising; *The Life of Cattleman Ray Fryer*
(Central Queensland University Press)

From the Gulf to God Knows Where; *Living in Australia's Outback; Volume One*
(Central Queensland University Press)

Foreword

Maybe It'll Rain Tomorrow is the perfect title for Marion Houldsworth's Volume Two of *From the Gulf to God Knows Where.* Rain is a lifeblood and a ubiquitous topic of conversation in the bush. It can mean the difference between success and failure; life and death. 'Maybe it'll rain tomorrow' is a catch phrase used by country people and expresses the optimism and courage they show in the face of often almost overwhelming adversity.

It mightn't rain for years but the trick to surviving, as Hughenden grazier Toby Rogers points out, is imagining that rain is only a day or so away. In the meantime bush people have learned to cope. In the Kimberleys, stockman Cliffie Robinson knew he could rely on the local Aborigines' knowledge of hidden waterholes. Young bush mother, Elaine Cluff, boiled muddy creek water for her family for months, only to see the horrified look on the face of a hospital nurse at seeing her baby daughter's cloudy bottle.

And as if prolonged drought wasn't enough, there was also the flip side; getting too much rain with its inevitable consequences. Pioneering family member, Helen Clark, vividly recalls experiencing a cyclonic flood on Mellish Park Station in the Gulf when she and the family took refuge inside the roof of the homestead as flood waters rose. Kerry Kendall recalls the heroic efforts of getting a sick stockman across a raging creek on Dotswood station to the Flying Doctor's aircraft and so saving his life.

So it's not surprising that drought and rain figure frequently in many of the wonderful stories that make up this book. Each told in down-to-earth manner, they demonstrate how bush people have learned to take such major challenges in their stride. This book is a celebration of their resilience and achievements. Drovers especially, moving mobs of cattle vast distances - tough and dangerous work demanding outstanding horsemanship - developed a special affinity with the landscape and have become part of the Australian legend.

These are stories that are told with warmth, humour and compassion. Marion Houldsworth has great admiration and respect for the people she writes about. It shines through her work. The book is eminently readable and is rich with interesting and amusing anecdotes. It is a tremendous read and a fitting sequel to *From the Gulf to God Knows Where,* Volume One.

Adjunct Professor Ross Quinn PSM
Central Queensland University

Acknowledgements

Once again I am grateful to Professor Bill Gammage and Bruce Simpson for permission to use some of their material from the Australian Drovers' Project in the National Library in Canberra. I hope that I have done justice to Bill's and Bruce's material and that the voices of the drovers and cattlemen who have passed away can be heard again in this, the print version, of their life-stories.

Ray and Betty Fryer of Tabletop Station have again shown their customary enthusiasm for backing-up my research for this project. Without their wide network of friendships across the Outback I would never have met some of the wonderful people whose stories go to make this series.

Two of the kindest hearts of the west are those of Liz and Col Flood, of The Drovers' Camp, Camooweal, always there with support and hospitality, and staunch in their belief that the old drovers and stockmen who return to Camooweal as though to the days of their young manhood, are the wonderful people they are. Without them it would not have been possible to make the long trip to Wyndham, W.A. for the Scattering of Ashes service for dearly loved writer of CQU Press, Bobby Buchanan, an unforgetable experience on Five Rivers Look-out for all of us who were able to be there.

A special tribute of thanks to Jan Cardnell of CQU Press for her meticulous proof reading and advice.

Friends are so special. Thanks again to Beryl and Ron Quelch for their unfailing support and hospitality in Townsville. Also to John Newan, Melinda McKerney and Rachael Kallis for their decorative art.

No writer should commence a book without a friend who is a technical wizard in the Terra Infirma of matters pertaining to computers. John James has been invaluable. Without his skilled back-up I would long ago have reverted to quill and ink. Thanks, John. And also to outback photographer, Hugh Brown, of '*Living Colour*', who has again generously gifted the use of one of his superb images for the cover design.

As everyone across the Outback will be aware, CQU Press Outback Books suffered a catastrophic blow with the death of its Founding Publisher and Editor, David Myers, 'Old Silvertail', in March this year, when David lost a valiant fight following brain surgery. Writers of Outback Books know what a debt of gratitude we owe David for his inspiration in setting up the press so that the people of the Outback might have a voice with which to record their story. Although it is hard to imagine how it will be possible to carry on without David's drive, humour and inspiring leadership, it is doing so, enabling the story of the Outback to continue to be heard, that will be an ongoing tribute to his memory.

Adjunct Professor Ross Quinn has graciously and generously undertaken to edit *Volume Two* of *From the Gulf to God Knows Where* and I am deeply grateful to him and also to Vice Chancellor and President Professor John Rickard for his faith in the value to Australia's cultural history and sense of national identity of the press David Myers founded.

The Jabiru

Dedication

To honour the memory of

David Allan Myers, AM

1942 -2007

Writer, Poet, Publisher

Whose vision splendid of founding

Central Queensland University Press, Outback Books,

enabled the people of Outback Australia to have a voice with which

to record their story as part of the national heritage.

For his services to Australian Literature,

David was appointed a Member of the Order of Australia, in 2004.

'They shall mount up on wings as eagles.' *Is, 40:31*

INTRODUCTION

If the people you meet in this book aren't yet old mates, they should feel as though they should have been, before you put it down. Mateship, that quintessential expression of what it is to be Australian, the give-a-hand co-operativeness, the humour, the 'life-enhancing, nation-building force of it'[1], is the underlying theme of this book.

My drive to collect these stories stems from knowing that time is shortening. Before long they will be lost forever and with them will go the chance they give for us to learn from the generations that have gone before; the humour, the drama, the long-forgotten technologies, all the gallant, unassuming tales of the courage of ordinary people, the triumph of the human spirit in adversity.

Wonderful material comes to light. Did you know – did anybody know – that chewing the leaves of turkey bush can cure dysentry? That a broken axle can be welded in a hollow tree? That green bananas make a substitute for mashed potatoes? So much Bush know-how lost forever if not recorded.

Then there is the humour; the Redcliffe cook's method of putting the squidges around a pie-crust; 'Wagga' Darcy, treed by a rampaging buffalo without the benefit of his trousers; Wayne McCulloch's stand-and-deliver with a bull 'tall as m'self with a head like a forty-four gallon drum.' Humour in every situation, if not at the very moment, then later, recalled around the camp-fires of the stock-routes under skies ablaze with stars. And never ask an outback cattleman, 'Do you remember me?' He will answer, 'Yair! I'd know your hide if it was hanging on the back fence!'

For courage, it would be hard to beat that of young Alice Hopkins. Left in charge at night with a tentful of little children, surrounded by snorting buffaloes, she ordered the children 'Hide under the bed!' while she herself 'stood in the door of the tent with the gun'. Alice would have been thirteen, maybe fourteen.

For drama there is the capsized boat in Kerry Kendall's '*The Young Ringer*'. The old camp cook's 'I'll stay with youse and whoever knocks up, I'll bloody take over from' is worthy of inclusion in the annals of Australian mateship.

There are more women's stories in this book than in Volume One. Recently I was at Sussex University, involved in a Day School on Oral History. My topic was *'The Challenge to the Oral Historian of Collecting Material in Australia's Outback'*. I accompanied my talk with images of boulder-strewn ravines in the Kimberleys, crocodile infested rivers in Arnhem Land, of waiting for the billy to boil in a Barkly wind, of homesteads and cattle grids, distances and dust. I did not neglect to mention the need to keep an eye open for cattle on the road, for kangaroos, and gullies for comfort-stops - and at comfort-stops

[1] Bruce Campbell, A.M; Founder and Chairman of the 2002 Year of the Outback.

a wary eye for death adders. Graphics presentation over, I thought I had made a decent fist of it and expected smiles of appreciation. But, No! From the mainly female audience a cry went up; 'Why aren't there more women's stories in your books!' the hostility almost palpable.

Useless to explain that in the era of which I write – the Droving Days - an unknown concept in the UK, of course - it was the men who sat around the fire at night after the long day's stage with the cattle, swapping yarns of mates they had known, great horses they had ridden, rushes they had turned, all told with laconic understatement. Bushmen hate a skite; 'blowing yer own bag' is scorned. Over the years men became polished yarn-tellers. Some of the stories developed a patina from re-telling but were none the worse for that. A good yarn is a good yarn, no less for having been heard before. Mates encourage one another with 'Give's the one about ....'

So, there are more women's stories in this volume. Edna Zigenbine's account, in such unassuming language that only the discerning reader will recognize the challenge involved when, scarcely more than a girl, she took over the mob from her sick father. Then there are Elaine Cluff's three day search for her little lost boy, and the tragic disappearance from Mallapunyah homestead of the Darcy children's mother, a mystery unsolved to this day.

And how better to exemplify the truth that what you do in your time of trial can be your greatest triumph, than Phoebe Atkinson's, '*Bred by a Bloody Woman*!' There won't be a man who does not finish Mrs. Atkinson's story without taking his hat off to this remarkable North Queensland cattle woman.

Some of the stories deserve a place in Australian literature with Lawson's and Paterson's. What is literature but something that conveys the learning-experiences of life from one human being to another, of essential truths that we recognize. The best thing about them is that there is no pretence. Wisdom does not require special vocabulary or syntax. Men and women are speaking of the reality of their lives, and from the small details you can fill in all the bits you know would have been there. Brenda Wilson's exasperated 'Don't mention the bloody ice-cream again!' conveys more of the sense of dust, heat, isolation and the incessant hard-work of life at Fitzroy Crossing than pages of elaborately laboured prose. Our laughter at such an unguarded moment is an acknowledgement of some latent aspect of our own reality. A good story releases from the subconscious the stories in our own lives.

The particular charm of Oral History is that it enables us to tune in, as though on some cosmic radio, to a moment in time in the lives of people long turned to dust but whose words are preserved for us to hear, to a microcosm of life in which a very real human drama is taking place. When fifteen-year old Reg Hart returns from his first droving trip and his mother greets him; 'You're thin, Boy!' you are there in the warm little kitchen to share the moment. You hear Reg's wry, 'Yeah! Look at the dog! He's leaning up against me!' and begin to understand what the Great Depression meant to those who lived through it. But, oh! That warm kitchen! Those welcoming arms! Don't we all at times long for the conventional certainties that, despite the poverty, sweetened the lives of earlier generations? Good literature addresses the human heart.

The Outback has produced a type of people that believes that the hours of daylight are for work, that a man grabs his hat and heads for the horse-yard, the tractor shed, or the back paddock, before the sun hits the horizon. He expects his day to have problems but is confident he will think of a way around them and that what is right to be done cannot be done too soon, so get on with it. He has learned not to dismiss ideas that at first don't fit the conventional wisdom. Reay Atkinson built his dams in natural hollows that became permanent water-holes. Mac Core remembered his grandfather, William McDowall's introduction of the tick-resistant Brahman strain into the north, despite the head-shakings that 'Them yaks'll never breed'. Phoebe Atkinson took her issue with the terrible roads of the outback to 'Nugget' Coombs, – 'His name used to be on the bank notes' – in Canberra. Before long the construction of the Beef Roads was underway. True men and women of the Outback, energized by the heat and light and the illimitable distances, they believed that all it took to bring the impossible to pass was the courage and determination to get on and do it.

In an increasingly over-crowded world community, small nations need to maintain a sense of their own identity. The Australian sense of the mateship of the common man is the core value of our nation, of who we feel ourselves to be. It is my hope that the stories in this book will play some part in reinforcing that sense of what it means to be gladly, proudly Australian.

CONTENTS

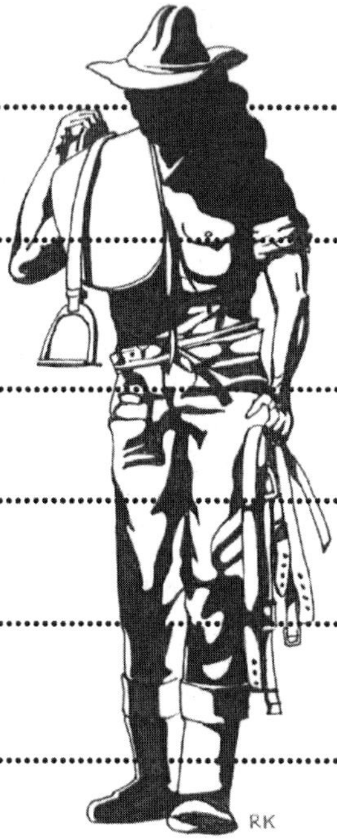
RK

1

Kate Darcy Teece

ॐ ॐ ॐ

Introduction

For the Darcy children of Mallapunyah, all fifteen of them, their childhood must have been as close to that of the Swiss Family Robinson as it is possible to get without actually being on a desert island. Their desert island was a chain of crystal-clear water-holes surrounded by magnificent paper-barks, far removed from civilization, somewhere off the lonely back-road between Borroloola on the Gulf, and Camooweal on the Queensland border. It was a life of self-reliance in a bush-timber homestead built by their ingenious, irrepressible father, eating meat, milk, eggs, fruit and vegetables which they produced themselves. All the children could ride like the wind. They could muster, break-in, build yards, put in fences and tend the gardens that became famous for their fecundity and abundance. The girls 'could do anything that a man could do!' which was fortunate, as all seven of them had been born before the boys, who with seeming circumspection, delayed their arrival till later. But all the children knew the joy of work and pitched in with unstinting enthusiasm to develop a property literally carved from the wilderness.

There was simply nothing, it seemed, that the Darcy family couldn't take in their stride, until the fatal day, in 1944, when their beloved mother and 'one of the little ones' disappeared without trace, never to be seen again, despite a month-long search by hundreds of volunteers. The story of Mrs. Darcys disappearance has become a legend, spoken of in subdued tones; another life lost to the heat and vastness of the inexorable Outback.

I first met Kate Darcy Teece when, frail and ill, she was hospitalized in Cloncurry with a serious heart condition. So it was a joy, some time later, to learn that not only was she recovered and 'back to her old self' but that her stalwart husband, Ab, had undertaken to tape-record some of her girlhood memories on my behalf. Ab had always assured me, 'Kate would give you a good story!' We were able to fill in extra details by long-distance telephone around the globe. A problem is something that you think of a way around.

I learned to love this wonderful lady and her gift for telling the stories of her girlhood on Mallapunyah; racing the billy-goats, diving into translucent water-holes; tending the luxuriant gardens, doing Correspondence lessons around the freshly-scrubbed verandah table. Most of all I loved Kate because she could still remember, and recite by satellite-link phone around the world, the poetry with which she and her brothers and sisters had entertained themselves by the long-ago camp-fires of their youth, 'Out on the big McArthur Run'.

The Darcys of Mallapunyah

Kate Teece – nee Darcy

'Seven girls! We could do anything that a man can do.'

Somewhere along the road between Camooweal and Burketown, there's an unmarked grave. That's where my Dad's father is buried. He was a carrier with a horse-team and wagon of his own but along the road he took sick and died. He was buried by the next carrier that come along. There were no stones to mark the grave so no-one knows where it is.

But I'll start my story at the beginning. My father was born in Hughenden in 1890. He had two brothers and four sisters. Then the whole family moved up to Camooweal and the kids grew up there. As a young man, Dad moved to Brunette Downs on the tablelands in the Northern Territory, two hundred and fifty miles out of Borroloola. He got his own horse team and wagon and started carrying. On the road he would walk along beside his horses. It was on one of these trips that he met my mother. She had been on Brunette and she'd married this man. He died and left her with two small children. So she was riding along the road to Borroloola trying to get to Darwin to put the eldest one, Alice, into the convent there. Her father had been a ship's captain and she'd been to the convent herself. She could write a beautiful hand. And along the road she came on Dad and his team. He said to her, 'You can't go all that way on your own. It's a hundred and eighty miles. You'd better come along with me.' So she went along with the wagon and when they got to Borroloola she thought, 'Maybe this is what love is?' That was the beginning of the relationship.

Mum went on to Darwin to put Alice into the convent and then she went back to Borroloola. By that time Dad was back again to get another load. They were married and after that they hauled up and down the road, the two of them together. They had a bunk on the wagon and Dad built a cage underneath the wagon and they had chooks. And at night when they came to the place where they were going to camp, he would open the door of the cage and out all the chooks'd hop and they'd feed around and then when it got late they'd get back in again to roost and Dad would shut the gate and they'd be ready to travel again next morning. So they always had fresh eggs along the road.

Then they come to a place called Top Spring, a little rocky spring off the Borroloola road which was the furtherest water, and they stayed there. My eldest bother, George – but he was always known as Wagga – was born there. Not too long after that they shifted along to a better place at Kilgour Gorge and they put up a hut there. Mum made the walls of ant-bed and stone and Dad put a roof of iron on and she had four children there, myself, May, June and Ethel. We lived there for five years.

In 1928 someone told them about this big spring which wasn't too far away so they took a ride round and looked for it and found it. That was Mallapunyah. So towards the end of '28 they packed everything up, chooks, dogs, cats and kids on the wagon, the whole lot, and the goats and horses run along behind the wagon, and they drove across to Mallapunyah.

When they got to about two miles out, they could see that there was a big sandy patch going down into the water at the springs so Mum and Dad told Alice – she was back from the convent by then – to take us kids down and walk ahead of the wagon. And we found this lovely running water. And we decided we'd have a swim there to cool off. Alice thought there might be alligators there, so she put one of the younger ones in and we waited and nothing happened, so we all got in and had a good bath and a cool-off.

We lost a kitten there. When we came back to where our clothes were, it had gone. We'd lost its mother the night before. But then Alice went back the next morning and found it. But while we were swimming, the wagon caught up. They went up a bit and found a suitable place and made camp there. But Dad, he could only stop one night because he had to keep going. He had to go back to Borroloola to get another load before the wet season set in. He put the tent up and then went. And Mum went out with him for the one night and us kids were all in the tent. And during the night the wild bulls were kicking up a noise on the other side of this tent. Alice made us all get under the bed and she stood at the mouth of the tent with a gun.

Next morning it's all quiet again and Mum came back. Then Alice and Mum got to work and put up a bit of a bark hut. They got the bark off the big paper-bark trees that were all around the springs. They'd cut the bark across the top as high as they could reach and then strip it down. You could get big sheets of it. The hut didn't have doors or windows; only curtains where doors would have been. But it was alright, that hut. It leaked a bit here and there but it did us until Dad came back.

Dad took up a miner's lease around the springs, just a square mile of country. Mum got the first fruit trees round from Queensland Pastoral supplies on the boat into Borroloola. We had plenty of water for those fruit trees from the springs and the soil was good black soil. Mum made channels from the springs that used to trickle down to the fruit trees. That was the beginning of our gardens.

About twelve months after, Dad got a load of iron and made a house. This was about 1930. The house was a nice bungalow; four bedrooms and a sitting room with a veranda all round. The veranda was very handy and every time another child was born they put another bed on the veranda. We lived in that house for years. Dad made all our furniture. Mum and Dad had shop-bought beds but he made the beds for the rest of us himself.

Dad could make anything! He was clever. He made his own horse-shoes. He'd get the ready-made ones for the camp horses but those big draught-horses, he couldn't get the sizes to fit them, so he would make them. And if he broke an axle on the wagon he'd get a hollow tree and he'd put a fire at the bottom to get the heat going up the hollow and he'd put the axle through and he'd weld the axle together like that. That's how he'd mend the axle along the track, but once he got back to Mallapunyah, he had a forge there and us kids used to have to pump the bellows for the bloody thing! Take it in turns. Dad could weld anything. He learned to do black-smithing from an old fellow that showed him how when he was young and he always kicked himself that he'd not taken more notice of what the old fellow could have taught him.

Back in the earlier times, in the '30's and early '40's, we used to see quite a few natives wandering around there, semi-wild they were, with not much clothing on. I remember one old fellow in particular, Friday. He used to live at the gorge and we used to go and camp at the gorge to muster our horses. And away on the hill we'd see Friday standing with a woman's skirt on; poor old fellow, he had no trousers. We'd make our camp, make our fire and the next thing we'd see Friday sitting at the fire and we wouldn't even see him coming. We'd say, 'How you doing, Mate?' And he'd say, 'Oh! Me orright!' He'd share a meal with us and away he'd go again.

Another old fellow that used to help round the place was Millabulla. He was a lovely old chap. We knew him well. He had speared a white man that was trying to steal his wife. They'd taken him away and put him in gaol for a little while but he was let off lightly. He was round our place a lot.

There were other native families there too, and some of the women, when their child was born, they'd turn up to ask Mum to give it a whitefella name. And Mum would give her the name. I remember one, a little girl, she called her Nancy, and she grew up to be a very good person. Then they used to bring stuff in to trade with us; dingo scalps, or fresh fish. They'd trade them for fruit and vegetables and tobacco and sometimes a bit of flour or tea and sugar. And they'd bring in a billy of honey; anything that they thought we'd want, and we'd give them something for it and away they'd go again.

The blacks never stayed around too long. They didn't have a permanent camp. They might stay there for a month or so if the lilies were good, but then they would pack up and move on somewhere else.[1] There were a couple of old fellows that used to come and give Dad a hand sometimes. He'd give them some 'bacci and away they would go again.

While Dad still had the team on the road he had two natives, a man and his wife, Demon and Jackie Jackie. Demon brought the spare horses along and Jackie Jackie did the work around the camp and the cooking. Dad had a lot of respect for those two people. They used to work for him every year when he was carrying.

Our family was; Alice and Bill – Alice and Bill weren't Darcys; they were Hopkins from

[1] Waterlily tubers were a staple of the Aboriginal diet.

Mum's first marriage. Then George, named after Dad, but he was always called Wagga – and then Grace – she was always called Bubba – myself – I didn't have a nickname – then after me came May and June – they were twins; after that there was Ethel – always called Jackie; and then another set of twins, Jim and Tom. And then Annie, Mick, Norman, Fred and Bob. Bob was the tail-ender, born in 1940. Not one of us was born in hospital. The whole fifteen, we were all born wherever Mum and Dad may be. As quick as we were born, Mum would be up next day doing her work.

For milk and mutton we'd have up to five hundred goats at a time. We'd kill for mutton, and milk a few milkers. And, my word, we rode them! Poley Jack and Dollar were the best riding goats. We'd put them in carts, too. Dad made the carts for us out of boxes and he'd put wheels on and we'd have billy-goat-cart races. Norman was the best cart-goat. He could run! Wagga would be driving him. We used to have to yard the goats of a night because of the dingoes, but most times they would come home on their own. But sometimes, if a few of them stayed back, we would go out and look for them and bring them in. We all took turns doing these things.

The chooks used to roost mainly in a big old tamarind tree. They were the white sort for a good while, but then Dad got a black rooster we called Sid. We made nests for them out of hollow logs, and they'd always go back to lay in them. If they laid away under a bush somewhere around the flat, us kids'd look for the nests and get the eggs wherever they were. If ever the dingoes came around after the chooks, the dogs would get after them. We always had about six dogs.

One dog we had was called Stumpy. He must have been fairly intelligent because, one day, he comes up to Mum at the house and he starts whining, trying to tell her something. Straight away Mum knew something was wrong at the yards. When my brother came up to the house, Mum said 'What happened down there?' 'Oh!' he said, 'Nothing much. The horse threw me, that's all. Saddle and all.' And Mum said, 'I knew! Stumpy was trying to tell me! I knew something had happened.' But we must have been lucky, because we were so far out and there was no doctors if anything happened. We were a hundred miles from anywhere. But nobody got really sick; nobody got badly hurt. We could of, because us kids tried to kill ourselves plenty of times. But we didn't.

Mum and Dad knew a lot of bush remedies and bush ways. Dysentry plant was one. Turkey-bush was called dysentry-plant because if you got the young green leaves and chewed them and swallowed the juice, it was an instant cure! And it had a nice taste, too; like water-melon juice. During the war when we couldn't get coffee we used to gather the berries off the turkey-bush; it grows about knee high in that red country; not black soil, but wherever you see coolabahs you'll generally get turkey-bush. We'd gather the red berries and put them in the oven and roast them, then we'd put them through the mincer, and that was our coffee! Beautiful coffee, it was, too!

Dad used to go away on trips because he was still a carrier; from Borroloola up to the tablelands. That was his run. He'd only carry in the dry times. Once the Wet came, he would let the horses go, and they had a spell until about April; then away he'd go again. He'd be away for about three months. When he was coming we'd all be dressed up in our best. It was a big day for us and we'd walk out and meet the wagon. He'd put us up on his bunk on the wagon and we'd ride in. That was very good. We did this up till 1932; that was his last trip with the wagon. Then he went down to Townsville and got himself a car. He learnt to drive that thing coming back. He'd hardly seen a car before but he taught himself to drive and drove it right out to Mallapunyah. Then he turned that car from a sedan into a ute. By that time we had a good vegetable garden going and he started carting vegetables up the tableland to sell to the drovers. He made a living out of that for years.

We'd get our mail once a month; the pack horse mail from Camooweal to Borroloola.[2] It was a long ride for them. Later on they ran a truck out for the mail. The wagon days were over then. They ran the truck in the dry time and pack-horses in the wet season. One of the mailmen was old Jim Grace and he told Mum about the Correspondence School in Brisbane. So Mum wrote down to them and that's how we got our schooling. They were really good, the Correspondence School. They seemed to understand us lot, and we did marvellous school work with them and we got the taste for it. We would clear the breakfast things away and then we would all sit around the table and do our school-work. We found it tough for a while at first but once we got the hang of it, we liked it. I really loved history. And I loved poetry, too.

Mum used to send away and get material and make our clothes. We made our own hats. We made pretty well everything; clothes, hats – the hats were made out of pandanus. We'd put a lace of leather or rag that tied under our chin so they wouldn't blow off when we galloped. Dad was a blocky sort of a bloke, not very tall. Mum was tall. That's where we got our height from.

In 1937 Dad took a mob of draught horses to the Hughenden sale yards and that was when he bought his first wireless. A big cumbersome thing with wet batteries and dry batteries but it talked and we thought it was marvellous. We could hear people way down in Melbourne. And when the war-time came we could listen and hear the war news. We also had a seven day clock with a pendulum and it was marvellous, but later on we had a big flood that came right through the house, very deep, and took the clock away. And Dad used to like his rum and in that flood he was laughing because the water came through the house waist-deep and he said, 'No need to worry about getting water for my rum!'

Back in the 'thirties before the war started, there used to be men come right out to where we were, looking for work. Some of them had pack-horses and packs. Some of them were on foot. If they had pack-horses, they were called a bag-man if they were walking on foot they were swag men. Some of these bag men and swaggies used to camp near our place

[2] *Miller; Lillian Ada; The Border and Beyond;* The Camooweal/ Top Camp/Borroloola mail run was a monthly service by pack-horse, and later fortnightly. Passengers were taken by arrangement. This service was fraught with dangers through some very isolated, tough, frontier terrain. The route followed the Old Tableland Stock Route, through Avon, Rankine, (sic) Alexandria stations with pack-horse changes at various staging camps. Alex Grant, Count Biondi, Jack Fuller – who used a sulky – Jim Grace, Bert O'Keefe, Clarrie Hudson and the Booth Brothers all operated the service at one time or another. In the Wet it was always a pack-horse service. On one occasion Charlie Biondi stopped to give his horses a drink in a spring alongside the mail route, and there, floating face down in the water was a man with a spear in his back. He didn't draw rein until he'd made it safely to Walhallow station. In the early 1930s mail contracts were worth about £250 a year for three years.

because there was no work to be had, especially in the wet season. So they'd stay there and they'd help Dad. Dad would give them three meals a day. They'd do quite a bit of work for just tucker.

One day my sister and I were riding on the agricultural horses and we saw a lone horseman. There was no road there where he was, just bush. We wondered who he was and what he was doing. We started to ride over to see what he was up to. And this man let's out a yell; a cooee. Well, I was only about seven and I was frightened. I wanted to run away. But Alice was older than me so we rode over and we saw that he was just an old man and he was in a bad way. He told us he was searching for his son. His son was supposed to be fetching the pack-horses along behind him and he'd got lost, and he was just a kid. This poor old fellow couldn't find him anywhere. We took him home and Dad gave him a fresh horse and the next day we followed the kid's tracks along. He had gone off the road out on to a water hole to water the pack-horses and camped there the night. But we saw he was going in the right direction so we let this old man follow after him. We knew he'd catch him up before he got too far along. But in the meantime, there was a yard-builder coming along the other way, and he saw the boy coming along on his own and he stopped him. He knew he was too small to be travelling along on his own. So he was taking the boy along with him when his old father caught up with him and took him home to where his mother was.

Another time, when we were out on the stock camp, I was riding around and saw a man coming. I thought, 'I'd better have a look at this fellow!' so I rode over to him and asked him what he was doing. He said, 'I lost all my horses. My camp; my swag; every thing I own is gone! They galloped away from me!' 'Oh!' I thought. 'You are in trouble!' I said to him, 'You'd better come down to our camp. We'll give you a feed and see if we can help you find your horses.' So he followed back to our camp. And there were his horses in with our horses around the camp. Was he a happy man to see his horses and his swags and his packs again! He camped there the night with us and next day he went on his way.

And friends of ours, they would come down for about two months right through the Wet. He had a wagon, that fellow, and three small children and his wife. We supplied them with milk, eggs, fruit, meat, and they had a good time there at our place. They'd come every year and play cards with Mum and Dad. They'd stay right through until the Dry came then they'd get their horses up and go back to where they come from.

In 1941 Dad took up a grazing lease and it already had cattle on but they were all really wild, no branded ones. We had to put up a yard before we could start to muster. That same year was when I first met my husband that was to be. He was only a bit of a kid and I was a bit older. I thought it was beneath my dignity to take much notice of him. Him and his family were going through to McArthur River to pick up a mob of bullocks, and they had been two or three months on the road. We always took visitors to have a look round the gardens; the mangoes and pawpaws and all the trees were very interesting for them. They needed more horses and Dad sold them half a dozen. Then they went on to McArthur and picked cattle up and took them. It was about this time that we started building the yards.

Then in early 1942 we started to muster the cattle. And I tell you what! That was a bit of fun! They were wild! They didn't like being yarded but we got on with it. We branded about five hundred that first year. We were doing well. Then we started putting in dams and paddocks with ploughs and draught horses. Dad was still working those big draught horses from his team. Old Dad did a pretty good job, when you come to think of it, because Wagga was the only boy old enough to work. All the rest of us were girls. There were fifteen in our family, seven girls and eight boys but the girls were all born first. The boys were too young to do the work. Dad couldn't afford to pay men. We had no money. But us girls went on ahead. We could do anything that a man could do. We could make yards and put up paddocks. We shod our own horses. We could kill a beast for meat. Do anything at all! Anything a man did. But then later as the boys grew older they started working too. Tom turned out a good horseman. Jim turned out a good mechanic. Holidays were unheard of. Nobody had a holiday. Up till then the only outing we ever had was up to Brunette for the races and we used to look forward to that every year. There was a dance hall there and some of us tried to dance. We had quite a good time at the outing.

In about '42 the army sent a few soldiers to our place to see if they could buy horses off us. The army used to have horse-patrols to patrol the coast line in case the Japs came. So these soldiers come and we yarded quite a lot of horses in the yards for them to choose from. Two soldiers were giving us a hand to draft these horses off. Then, when we finished drafting in the yards about midday, just on lunch time, we said to the soldiers to come down to the house to have lunch with us. So we're walking down, one soldier out in front and we're walking along behind him. And he comes to the gate to the house, and as he opens the gate he steps aside and he says, 'Ladies first.' Well! We'd never heard of' 'Ladies first.' So we step aside next to him. He looks at us and he says, 'Ladies first!' We're still lined up beside him. Then he says, like a sergeant would say, 'Ladies! Go through!' So we all went through! That's the first we ever heard about 'Ladies'. I bet that soldier is still laughing about it.

In the war time we couldn't get petrol for the car. So Dad made a gas burner, a charcoal-gas burner it was, and he ran the car on that. The only problem with that damned thing was it wouldn't start with the self-starter. You had to push the car to get it started with the gas. Us kids used to push it and once you got it going it went alright; it would go anywhere. But you had to be careful when you pulled up along the road. If the grass was long and dry when you stopped, the flames from the burner would come out and set the grass alight. We almost started a few bush fires through there but nothing drastic ever happened. But I tell you what! We were all glad when we could get petrol again after the war!

And Dad couldn't get tobacco in the war time. He was the only one in the family that smoked. So we grew some tobacco and he made it into little blocks. He made a little press and he used to put the leaf in, and then bit of metho and a bit of honey and then some more leaf. Then he'd screw it down, and made little blocks of tobacco like that. He had a pipe and he smoked this tobacco until he could get bought-tobacco again.

We made our own butter. Made our own jam; mango jam; pawpaw jam, and pickles and chutney. And jam from bush figs that were growing around the place. Bananas, well, of course, they were almost growing wild. We used to dry the bananas, and they would last for months, and we loved them. We'd split them and put them up on the iron roof in the sun. They'd take about a week to dry. The birds didn't touch them, or the flying-foxes. And green bananas, before they started to get ripe – they had to be mature and green – we used to boil them and they'd pop out of their jackets and they were white. We'd mash them up we'd put a little butter and salt and pepper in and they were just like mashed potato.

There were flying-fox camps in the big old paper-barks along the springs. Mobs of them would come out in great big clouds just on sundown and circle around and off they'd go. The blacks used to eat them. They were part of their diet. They loved them. They'd put them in the ashes and chew the meat off them. We never ate them but we'd shoot them and boil them and give them to our chooks. The chooks liked them. We grew a bit of sorghum for the chooks, but mostly they ran fairly wild and found their own food. We always had plenty of eggs. But there were big brown pythons that would come and take them. So May and I would go out with the .22. She'd hold the torch; shine it up into the trees, and I would do the shooting.

We never had mosquitoes. They didn't seem to breed in the springs. But it was beautiful water. There was miles of water there. We were swimming all the time. And in big deep holes; deep for a kid. It was a wonder some of us didn't drown. But nobody did. It was called Mallapunyah before we got there. We tried to find out from the blacks what 'Mallapunyah' meant but none of them seemed to know. Friday knew lots of other places that had Aboriginal names; Milangetcha was right out on the McArthur River, and Oombaloonga was where a creek came in. And what the blacks called the McArthur River was Weag, which means 'running water'. The McArthur heads[3] up from what was called The Jump, up towards Walhallow station on the tableland. It doesn't come down through the dry but further down, where it starts to run a bit from springs and creeks, that's Weag, 'running water'.

We had a big long dining-table and we all sat around that at meal times with a form on each side. It had to be a big long table because there were a lot of us. And we'd sit around that three times a day for our meals and I think it brought us closer together because everybody talked at meals, and after tea, at night we'd play cards. Dad made that table. He

[3] rises.

must have got the planks for it round on the boat into Borroloola because it had beautiful pine boards. We'd scrub it and it would come up beautiful. And when we were sitting around it of a night time playing cards we had carbide lights. They give good light.

We entertained ourselves. And when we were camped out in the bush and there was nothing much to entertain us we had a book of poetry and we'd learn poetry. There is one I remember that I got out of the '*Register – the North Queensland Register*' – written by Dave Gilfoyle, called *The Big McArthur Run*. I'll give you a verse of that.

Out on the big McArthur run
Out where there's action, thrills and fun,
Out where there is no strife or fuss,
Where the outside world don't trouble us,
We ride to muster, draft and brand,
And stick to the jobs that we understand
On the big McArthur Run.

We had a big garden. It was well known all over the Territory, our garden. In the Dry we used to muster cattle and horses, and all that kind of work. In the wet season we worked in our garden. We'd plough the ground, put in our pumpkins and potatoes. We'd plough the veggie patch and grow cauliflowers and cabbages and all the other veggies too. We were pretty-well self-supplied like that. The garden was irrigated from the springs. The water run down all the channels and we'd ditch it and turn it with a spade where we wanted it to go. So that's how we put in our wet seasons. We were pretty-well working all the time. Some of us in the garden; some of us up at the yards breaking in colts; our horses and colts, just working them out of the yard.

We had a fair bit of fun on the place too. Once we had a little grumpy stallion called Towser and Alice was breaking him in. She let him out too soon, I think, with his mouthing gear on and his saddle and reins and everything. He came out so fast he jumped clean over the six-foot yard fence. He cleared it and he was gone, saddle, reins, everything! So we had to catch horses and get after him.We couldn't find him that evening so we gave up. Next day we went down and we rode around the waters. We knew he'd have to drink. We found where he'd trodden the reins in the mud for a drink. We followed him out from the waterhole and we found him. Towser wasn't galloping any more! He was tired! We took him home and broke him in and he turned out a pretty good little horse.

Another time I was on to some brumbies racing through the scrub. I told my horse to 'Go!' and he did, and I hit a tree. Broke both my arms. Luckily my brother was behind me. He came up. I couldn't get on my horse with two broken arms so he helped me up. I rode home, ten miles, with two broken arms. Mum soon got on to it, and put splints on my arms. That stopped me for a while. But it wasn't long after that I come alright again.

A lot of funny things happened. Sometimes they were dangerous. One particular bull, my brother threw him, and when we let him up, this bull wanted to kill the lot of us! For a while he couldn't get up so fast and we would just gallop around in a circle round the mob, so he wouldn't get too far away from them and then he'd go back in. But the further we went, the faster this thing got. He got after me and I wasn't on a very fast horse and my brother was laughing and yelling to me, 'Where are you taking him? Turn him! Keep him circling!' If I'd tried to turn him he would have got me! And this thing's chasing me and chasing me. And my brother keeps on laughing! 'Where are you taking him? Keep him circling! Turn him!' And I'm riding like I've never ridden before to keep out of this thing's reach! Eventually this bull's out of wind and down to a trot and we get him back into the mob again. But as soon as he's got his wind, out he comes again! Only this time he's after my brother! Wagga was a big fellow and he was on a very small horse, Havelock. And this bull is right on Havelock's tail. And now it's my turn to laugh! I keep yelling to him, 'Where are you taking him! Turn him! Keep him circling!'

Another time my oldest brother and my youngest brother were riding along and they saw fresh buffalo tracks. Buffalo tracks are a bit different from the yellow cattle. My youngest brother said, 'I'll throw this fellow when we catch up with him.' My eldest brother said, 'No you won't! You'll let him alone!' 'Oh! No!' young Bob says, 'I'll throw him!' And, just then, they looked up ahead a bit and there was this buffalo, just standing. The buffalo takes off and young Bob goes after him. My eldest brother's coming along behind. Young Bob runs the buffalo about half a mile and then it stops and turns. Young Bob, he doesn't get off to throw him; he just sits there. My eldest brother comes up and the buffalo takes one look at him and he goes straight for him! He runs my eldest brother for over a mile! But he couldn't catch him. And young Bob is coming behind, laughing like anything.

Another time Wagga was camped on his own at Kilgour camp[4] and he had some dogs with him. It was a very hot night and he took all his clothes off. The mosquitoes were bad and he only had a pair of shorts on under the mosquito net. During the night the dogs started to bark. My brother woke up and he saw this big buffalo coming. Well, he flew out from under the net and up the nearest tree. And in his haste, while he was getting up the tree, he lost his shorts. So he's up the tree without a stitch on, and the buffalo right underneath him and the mosquitoes biting. He thought, 'I don't know! How long do I have to wait here for this thing to go away?' So he said to the dogs, 'Go on! Get hold of 'im! Get him out of it!' The dogs got after the buffalo and it galloped off. So my brother gets down from the tree and gets back into his swag. Then he sees the buffalo didn't go too far and it's coming back. So he throws his swag over the stockyard fence and puts the rails up. He gets back into his swag inside the stockyard and lays down and goes back to sleep. He reckons the buffalo can't get him in there!

Another time Dad and Frank McMahon, the manager of Cresswell, adjoining Anthony's Lagoon, had a couple of bottles of rum. They thought they'd make a night of it. Around about midnight this Frank says, 'I'm a bit drunk, George.' Dad says, 'Well, get under the shower; that'll sober you up.' So this Frank gets under the shower. He sobers up a bit and he calls out to Dad, 'I can't find me shirt!' Dad goes in and he looks and he can't find the shirt, either, only a pair of trousers. 'Ah!' Dad said, 'Go to bed. We'll find your shirt in the morning.' When Frank comes out of the shower Dad notices he's got his shirt on upside

[4] Kilgour camp, 'a fair-sized water-hole just off the old Borroloola road, where teamsters and anyone travelling through would camp', was about thirty miles from Mallapunyah homestead.

down for trousers, one leg each through the sleeves. Dad takes him out to his bed and when Frank wakes up in the morning he's still wearing his shirt upside down for trousers.

Another time, Dad and a policeman who'd come in from out beyond, got on the rum. About midnight the policeman decides he wants a hair cut. 'Ah!' says Dad. 'I can fix you up! We got a pair of clippers here.' So Dad gets the clippers and goes straight over this fellow's head with them. Then he takes a look and he says, 'That's no good!' So he has another go the other way. He cuts half this bloke's hair with the clippers, and leaves the other half on. In the morning the policeman wakes up and he gets a look at himself in the mirror. He says, 'Gawd! George! You'd better finish the job, eh! Cut the lot off!"

Then in 1944 disaster struck. We were all out building a paddock, about thirty mile away. Mum and the little children were there at home on their own. We had a donkey and this donkey strayed and Mum and one of the little ones walked out from the homestead to look for it. But she never came back. The children that were there went looking for her but they couldn't find her. Then a policeman came along. He was on patrol and they told him. He rode out and found us where we were working. When we got in, there were a hundred men there, including black trackers and everything, but we couldn't find a trace of Mum, or the little one she'd taken with her. And even after the search parties left, we didn't give up. We kept on looking for them, searching for them, but all we could ever find were the tracks of the search parties, and never a trace of our mother. We searched for about a month, but never a sign. We looked in every nook and cranny on the place that we knew of, but still nothing. To this very day it is still a mystery and we never knew what happened to her.

After all the searching and never finding anything of Mum we decided we'd have to get back to work again. We worked long. We mustered cattle. Sold some more bullocks. We were building the herd up all the time. Then later on, 1947, my elder sister left home and went cooking on Anthony's Lagoon. So I had to leave the stock camp and come into the homestead to look after the smaller children. I had May there, too, helping me. I did the cooking and she did the schooling. Then in 1949 she went to Cloncurry and got married. That left me with the children so I took over the children and the cooking as well.

We were making good headway. We were selling more bullocks and things were starting to look up. The herd was getting bigger and we were putting in more fencing and more dams. My sister and I put an airstrip there, with horses again; those big draft horses were still working. Then we had a mail plane land there once a fortnight.

Then we got a bulldozer. That made the work pretty easy, much easier than horses and ploughs. Dam-sinking was easier with the bulldozer than with horses. Everything was looking up. The younger boys were getting older. We had only two younger boys home then, Fred and Bob. All the rest were out in the camp working. It wasn't long before Fred got to work too, and then there was only Bob at home for a while and everything was just an upward way. There was no stopping us then.

In early '53 two of the Teece Brothers, Ron and Ab, came back again because they had a block of country, Rosie Creek, south of Borroloola. They were there for a while mustering their cattle then Ab decided he'd contract for Anthony's Lagoon, adjoining our place, to do some fencing. They were there quite a while and we got to know them pretty well. Christmas 1953 they come over and had Christmas with us. When they finished the contract they came back to Mallapunyah. And that's when Ab and I got married, August 1954.

Ab and Kate's wedding day at Mallapunuah.

We were married at the front garden gate. The parson had come out from Tennant Creek. They'd come through occasionally and when he came one time Ab fixed the date for him to marry us the next time he was coming through. I had a blue dress on and three of my sisters; Ethel that was always called Jackie, and Anne, and Grace that was called Bubba, for bridesmaids. All the family were there and people came down from the stations. I made my own wedding cake, a big fruit cake, iced. And there was plenty of beef and vegetables and fruit.

We come away in Ab's old truck. We only got about a hundred and eighty mile on, right out in the middle of the black soil plain, and we broke-down – there in the middle of nowhere. We were there three days. Luckily we had plenty of food and water. We waited until a vehicle came and we went into the station with him. Then the manager brought us on to Camooweal. From there we went on to Townsville and had our honeymoon; a week on Magnetic Island; three weeks altogether. We bought a truck there, another Chev and come back out to Mallapunyah. We bought a part for the other old truck we'd left on the plain. Ab put it in and we brought the two trucks back to Mallapunyah. That old truck is still there to this day.

I enjoyed my young life at Mallapunyah. Out in the stock camp. Always on horses. Running wild cattle and wild horses. Mustering cattle and breaking-in horses. It was an exciting life. We had no cars to get around in. It was all on pack horses. There were no worries about anything; always something to laugh about; plenty to eat; plenty of beef; no money worries, nothing at all to worry about. There with my family. I loved the life.

2

Ab Teece

ॐ ॐ ॐ

Introduction

A tall well-built man that could give John Wayne a run for his money, Ab Teece is another of the almost legendary drovers of the north. On the night of the dance at the annual Camooweal Drovers' Camp Festival in 2005, I virtually kidnapped him from the barbecue outside the historic Town Hall. We were leaning against the side of a 4WD, balancing plates of steak and salad and trying to talk above the Progressive Barn dance in full swing inside the hall. I knew Ab was telling me of his droving days but it was impossible to hear. I said, 'I'd like to tape-record some of your memories. Supposing we go over to Lorna Freckleton's where it will be a bit quieter?' The Freckletons are a noted Camooweal family, their grandfather having been one of the early settlers. Most tourists passing through the archetypal one-pub township, seven miles from the Northern Territory border, take the time to step back in history at Camooweal's Heritage Museum, housed in Joe Freckleton's corrugated-iron store, with its century-old flagstone paving.

So, sitting at the table on the homely back verandah of Lorna Freckleton's Guest House, Ab Teece and I recorded his life-story. The opening incident is remarkable. And if Ab says he can remember it, then he can remember it. Ab is not the sort of man to dramatize. Miles Franklin, recalling her early years in 'Girlhood at Brindabilla', remembers being hoisted in her father's arms at the age of nine months. Ab's memory of falling out of the sulky into the creek at a similarly early age is equally remarkable, and as a story, it has the edge.

Despite Ab's having had only a couple of years schooling, in the telling of his story, his lack of formal education does not diminish his ability to give an account of his life and of his days in the droving industry in a spare and compelling style. The story of his determination to educate himself as a young adult, ranks equally with those of his long overland treks and other feats of physical endurance.

When Ab finally gave the droving game away he ran a saddlery and western clothing store in Cloncurry for many years, becoming one of the town's most highly respected businessmen. Now, at last retired, he writes bush poetry and songs for the Country Music festivals he loves to attend.

Bringing The Bullocks Along

Ab Teece

'Your night horses, they're your key horses'

If you fall out of the back of the sulky into a flooded creek and get washed away, it's the sort of thing you remember. The thing is, I was only six months old at the time. But I remember it distinctly; Mum grabbing me by the leg and pulling me up out of the water.

See, I was born in Cloncurry, in 1928, in the June, and my parents decided to shift to Mount Isa, so it must have been the wet season time, around Christmas, because they had animals; goats and cows and horses. To shift them there would have had to be water through the hills. And they come to this flooded gully and they had a lot of vegetables and things swung under the sulky on wire-netting. And the sulky went into the gully and trying to get up the other side, the belly-band broke and the sulky tipped up and I fell out into the water. And that's something I remember; the falling out and being washed away and my mother grabbing me out of the water by the leg; saving me. And the water would have been pretty muddy; and Dad going crook about the harnesses not done up properly.[1]

My parents took up a bit of a place outside Mount Isa that they called Hazelvale, after my sister, and they were dairying there. Mount Isa was a pretty rugged sort of a place in those days; nothing there, just a lot of tents and make-shift buildings. And one time, when I was about three, us kids had to take the milk churns in the utility to wash them, and I was sat in the back, and as my brother was backing it, my sister pulled the two pins out of the tail-board and I fell out backwards. The utility went over the top of me. That broke my leg in three places and four ribs. So they put me in hospital but I wasn't a very good patient. I used to pelt the toys and things at the nurses. When they took me home I had to learn to walk again. That went on for maybe three years.

I was living with a couple of aunties in town and supposed to be going to school but I'd think to myself, 'I don't want this going to school!' and I'd take off up the river looking for m'dad. They'd all be out looking for me to take me back. One time I hid under the house – it was low to the ground – and the aunties were trying to get me out. I kept them at bay throwing rocks at them. Finally, one come one way and the other come the other way and they got me out. So back to school I went. One had hold of me by the hand dragging me and the other is coming along behind with a big piece of pine-board! I was about six or seven,

[1] This incident is similar to Ray Fryer's account, in *Red Dust Rising,* of his having been born after the britchan on the sulky in which his mother was driving to hospital, broke and the sulky rolled back into the creek, and is yet another example of the resilience and hardihood of Australian bush mothers.

just a wild kid; didn't like being hemmed in.

In 1935 the family split up. My mother went one way and my father said he'd go up the Gulf fishing and he took me with him. So that ended my education. But my dad was mad on copper; always in the hills looking for copper, so he give the fishing away and went digging copper. We battled round the countryside for years.

Then Dad and m'brother, Clive, who was two years older'n me, was living in this old hut on the bank of the river. I'd have been ten. Then Dad heard about this copper-show, so he took Clive with him and off he went to have a look at it. He left me there at the hut. So I was there on m'own for a while. I wasn't frightened; but I never had much to eat. No lights of a night time, only the fire. I used to get water out of the creek. But one day this old pensioner, old Bill Boland, went past, and he said to me, 'D'you want anything from up town?' I said, 'Yeah! Get me a loaf of bread and a tin of treacle.' So that give me a bit of a feed.

Another time I went down to old Bing Sing's garden. He had a good sort of a cabbage growing there and I crawled in along a bit of a gully under the netting fence on m'belly and pinched it and took it back and boiled it. Little did I know at the time, if I'd went and told old Bing that I was hungry he'd have give me a feed. He was a good old Chinaman. Modern kids wouldn't be able to imagine what us kids went through in them days.

I never had much in the way of clothes, just the one pair of shorts and a ragged old shirt. And this day I wanted to wash them. So I took 'em off and I'm getting round in this old coat. And this woman come past in this little car, and she sung out to me, 'Ain't you hot in that coat?' And I said, 'No. I aint hot.' But there was this big-mouth kid there and he sung out, 'He only got a coat on because he got no trousers on!' And some time later, the Old Fellow and Clive come riding back late one night, so everything was right again for a while.

Then I had a couple more years education when my brother Cec come back and seen that I was just helping Dad digging this bit of a copper-show. See, the Old Man was mad on copper. That was what he was after all his life. That was all he knew. But Cec told him, 'We've got to get old Ab here a bit of schooling!' So he took me into Mount Isa and I stopped with an old dairyman there, a good old man, and stuck it out for a couple of years. I might have got to about Prep Two or Three. I couldn't really read or write.

Then my Auntie and Uncle up in the Gulf had this station, Mayvale, and they took me up there for twelve months. They didn't worry about whether I was educated, as long as I worked; cattle-work. I was a good rider.

When I was about twelve, Dad and Cec decided to get a droving plant together and I went droving with them. That was when first I come out to the Territory. In 1941 we went out to Mallapunyah on the Macarthur River and I met Kate Darcy, the girl who in years to come would be my wife. She was one of the Darcy girls. There was about ten or twelve of the Darcy family at Mallapunyah. I'd heard of this family that had big gardens. I was only a kid and when we finally got there I was looking for fruit. There were four or five boys and about the same amount of girls; five sisters; Grace, Annie, Jackie, June and May and Kate. Kate was the second eldest. I looked at her and she looked at me. She didn't like me a real lot because I was only a bit of a kid and she reckoned I was a 'cheeky fella'[2], after the fruit, see. I wasn't too worried about chasing girls in them days. I was only about thirteen.

We went up to Macarthur River station and we took delivery of the bullocks; 3rd May, 1941. We brought them down to Brunette and the mid-winter rain set in, and it was cold! And, hell, it rained! A couple of bullocks died of the cold. We had a wagonette, pulled with about four horses, and it was too boggy for it to move so we couldn't go anywhere. And we've got no clothes; not prepared for wet weather. I had a pair of half-worn-out old boots and I lost one of them in the mud and the other one got burnt up against the fire, all shrivelled up. So I'm riding round the cattle with no boots on in the cold. Then we went on till we got to the Ranken and followed the Ranken stock route down until we come to Urandangi and then on to Boulia. Then on, until you cross the Channels to Windorah. But a cold trip all the way. Afterwards you can see the funny side of things. You only think of the good times.

When I was about sixteen Cec and I went up the Territory with Albert Hooker, way over to the Western Australian border, and brought fifteen hundred head of bullocks in from Mistake Creek. Mistake Creek would have been a Vestey's place in them days. It wasn't much improved; just a pretty-run-down old place.

Albert Hooker's father, Eddy Hooker, was the cook. Percy O'Keefe was the horse tailer. Then there was Ronnie Dwyer, Bill Flannagan, Clive, the brother, and m'self. You had to have six men in your plant to move fifteen hundred head of cattle, four men with the cattle and the horse-tailer and a cook. You'd cut your dinner and have it in your saddle-bag and the cook would go ahead, usually about eight or nine mile to the next camp and the horse-tailer would take the horses along. Each man had about four or five horses and you'd change horses each morning and spell the fellow you'd had. It wasn't hard on the horses because you were just poking along, steady and slow, the cattle feeding along as they go.

Those Mistake cattle were bad cattle, scrub cattle. They used to rush two or three times a night the first weeks we had them. One particular night they come racing along and almost run over the top of the camp. Of course, you kept your fire going and if they did happen to head towards the camp well, the fire would split 'em. But when we got to the Murranji they behaved themselves and never rushed once. The Murranji's a pretty scrubby sort of track but the bullocks were good, right the way through. They seemed to like those bullwaddi, lancewood scrubs. But then out on the open downs they were rushing all the time. And

[2] Northern Territory slang for no-good, dangerous; e.g. *cheeky-fella snake*, extremely venomous; *cheeky-fella yam*, not edible.

they'd come straight towards the camp. We kept the fire going to split them. Every man going on watch would stoke the fire up. We had them on the road five weeks before they started to settle down. The last time they rushed was at Anthony's.

There were government bores and watering points along the stock route every eighteen miles. And what you did was, you watered your cattle and walked them out, six or eight mile, and camped. That's the first night. The next day you'd be on water for your dinner camp. They'd have a big old drink and then you'd walk them out again.

When we came off the Murranji into Newcastle[3], we stocked up with supplies, then come on down through Anthony's Lagoon and kept going till we got to Camooweal; a fourteen weeks trip. We took them out to Morstone and delivered them and picked up another mob of Mistake bullocks that was brought in the year before, and took them to Dajarra, about a four week's trip. They were trucked from there. That would have been 1942.

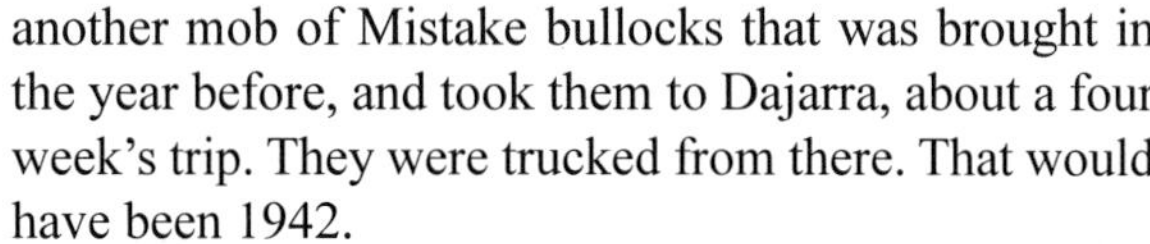

Then the next year we went from Camooweal through Boulia down the Georgina to a place called Tanbah in the Channel Country and delivered a mob of bullocks there. And that's when we got our own droving plant together, me and the brother and the old Dad and we done a few trips, nothing big. And after that I started to branch out on m'own, mostly around Hughenden, and down the Diamantina, taking station cattle.

Then Clive drew a block of country, Rosy Creek, out from Borroloola. He thought it would be good country and he talked me into going up there with him. But when we got there we found it was no good; no cattle and too much scrub. So I took a contract fencing job. And that's when I started to get together with Kate again. She didn't look too bad to me this time. I'd go down to Mallapunyah to see her. And I did a bit of work for her old man, but not for money. And Kate and I got together a few times, at Christmastime and so on. Kate wanted to get married. She must have had it in mind that she wasn't going to waste her life up in the Gulf and that I didn't look too bad after all.

We got married on Mallapunyah. I asked the preacher to come there and do the wedding. So we got married in the front gate of the house. The preacher decided that would be the

[3] Newcastle Waters, a beautiful permanent water-hole on a water-course which flows south into Lake Woods, is home to an abundance of bird-life, and was named by explorer John McDoual Stuart in 1861. The tiny township on its banks, a few miles west of Elliot, was once famous as the junction of three stock routes, the Murranji, the North South and the Barkly and was a welcoming meeting place for drovers coming in with their mobs. Little remains of the township today but a tiny school and a scattering of semi-abandoned corrugated-iron homes. The remarkable old bush pub, the Junction Hotel, still stands and seems to ring with the hearty voices of long-departed drovers slaking well-earned thirsts after weeks on the road. A life-size bronze, *The Drovers' Cook*, by sculptor Eddy Hacket, was erected in 1988 to commemorate the drovers and the droving days.

best place. He told me, 'You'll stand there and the bride can walk up there.' He had it all worked out. Her father gave her away. She wore a nice sort of dress, and things in her hair. The girls done her up pretty good. My best man was Harold Edwards, a friend of mine. He'd been digging copper around the place. We had quite a party afterwards. The manager of Cresswell, he was there, and Cliff Nissen, the engineer on Anthony's; all the locals, they all turned up. We had a honeymoon in Townsville at Picnic Bay on Magnetic Island. That was in 1954. We've been married over fifty years now and we're still good mates.

After the wedding, m'father-in-law, George Darcy, he give me a mob of bullocks; three hundred and twenty head. He said, 'Take 'em away and sell 'em, Boy. Pay me when you see me. Twenty pound a head.' I sold them the same day for thirty-three. We went down to Hughenden and I did stock work round various stations – head stockman mostly – Chudleigh Park, Mt Emu, Dutton River, Mount Sturgeon and Charlotte Plains up in the basalt country. Some of them places had wild cattle, especially on Charlotte Plains. It was hard country to work in but you took pride in your work. But then Mount Sturgeon had a mob of about twelve hundred bullocks and when the place was sold they give me the job of taking the cattle away. I said, 'Well, I'll take these bullocks down on the road.' So I got a plant of horses together – beautiful horses, too. You could stand on the back of the truck in the morning and count your horses coming back. Never seen horses like it before. We took those bullocks down to Brighton Downs. That was the year that President Kennedy was assassinated.

Kate used to go on the road with me, cooking for the camp. One trip, from Mount Sturgeon, we got along the road and of course, a few of the men pulled out, which happens. One will pull out and another one thinks, 'If he's going I'll go too.' So I finished up with just one man with the cattle and the horse-tailer and Kate doing the cooking. But we went along good. Beautiful little bullocks. Put the horses with the cattle and when the horse-tailer caught up, Kate would go on dinner-watch for us and that'd leave the boys have a good long dinner-camp to catch up on a bit of sleep.

Kate used to make good bread on the road; and a lot of dampers, too, of course. She had the two-ton truck, a Ford. She can't drive but she was only doing five mile at a time. She'd go five mile and then we'd pull up for dinner and then go five mile after dinner. She didn't mind that. She'd go up ahead and get the billies and the dinner all ready and then she'd have a sleep in the truck. Then when she heard the cattle come up round the truck, mooing, she'd get up and light the fire and we'd have dinner. Then after dinner she'd go another five mile on to night-camp. Cooking for drovers is pretty easy. You've got all day doing nothing. No housework!

One particular day, we were going along early in the morning and my horse, a bit of a colt, started to root. He put his foot in a hole and fell. Then he raced away with m' saddle. And the only man with me raced away after m' horse, naturally. He was gone about an hour and a half. And I'm there on me own on foot with twelve hundred head of bullocks, chucking sticks and bits of dirt at them to move them along. But they were good little bullocks and they're just feeding along and I'm behind them. My main worry was that someone would come along and see me and they'd think to themselves, 'This must be a new way of droving!'

Then I got the job managing a little station outside Hughenden, Dunraven. We were there a good while. We had four children and then the smallest one, one of the babies, got bronchitis and ended up dying. We lost him. We found it hard. But other people had it just as hard, I suppose. One of the saddest cases I heard was Old Jimmy Alexander, on his way out to Brunette on his truck. He got bogged down. One of his kids got sick and died and he had to bury it, there and then.

My brother nearly lost one of his kids, young Smiley. They were mustering and he went racing away just on sundown to block a mob of horses. The pony fell with him and he broke his leg. He lay there all night – a cold windy night – out on the black-soil plain. A whole lot of searchers come out from Kynuna and they finally got him. To lay out on the black-soil without a blanket would be bad enough but to lie there all night with a broken leg! That must have been bad.

I had a bad rush one night coming from Helen Springs. And about two days out, I was on watch and I got a bit slack. I never kept the fire going and it died down. The bullocks rushed. They never went near the camp; they rushed the other way, out across the plain. But a windy night and the men didn't know I was on me own. And I raced up ahead of the cattle trying to swing them around. They split up and I was yelling – must have been an hour and a half – trying to hold the mob together. I didn't know where the hell I was; just galloping round an open plain. Then one of the boys woke up and threw a bit of wood on the fire and got it going. I seen the fire blaze up and I realized I'm going to get help. Without the fire you've got no idea where you are, or which direction the camp is. We lost a couple of hundred head of cattle that night but we scouted round and got them all back together again.

That's the funny thing about cattle; you can have a mob out there on the flat all camped and quiet and within split seconds they can be on their feet and going. They all seem to know to go the one way. They all go together. Something stirs one up, a snake or a rat or something, and a thousand bullocks, all camping peacefully, are on their feet galloping. A good stockman, he knows, when he's riding round the cattle, if they go and they're come towards you, you get your horse out of the road. Then you can get your horse up ahead and try to wheel them round. That particular night I was riding a terrible good horse. When they jumped she knew to get out of the road of them coming and then she just grabbed the bit and took the lead and swung them around. She was a terrific mare. She really knew what she was doing. It can get a bit hairy at times, if there's broken gullies or a fence or something, but a good man, he will have a look around before he puts the cattle on camp at sundown and he will know, 'Well, there's a big gully over there,' and so on, and he will remember where that is. Your key horses were the night horses. They had to be good.

Before I was Boss Drover I was nearly always on midnight watch; twelve to two and then you go and wake the boss up. He rides round the cattle till four o'clock and then he wakes the men up. The midnight watch is the worst. Cattle all get up about midnight for a bit of a stretch, even quiet cattle, they get up and walk around a little while and stretch and then they'll settle down again. You have to sing to them because when you're riding round a mob like that, if your horse puts his foot on a stick and it cracks, or if he trips, it will frighten the cattle. So you have to ride around making a noise singing. You sing all the old favorite songs; 'Suvla Bay' and 'Rusty It's Good-bye' and 'Shep'. And one particular time when I was Boss Drover I had a man, a white man, with me, a bloke named Johnny Wade, and he was a real good singer. He'd ride around the cattle singing and he was that good you'd try to stay awake to listen to him. After you've been a week on the road, you always seem to wake up when it's time for you to go on watch. You'd wake up and think, 'Is it wake-up time yet? Must be a while yet.' But sure enough, it would be time for him to call you.

The longest dry stage I ever did was forty mile, down near Palparara. Doing a dry stage you've got to water them and go out as far as you can before you camp that night. Then next day you poke them along as far as you can. You have a dry night that night. The next day you'll get on to water. A lot of people think you've got to flog bullocks along to get them through a dry stage, but if you just let them feed along, poke along, they'll be OK. Keep the lead away and let the tailers walk.

In your plant you might have forty or more head of horses, four for each man. You'd hobble them out of a night-time. You'd put a bell on the ones you know are likely to clear out. A lot you wouldn't put hobbles on. You know they're not going to clear out and you don't want them hobbling around all night. They'll hang around with their mates. I'd use mainly green-hide hobbles. They're about the best you can get; easy to make, and cheap. I'd make mine myself; a little chain about six inches long with a swivel in the middle. If you've got a bit of a rogue horse that wants to sneak away you'd chop a little bit off the chain to shorten his step. If you keep your hobble straps greased up pretty-well, they get really soft. Otherwise they chafe them. I'd use the fat off the beef-bucket.

I done a bit of rough riding in my time. When the rodeos come I'd travel anywhere, Alice Springs to Darwin, just to ride buck-jumping horses! I was young and stupid. I done everything to kill m'self off a horse and just couldn't do it. In 1959 I was on the committee that started Mount Isa Rodeo off; about six of us was practical men, the rest was doctors and lawyers, and the manager of Mount Isa Mines, Jim Footes. I helped plan the yards and Theiss Brothers built them; all steel yards; steel out of the mine. One ride I top-scored. Another time the horse bucked over on top of me and knocked me

Ab was involved with the establishment of the Mount Isa Rodeo Association and a keen participant. Once, regaining consciousness in the ambulance to hospital , he asked, 'Do I get a re-ride?'

out. When I come to I was in the ambulance and Kate reckons the first thing I wanted to know was, 'Do I get a re-ride?'

I used to have a bit of a reputation as a grass fighter. I'd love a fight. I'd go up town hoping to get one. One time a bit of a fight started in the Grand Hotel. Then someone said, 'Police!' So away we go, all different angles. And I must have broke me hand, or bruised it bad, because I had it all wrapped up. The next morning I went up the Shamrock Hotel and I get m'self a beer. So I'm leaning on the bar and I look across, and there's the Sergeant of Police. 'Teece!' he says, 'I'll give you fight! I'll do you one hand!' I says, 'Yes, Serg!' Then I get the beer into me and the next thing is he says, 'Well! Come on! We'll go across to the Grand Hotel and you can apologize to Ted Savage, the publican.' So over we go and I say, 'I'm sorry, Ted, that we had a fight here last night.' He says, 'It's right! Don't worry about it!' So then, me and Old Serg we get on the booze together. He was supposed to go on duty about two or three o'clock but by then he's drunk. So some of the boys got hold of him – a big old fellow, he was, Old Serg – and put him in a wheel-barrow and they wheel him round the back of the pub out of sight and plant him in among some bushes. So there's Old Serg, choked down[4], and the Senior Serg looking everywhere over town for him!

I went up to the Territory once working for the Americans on Goodparla[5]. There were some good men amongst them. But they wouldn't draft their horses off. The horses didn't know anything about being drafted. They'd never been taught. Americans didn't know anything about walking up to a horse and catching him and slapping him across the flank with your reins to make him face up. You had to catch him with a rope. They'd go into the yard with a mob of horses with a rope and they were smart men with those ropes. They'd see the horse that they wanted and they'd spin the rope and the horse'd just have to put his head up and they'd have that rope on him.

But all the time, I was determined to better, m'self. I was always the young brother, the no-hoper as far as the other brothers were concerned. I'd started off working and I couldn't read and write. Couldn't read and write! So I decided to teach m'self. I started reading cowboy books, which I could relate to; hills, cattle, guns and all that, just little western stories. In 1950 I decided to join the army and I had to have an educational test and I passed it! I was in for two years until just after the old king died. The night the king died I was in Concord hospital and I was a bit delirious and I could hear these cows and calves bellowing and I thought to m'self, 'Well, that's it! I've had it!' I thought it was my end had come. I never found out till years later that Homebush trucking yards was just across the way from the hospital!

So then I come back to the west, stony broke. I'd been drinking a bit and lairizing around and I never had a feed all the way to Mount Isa. When I got off the train there was an old half-caste bloke there I knew, old Eric Ranken – I'll never forget him – he took me in, bought me a beer and he give me a feed and he got me a taxi out to Yelvatoft where me brother was managing. I never looked back after that. I got on my feet. And about twenty

[4] Dead drunk.

[5] Goodparla station, north of Pine Creek, owned by an American family, specializing in breeding buffaloes for the overseas meat market.

years later old Eric turned up at home one night and he said, 'Can I get a loan of $20 off you?' I said, 'Yeah! Eric! I can give you anything you want. I'll never forget what you done for me!'

I became a saddler; self-taught more or less. The brother Cec was a bit of a saddler and I picked it up from him. I always wanted to be a saddler, so I started making saddles, work trousers, town trousers - good ones – shirts and coats. I had m'own label. '*The Rodeo Saddle Shop*' with a picture of Australia on it and a little spot for where Cloncurry was. And I reckon that's something; a boy with no education, no training. We were in that shop for must have been twenty-five years and doing good, too. And I had the little secretary and she used to do the books, because I had no education in that side of things and she thought we were making a fair bit of money so when she got married she said, 'I'd like to buy the shop.' So I said, 'Righto!' and I sold it to her and retired.

Now I get around to a fair few poetry festivals and music festivals. I go down to Tamworth and sing. I go to the Oasis Hotel and for the ten days I'm there I sing every day, mostly my own songs. I've written quite a few. I've met a good crowd down there; Slim Dusty, Michael Cook; the whole lot of them. All top artists, and they treat you good, too.

The droving days are gone now, but if you've got good horses, in a good season, droving was a good life. Any drover, if he was a good drover, looked after his plant and looked after his cattle and they got quiet and it was a pleasure. Those old drovers, on cattle camp of a morning, they'd stir the cattle up and they didn't push to get them away. They'd leave them stand up and stretch themselves and stand around a bit and leave all their droppings on camp so that the next drover that came along, he could see how well fed your bullocks were. They took a pride in it, and pleasure.

There were hard times. And there were bad cattle. But there's a catch in everything, whatever you do. If droving was easy everyone would have been droving. Even today you might be driving along the road and you see all these miles of waving grasses and you think to yourself, 'Yair! I wouldn't mind having a mob of bullocks out there right now, bringing them along.'

3

Cliffie Robinson

ॐ ॐ ॐ

Introduction

Cliffie recording his story at Bohle River

Sharks, crocodiles, mustering wild bulls in the Kimberleys, netting 'muddies', fishing for barramundi in the Daly, developing his unique art style; these laconically recalled memories of growing to manhood in Australia's north read like Ripping Yarns.

I had been told that Cliffie Robinson lived 'at the mouth of the Bohle in a bit of a place he built himself', and that 'Cliffie'll give you a good story.' 'The mouth of the Bohle', just north of Townsville, seemed more to promise sand-flies and mosquitoes – being an area of horizon-wide tidal flats, salt water creeks, mangrove swamps and tea tree sand-ridges. A four-wheel drive later, 'Cliffie's place' turned out to be idyllically situated up-river, among groves of palms, pandanus, ironbark and white gum, and the 'built-it-himself' a generously large, timber and corrugated-iron-roofed, open-planned living-area, agreeably furnished, lacking only walls. And, really, who needs walls in North Queensland? Clifford himself, far from being the mahogany-skinned diminutive ex-fisherman that I had imagined, was a tall, engagingly charming man who, in a dinner suit, would not have looked out of place at a civic reception at City Hall. When I admired his home, Cliffie delighted me by saying, 'Well, come and have a look at this!' and showed me that one of the timber supports of the building was in fact a living tree, growing insouciantly through the roof. He 'hadn't had the heart to cut it down' when work was underway.

Having, myself, grown up in Townsville in the 1940s, it was not long before it began to dawn on me that this Cliffie Robinson, well known in the north for his remarkably individual art, was one of the Robinson family, original First Settlers from the days of Robert Towns, the *St John Robinsons of Mount St John and the Mount St John Zoo, without which no 1940s childhood of Sunday afternoon visits, in best bib and tucker, to see the crocodiles being fed, would have been complete.*[1]

Recording, transcribing and editing Clifford Robinson's story was an experience in itself; his recall of the details of growing up at the zoo evocative of an era when children were no less happy for the hard work they were expected to do. That after-school 'bread'n sugar' or, for a real treat, 'bread'n-condensed milk'! Admirers of Cliff's art will value the detail of the model animals fashioned from gully-clay that presaged his development as an artist. The account of his midnight swim to rescue the boat off the Daly River, with 'two knives in case I dropped one', in expectation of being 'grabbed by a croc at any moment', is told with superb economy of words but is as spine-chilling as any in more polished literature. Clifford Robinson continues to uphold the fine tradition of four generations of the Robinson family's determined individuality and achievement in North Queensland.

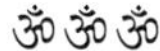

Taking A Few Chances

Clifford Robinson - Artist

'Red eyes everywhere! You've never seen so many crocs!'

There were three women in the boat being rowed ashore. It was 1865 and they were landing in Cleveland Bay at the new settlement. The three of them drew straws to see who would be the first white woman to step ashore. My Great-Grandma, Catherine Colven, got the short straw, so she was the third woman ashore.

She had arrived in Australia, an Irish immigrant girl from County Armagh. She and her brother left Ireland because of the potato famine. Her brother, who was a chemist, died on the way out and was buried in Cape Town so she came on alone to Brisbane. She was twenty-four.

When the ship arrived in Moreton Bay, she got a job as a maid at Government House looking after the kitchen and the dining room. Then she heard that there was a new township being formed in the north on Cleveland Bay. Robert Towns was starting this place and was going to start a hotel, the Criterion. They needed a woman to do the kitchen and dining room so she applied for the job and got it.

They came up the coast on the *Policeman*. It had a load of timber for an annexe to the Criterion. In those days there was a rocky bar across the mouth of Ross Creek and ships couldn't get in. They used to have to anchor out in the bay and row the passengers ashore. Later they blasted that bar to make an anchorage. So when they landed, the three girls went

[1] See; *The Morning Side of the Hill; A Townsville Childhood;* Marion Houldsworth. JCU Press, 1995, Chapter 11. '*Mt St John Zoo was always crowded with American troops taking photos in front of the crocodile pool, especially at three o'clock, feeding time....*"

to the 'Cri' where they were going to have these jobs.

When she been there about six months, Robert Towns came up. Apparently it was the one and only time he stayed in Townsville over night. He stayed at the Criterion and the next day they rowed across to Magnetic Island, as Towns said, 'to open up the Island.' The three women drew straws again to see which of them would be the first woman to step ashore. This time Great-Grandma drew the best straw and so became the first white woman to set foot on Maggie Island.[2]

Later she married a bloke called Heinrich Rubenstein, though later he changed his name to Henry Robinson. In those days they had to ride their horses down to Bowen to get married. This Heinrich was from Hamburg in Germany. He had come up overland from Sydney, as a drover or a cook, with ten thousand sheep for the Hanns as part of their first

COUPLE MARRIED 65 YEARS

An adventurous 90 year old man who has become a legend in his lifetime will celebrate his 65th wedding anniversary with his wife today. The legendary Mr. St. John Robinson and his wife Cecile were married beneath the mango trees at Springfield, Townsville, in 1906. For Mrs. Robinson it will be a double celebration as it is her 88th birthday. Both were born in Townsville. Mr. Robinson is a Boer War veteran who was in the relief of Mafeking. Now he is a successful cane-farmer living with his wife at 29 Paxton St, North Ward. During his wonderfully interesting lifetime he established Mount St John Zoo and Bird Sanctuary. He was the first Australian to breed crocodiles in captivity. He often rode his favourite 20 foot crocodile, Tarzan. His personality and feats of daring made the zoo one of the North's best tourist attractions.

Mr. Robinson was a noted horse rider in North Queensland. "I took ninety horses over to Mauritius and rode the buck-jumper on the sand when we arrived." he said. "The boat was the E.J. Spence, a sailing boat.' A volunteer for the Boer War, he and his mates from Charters Towers enlisted together. He remembers Lord Baden Powell riding his horse among the men who held their positions until relief came. But it is the land that has always been his first love. After selling the Halifax Hotel he and his wife took up land at the Bohle and Saunders Beach.

Extract from Townsville Bulletin, 1971

[2] Gibson-Wilde, *A Pattern of Pubs*; p. 143; When the Criterion opened in May 1865 it had '*three sitting rooms and twelve bedrooms.*' By August it was advertised as '*having two storeys, twenty-five rooms, a balcony twelve feet (4m) wide and a billiard table.*' The building had been erected and furnished by Black and Co. Black's partner, Robert Towns, objected to the installation of the billiard table saying it '*would not improve the moral code of society in Townsville.*' He also disapproved of the arrival of the first '*bar maids*', '*Misses Colven, Gilchrist and O'Dowda*', but on his only visit to Townsville he '*enjoyed their company on a picnic to Magnetic Island*'.

expedition. The Hann Highway is named after them.

Henry and Catherine set up a vineyard at Kissing Point and built a big house there. But they got wiped out in a cyclone so they moved in behind Castle Hill and started a dairy to supply the town with vegetables and milk. In those days, all that area had big lagoons. Their place became known as the German's Gardens and people would drive out there on a Sunday afternoon for an outing to buy fruit and vegetables. But being German and Irish they weren't the most popular amongst the rest of the population of Townsville. This was an English Colony, you know! And here's these bloody Germans and bloody Irish! So in later years, when World War One broke out, the German's Gardens copped a pretty-swift name-change to Belgian Gardens.

Granddad's brother Fred always claimed to be the first white baby born in Townsville but that's debatable because a Mrs Sandwood had a baby about the same time. Fred was great-grandmother's first baby, born about 1870. My grandfather was next born and named St John Robinson; the 'St John' after the Irish grandfather.

When great-grandma first took up Mount St John, it was in the middle of a big flood-plain area that ran from the Bohle River back to where the airport is now; probably about five thousand acres. Great-granddad also had a bigger property called Springfield, at Yabulu, where the nickel processing plant is now.

The blacks were pretty wild in those days and at Mount St John, great-grandma would sometimes see a big mob of them coming across the flood-plain from behind Cape Pallarenda.[3] That area was their traditional hunting grounds. So she had a stockade built on a natural mound there to be able to watch out for the blacks. But talk about the Stolen Generation! A big mob of the tribe ended up camped almost permanently at Mount St John. My Grandma would take a lot of the little girls and babies and their mothers in and feed

[3] The extensive lagoons and mud-flats of Townsville Common are now a World Heritage Wildlife Sanctuary to which bird-watchers from all over the world come to see the vast flocks of pied geese that arrive annually, the rare jabirus and the elegant display-dancing of groups of brolgas.

them and look after them, and when the tribe went walkabout over to their hunting grounds at Cape Cleveland, the girls wouldn't want to budge. They wanted to stay with Grandma. She always had ten to twelve of them at the house and they adored her like a mother and grew up almost part of the Robinson family.

So my grandfather, St John Robinson, grew up with the boys of the tribe working on the property. He could speak all their dialects and later when there was any trouble among them he would help sort it out. The authorities had mustered all these different tribes together and re-settled them on Palm Island. But you can't jam them all together like that. There were fights and murders and rapes and the police would wonder why. They would come and get granddad because he was the only one that could understand the language. He'd be called on to mediate because he could always find out what the trouble was and who had caused it.

Then as a young man he went up to Ingham and bought cane farms around Cordelia. He used big horse-teams to do all his ploughing. He'd married Cecile Saunders, the daughter of George Saunders, one of the first shire councillors, who'd owned Springfield originally. He and Grandma were married under the mango trees at Springfield in 1906.

Then he bought the Halifax Hotel. My Dad was born there in 1910. They served beer for threepence a pint mug, including a counter lunch. There were a lot of crocodiles in those days in the Herbert. A mailman got taken by a croc crossing it. No bridges, of course. Grand-dad was a good shot – he'd been to the Boer War - and used to hunt crocs. But then, before the word had even been invented, he became a conservationist. He was fascinated by these big reptiles. He built big enclosures behind the Halifax Hotel and started to trap crocodiles instead of shooting them. That proved to be a big draw-card. People used to come in their sulkies on a Sunday afternoon to see these big crocodiles being fed.

When granddad sold the hotel about 1920, he didn't want to leave his crocodiles behind. His mother had all that country around Mount St John so he brought them down in his old truck. It was a pretty rough old road and there weren't many bridges. But he got them through and started up a zoo. He got an order to have the area declared a sanctuary and built big lagoons where millions of ducks and geese would come. So that was the beginning of Mount St John Zoo. He was the first in Australia to breed crocodiles in captivity.[4] He had some big crocodiles there. His favourite was a twenty-footer named Tarzan. For Townsville people, that became their Sunday afternoon; driving out to Mount St John and walking around the enclosures at the zoo to see the crocodiles being fed.

Some of the Aboriginals used to camp down at the turn-off to Rowe's Bay. Their gunyahs were made out of sheets of iron or bags or whatever they could scrounge. The little trees they used to camp under are still there to this day. They don't appear to be much bigger and that's over sixty years ago. They had fish traps at Mosquito Creek. If they got a crocodile in the trap they'd rope it up and bring it out to granddad and sell it to him for a few bob and

[4] *The Morning Side of the Hill, p. 127. 'Once there was a huge crowd to see Mr. St John Robinson punt out in a dinghy to where a female crocodile had a nest in reeds in the middle of the lagoon. When he tried to remove some of the eggs the mother crocodile lashed her tail and charged. He had to fend her off with one of the oars. Everyone applauded but I was on the mother crocodile's side.'*

he'd put it in the zoo.

Granddad always had a couple of thousand head of cattle at Mount St John and when my brother John – he was the first, then Sandra, then me, then Alan – the four of us - were growing up, we had our own horses and were mustering from the time we could ride. Granddad was a tough old character and he'd been a noted North Queensland horseman. He had us riding everywhere bareback. He'd say, 'If you can't ride bareback you can't ride at all!' We had to be able to gallop bareback. He wouldn't buy us a saddle until we learned to get our balance. You got plenty of busters and the ground was pretty hard so you learned to stick on. Then he'd give us a saddle.

The homestead was right at the zoo; or rather, the zoo was built around the homestead. The house was a big two-storey place, a beautiful old house. Underneath, it had an ant-bed floor and the kitchen with a wood stove. The smoke would make the walls dark and Mum would make us whitewash them. And when she was cooking she wouldn't let the pots go black. Us kids had to scrub them with sand-soap; rub and rub with a bit of rag and make the enamel nice and shiny again.

John, Sandra and I were all born within three years of one another and we were the ones that got to do all the work. The other three were born later when we were a bit older and we had to look after them too. But it was a good upbringing. There are not many kids who are bought up in a zoo. And us kids, growing up there, well, there were always blacks about the place, and the gins in the house were like having extra mothers.

When I was about eight or nine I used to do a lot of clay-modelling of the animals. The black kids and us'd go around the gullies at Mount St John looking for clay. We'd dig it out; proper yellow modelling clay, just like plastercine to us, but it would set as hard as cement. You modelled things and left them to dry in the sun. The black kids would make little animals and they'd scratch a design of a turtle, or a fish or a bird on them and leave them to set hard.

I used to make models of crocodiles. I wanted them to be perfect so I'd get into the enclosures to model a big croc and I'd watch him and I'd put all these little buttons all along the back, the teeth - get the teeth perfect; everything perfect. The crocs didn't care; they weren't worried. When the models set hard I'd take them to school on a board so they wouldn't break and show all the classes and the teachers.

We went to West End School about five miles away. Mostly, Mum would drive us in the back of the old Chev, all piled in. No such thing as seat belts. Oh! It was good! In the afternoon at about half past three, a rail motor would go up the line to Ingham. It would stop in front of the school and we'd get on and it'd drop us off in front of the zoo. All we had to do was walk across from the railway line. When we'd get back home, we'd have a bit of bread-and-sugar, or sometimes bread-and-condensed milk, if we were lucky. Then we'd have to go and work at the zoo. There was no such thing as playing, although we made a game of doing it. We had to cut grass for the kangaroos and the monkeys; feed all the animals; sweep out the cages; clean their water dishes out. That took a couple of hours. Then John had to go and get the cows for milking in the morning, and put their calves in the calf-pen. We had to chop the wood; make sure there was enough wood in the wood-box near the stove, for Grandma, and chips ready to start the fire in the morning. The chooks had to be fed, the eggs collected. Everything.

At the week-ends, we'd maybe go up to the Fryers' place at Tabletop on Herveys Range. Grandfather and Gulliver Fryer had been friends since the early days of Townsville.[5] Sometimes we'd go further up the Burdekin to the Cores at Blue Range.

One day we were just getting home from school off the rail-motor as Mum and Dad were leaving in the truck. They were taking old Hughie, one of the Aborigines Dad had working for him, away to hospital. One of the crocs had got him. Hughie was a Palm Islander, a traditional hunter and he'd got into one of the croc enclosures to tickle barramundi. It was a pretty large enclosure, part of a big swampy lagoon with about five or six crocs in it. Hughie used to lie in the shade of the bamboo with his arm in the water and the barra would come and he'd tickle them on the belly and then just slip his fingers through the gills and flip them out. But this day one of the crocs grabbed him by the arm. Dad saw what happened. He grabbed the reaping hook and jumped into the water to fight the croc off. He tried to get the croc's eyes with the hook and pull Hughie out. He must have got its eyes because the croc let go and backed off. It was lucky the crocs weren't hungry otherwise they would have fought over Hughie and pulled him to pieces. But they were all well fed every Sunday. There'd be bus-loads of people come out from town just to see the crocs being fed. Granddad would call, 'Come on! Come on!' and all the crocs would come swimming across and he would throw offal from the abattoir into their jaws.

But poor old Hughie! He had a broken arm and a broken leg. He died in hospital two days later, probably of shock. Well, he was in his sixties. The crocodile had slapped him with his tail and knocked him into the water. They always break your legs when they come at you, even if they are up on the bank behind you and you're down getting a billy of water, they will just run past you and slap you with their tail to get you into the water. They don't attack you with their jaws. They swipe you with their tail to break your legs and then they come back and get you.

But Dad had to face a criminal charge of manslaughter for putting a Ward of the State in a dangerous situation, because Hughie had a bag and the reaping hook in there, as if Dad

[5] See; Marion Houldsworth, *Red Dust Rising*; CQU Press, for an account of the Fryer family of Tabletop station on Herveys Range, also *Beyond Blue Range* in this volume.

had sent him in to cut grass. But he had just gone in there of his own accord to tickle for barra. So Dad was found not guilty and was actually recommended the highest award for bravery for jumping into the water and saving Hughie. He got the Silver Medal from Sir Leslie Laverack, the Governor of Queensland.

So, after growing up in a zoo like that, as a young fellow of about seventeen, I went down to Sydney and got a job at Taronga Park Zoo. And to push the art side of things I went to Art School at Sydney Technical College. Then I decided I wanted to do a bit of travelling.

***The Kimberley Drover*; oil on canvas, by Clifford Robinson**

I got a job as a ringer on Dunham River station in the Kimberleys. When you are flying into Wyndham from Darwin all you see is just a never-ending sea of mangroves and salt flats. You'd wonder where the cattle get a feed. Cambridge Gulf is unreal. You never get to see the Indian Ocean because there's so much Cambridge Gulf. It's sixty miles from Wyndham to the ocean.

The cattle on Dunham hadn't been mustered for twenty years; all shorthorns, unbranded. There were no fences between El Questro, Dunham, Bow River, all those places. It was 1969 and one time we took bulls into Wyndham from El Questro and called in at the Six Mile pub. I said to the bar-maid, 'What's the score on the bloke walking around up on the moon.' She told me, 'That was over a month ago! That's over and done with!'

The main camp on Dunham was where a truck could get into. We'd take everything off the back of the truck and set up camp. Places that were too rough or too isolated, it was a case of swags and packs.[6] There were about thirty men in each camp, thirty natives and thirty white-fellows. The blacks never mixed with us; they'd camp a hundred yards away. They'd come up to get their tucker. The cook would just dish it out and put it separately and later you'd see a hand just come in and take a plate.

We had portable yards and we'd rig a ramp and run all the cattle up into the trucks. Depending on size, we'd load twenty big bulls or forty smaller ones, a go. Then you'd pull these yards and carry them to the next camp. A few times the cattle rushed. We could have cattle in the yards to load next morning and during the night they'd rush and take the entire side panels out of the yards. There'd be cattle still galloping next day to get back to where they'd been brought in from and you'd have to get round them and get them back. The pilot

[6] Pack-horses

of the mustering-plane would radio, 'There are bullocks still travelling out here.' And that would be twelve hours later.

We mustered in different mobs; seven would go this way, eight would go that way; all going out in different directions. I always went out with the blackfellows because they knew the country and you could learn from them. A lot of the other fellows wouldn't go with them; prejudice and that. But I liked mustering with the blacks. You'd always camp on a nice spring; they knew the waters; knew the springs. You'd ride up these little gorges and come to these little oases; only the blackfellows knew they were in there. We'd be on water and the white-fellows'd be on a dry camp! The blacks have got that instinct to spend a lot of time looking for bush tucker. You'd learn the different kinds of bush tucker and how to track; jump off your horse and study the tracks. It makes the day interesting. They'd get a goanna, break their legs, so they can't run away if they get loose, and tie it across their saddle at the back. And at night after the mustering you'd see them galloping home with the tail sticking out. I saw a lot of country like that and I enjoyed being with them.

We kept any of the decent cows and the station bought good bulls to put over them. We branded the calves; all bronco branding. The bulls and bullocks went into Wyndham to the meat-works; a pretty big set-up. At that time the Yanks were big on bull meat for the hamburger trade.

In the sixties, Wyndham was a proper frontier town with big old boab trees down the street, hundreds of years old. You could imagine the camels tied up there and the Afghans and all the camel-trains bringing in the gold from Hall's Creek. The main wharf was at the Big Loop but the old original wharf was opposite the town pub. In the late afternoon that big hill behind the town, all red boulders, used to warm up and you'd feel the heat radiating off it. The Six Mile pub was just a little old wooden place, out of town across the mud-flats. We had some wild times there when we came into town of a weekend.

The main street of Wyndham. Very little has changed since Cliffie's time.

You get some characters in those mustering camps. My mate, Johnno, would bring them out from Wyndham and he'd dry them out and put them on the cooking. They'd be okay for the first week or so and then they get *munjeri;* sour. One time one of them was sending a stores' order back into the station and he'd ordered methylated spirits. Johnno said, 'What do you want metho for?' This old bloke reckons, 'It's for the Tilley. To light the Tilley.' Johno says, 'We haven't got a bloody Tilley!' The old bloke tells him,

'Well, bloody well get one! I get up at two o'clock. I need a Tilley-lamp!' Poor old bugger! His skin was cracking. They get that way they'll drink anything.

One time out mustering my horse threw me and I busted three ribs. We were spelling the cattle for a bit in the middle of a big stony creek and there were little water holes where they were watering. But there were a couple of these cranky old bulls that kept charging out all the time, so you'd have your saddle-bag full of rocks and when they came out at you, you'd try to get them square in the head with a rock and then spur your horse out of the way. We weren't using whips because whips would have woken a lot of wild cattle up that we were there and they'd have taken off and we'd have lost them. The buggers can hear a whip-crack miles away, and they just go.

So I'd got off my horse to fill my saddle-bag with these stones from the creek-bed, and this bull come out of the mob at me. The horse I was riding was called The Bastard and he lived up to his name. When I went to jump on him, he straight away rooted me off. The bull got that much of a fright, he just took off but I'm on the rocks underneath him and all these stones in my saddle-bag are coming down over me. And I couldn't breathe.

I just kept riding for the rest of the day. Next day I was shoeing a horse and I knew something was wrong. I went to the boss and he said, 'Righto! Go in to the Sister today with Tom. He's taking a load in with the Leyland.' So I did. And a great trip, too! We were towing two trailers of bulls, and going in through El Questro, through the sand in Buffalo Creek, the second trailer wouldn't tow. Old Tom does his top. There was no way I was going to sit doing nothing, so there's him, and me with broken ribs, trying to dig sand away from these wheels to get her going. In the end we had to let the cattle in the second trailer go and pull the first trailer through and leave the other behind.[7]

I went to the hospital to get an x-ray. There was just the Sister-in-Charge. No doctor. They took the x-ray and had a look but they said there was nothing they could do; ribs just have to mend. So I booked into the pub. The sister said to me, 'Don't go and get drunk and fall over!' That was the first thing I did.

In 1971, I decided to take off and head for London. My girlfriend was already over there working as a barmaid. I had to get a job, so the first thing I applied for was cooking. I'd always liked cooking. Mum taught me as a kid of ten or eleven. She'd be busy sometimes and I'd put the roast on for her. I could do puddings as well, the ordinary basic ones; bread-and-butter custard, rice pudding, syrup pudding.

So I went for a job at a pub called the Watling Arms. It was built by Sir Christopher Wren in 1666 as an ale house for his men when they were rebuilding St Paul's Cathedral after the Great Fire of London.[8] They asked for my résumé. I said, 'What's that? We don't have resumes where I come from.' I said 'But, I'll tell you what! I'll work one day for you

---

[7] The magnificent gorge at El Questro is now the highlight of the tour for visitors to the Kimberleys. Clifford said, in recording his story, '*In my day they had no idea that it was there.*' Such are the impregnable fastnesses of the ancient mountains of the region.

[8] The Olde Watling , a tiny, bow-fronted, black-and-white timbered pub in Watling Street, five minutes from St Paul's Cathedral, is still very much open for business and appears not to have changed in the centuries since it was built, and certainly not since Cliffie wowed American tourists and Londoners alike with his 'good Aussie tucker' in the early 'seventies.

for nothing and you can see for yourself.' He said, 'Righto! There's the kitchen!' Well, they had all these big steamers and it's pretty easy to cook for Pommies. They'll eat anything; ordinary tucker; tripe and onions, steak and kidney pudding, oxtail stew, corned beef brisket and boiled potatoes with white sauce, stew with dumplings. And all these Yanks would come and they would say to me, 'Say! Where did you learn to cook traditional British pub food like that?' I told them, 'I was brought up on that kind of tucker and I love it!'

In London my girl-friend and I used to walk along Hyde Park every Saturday and Sunday and you'd see all these artists with their work along the footpath. I said to her, 'If I did some drawings I'd go halves with you if you sold them.' So I started drawing again. She'd sell them for about three or four quid each.

Cliffie signing a portrait of Banjo Paterson as a gift for the author.

And one day I looked in a shop window and I saw an electric soldering-iron. I'd watched the blackfellows in the Kimberleys burn designs on their boomerangs and didgeridoos with a hot wire; an emu or a kangaroo or a crocodile. They'd have about six or seven pieces of eight-gauge wire in amongst the coals. They'd pull one bit out and burn a little bit of the design and it would go cold and they'd put that one back and get another bit. I thought, 'I wonder how those old blackfellows would go with an electric soldering iron?'

Then I wondered if you were burning wood designs if a soldering iron would keep hot. So I went and bought one for three or four quid and I got some off-cuts of ply, and did a sketch with a pencil and started to burn. And the iron does keep hot. That was the start of it. I got some books out of the library about Africa and did some action-shots of lions on the back of a giraffe or a zebra, pulling them down for a kill. They sold well. I could have sold a lot but I could only do about one or two a week. I had to wait a month before we got enough to sell, but I knew I was on to something.

I came back to Darwin in 1975 after the cyclone to help with the re-building and then had a couple of years barramundi fishing on the Daly. You could only get in to the spot where we were fishing during the Dry, so in-between, in the Wet, I was sitting in the caravan one day wanting to do something to fill in time and I went and bought another soldering iron. Because, with paints, you leave the tops off your tubes and they all go hard; or someone calls in to see you and you forget to wash your brushes and they dry solid. But with a soldering iron, if someone comes in you just switch it off; you waste nothing and you start again when you're ready.

So I kept doing the burning on to board, experimenting, trying to perfect the shading. I thought the drawings looked too flat and I wanted to get a more three dimensional look so I put a complete wood-stain over the lot, then started to bring out the highlights with sandpaper, rubbing back areas that needed lightening a bit. Then I experimented with different wood-stains to darken the grain in places and I'd bring out the fine highlights with a Stanley blade or a razor blade.

But I noticed that over time, the wood-stained ones darkened underneath. So now I've discovered acrylic colours and I'm experimenting with them. You can use a medium to make the acrylic transparent so you can still see the grain of the wood but the colour holds and they don't darken. I think its going to be the final technique.[9]

So, getting back to after the clean-up in Darwin, I decided to go fishing with a mate down the mouth of the Daly. His daughter was on Stapleton station so we had a permit to go through. Unreal, it was! Even in a four-wheel-drive you had to put chains on! No kidding! We'd bog ten or fifteen times. There were a lot of buffalo around and we'd look out for a big fellow to shoot on the way down to get some steaks for a good feed. We'd hammer through the hide to cut a hole in it and we'd reach in and cut the fillets out. They were good eating. We'd chop the horns off and leave them on an ant-bed for the ants to clean up and sell them the next trip up to Darwin. We'd get fifty dollars for a big set of horns. The old bloke we sold them to used to do them up with a grinder and mount them and sell them round the pubs.

When we got through we'd set up camp under the banyan trees. Those old banyans were all planted by the Macassars, hundreds of years ago, big old groves of them.[10] We'd go

[9] Cliff has done portraits of many noted Australians. He had not long previously finished a commissioned series for the North Queensland Amateur Race Club, of Aboriginal jockeys.

[10] For centuries fishermen from Makassar, in what is now Suluwesi, arrived on the northern coasts of Australia at the beginning of the wet season and stayed until about March to gather sea-cucumbers, also known as beche-de-mere, or sea-slugs, which when dried, were a prized delicacy in China. The Macassars exchanged tobacco, iron and glass with the Aborigines for turtle-shell and labour. Many Aboriginal groups still commemorate their visits in ceremonial dance and art. Some Macassan words remain in coastal dialects.

around to the mouth of the Daly and get big barramundi, come back, clean and fillet them and pack them on ice and stay until we filled our ice-boxes. Then we'd bury the nets under the banyan trees so pigs wouldn't chew them up and take the fish up to Darwin and sell it. A couple of days on the grog and back down fishing again.

In the camp we had that much crab and barra we couldn't eat it all. We'd just eat the wings and take the fillets back up to Darwin. The wings were beautiful. And big mud crabs! They'd swim through the nets and get tangled. We'd have to smash them out because we weren't fishing for crabs. We'd just take the nippers; take a bucketful back to camp and live on them.

During the day when we were waiting for the tides, we'd pull one net, and if it was ripped we'd tie one end to a mango tree and the other end to the back of the truck, and stretch it out along the beach. Then you'd walk along with a wooden needle and mend the holes. We'd do one a day. Kept you occupied when you were waiting for the tide. You get big tides up there; the tidal variation must have been thirty feet at times. The mouth of the Daly was fifteen miles wide. You could just see the cliffs at the other side. It's still three or four miles wide for a good way up river, with a pretty big tidal rise and fall.

We had an aluminium boat, v-bottomed, because we used to go out into the open sea a bit and it could get a bit rough. There was a big rocky point to get round into the mouth of the river. One time we were coming back loaded up with fish and nets and we had about an inch of freeboard. We were riding these waves and Chris was getting worried and he's looking up ahead around the point. He said, 'We might have to go back and drop some of the nets off in the mangrove.' I said, 'If it gets any rougher around this point you can bloody drop me off in the mangrove, too.'

Turtles used to come up on those beaches and lay their eggs. You'd see their tracks. The pigs would root the eggs up. I don't go for turtle eggs myself. They never seem to set properly. They seem half raw to me. But the Aborigines! God! They liked them that much, they'd eat them raw.

There were plenty of crocodiles round there. They'd be watching the nets all the time. Big crocs, too. We often got them in the nets but we always carried a .303. When they were tangled up in your nets, you'd see what could be a log among the corks. Most of the time they weren't drowned because they float on the top and when they hear the boat coming they go under and take your net under. Then you've got to pull the net up and the next thing you see is their head and tail lashing. It puts the wind up you! You're trying to get a shot in with the .303. Then you have to untangle the net and get the carcass out. We'd skin them and salt the skin down and bury it in the sand and leave it there.

When you're going up the river on the night tide, you'd have a car battery rigged up to spot for the nets and you could see all these red eyes – crocodiles' eyes – everywhere, looking at you. You wouldn't have wanted to fall in. Never seen crocodiles like it!

There were some big sharks there, too; one time, a big hammerhead. We had put the net out on mud flats where there was about four foot of water and we could see this black thing miles away, this big thing, up in the air. I thought it was a snag that had washed into the net. But it wasn't a snag, it was the dorsal fin of this big hammer head shark, drowned.

They drown quick in a net. A shark has to keep moving all the time to get oxygen through its gills. That shark would have been sixteen foot long. The fin was right out of the water. We had to cut the net in places to get it untangled. We cut the jaws out – a big set! – for the crabs to eat. Later on, when they'd dried out we took them back up to Darwin and got a couple of hundred dollars for them.

Every net was two hundred metres long, but you'd join four, five, maybe six, nets together in one line. You could have a net over a kilometre and a half, sometimes. You'd anchor them, a big mud anchor at each end with a buoy and a couple of buoys in the middle so that other boats could see. But we never saw another boat the whole time we were there. If 'Fishies' – fishing inspectors – came and you didn't have your buoys at each end and buoys in the middle, well, you're in trouble. But the year and a half we were there – in the Dry, the only time you could get down there – we never saw one fisheries inspector.

You ran the nets parallel to the beach, about a mile off and they'd go out with the tide. As well as barra, you'd get salmon, big grunter and bream. We had about four big ice-boxes on the back of the truck and one was for 'mixed estuary fillets'. You didn't get as much for them as for barra but you'd still get a decent price so you wouldn't waste them.

And of course we knew we could have got into difficulties down there on our own like that with only just the two of us there. No wireless or mobile phones or anything. We more or less agreed; if something happened to either of us, he'd have to shoot me or I'd have to shoot him. That's the way it was. We never carried a life-jacket in the boat. You just took your chances. We didn't even think about the risk. You don't when you're young. I was in my late twenties.

At that age you take some chances. One night we'd been working like hell with a big run of fish and we were buggered. As soon as you got back to camp you'd have to fillet the lot them. You had miners' lamps so you could see what you're doing, working late. There were millions of insects. You're breathing through your teeth. Then you'd just grab a cup of coffee and kip down by the fire.

This time we missed the tide and we'd had to leave the boat right out and drag all these bags of fish across the mud flats into where the little fresh water creek ran out at the camp. Oh! It's a lot of work to drag them bags in, fillet the catch and stash it away in the ice-boxes. And here's the boat, anchored way out across the mud. Chris said, 'One of us had better keep awake and walk that boat back in or we'll miss the next tide.' I said, 'Yeah. You grab some sleep and I'll stay up.' But I went to sleep too. I thought I wouldn't, but I did.

The next thing I woke up, and I shone the spotlight out to sea. The boat was way out, bobbing up and down. I said, 'Oh! Shit!' and woke Chris up. He said, 'We've missed the bloody tide!' I said, 'I'll swim out and get it.' He said, 'Christ! Don't be stupid! There's guts and everything thrown in out there! Sharks and crocs will be feeding and hanging around for more.' I said, 'If I don't go out and get it we'll miss the next tide. All the fish in the nets will rot. We'll lose the lot.' The waters are warm up there.

So I got a knife on my belt and I put another one on my arm. Two knives in case I lost one. I said to Chris, 'Just keep the spot-light on that boat so I can see where I'm heading. I don't want to land up in bloody Africa!' I waded out up to my armpits for a while and then started swimming. Every minute I expected to be grabbed by a croc. Wasn't I happy when I got to that boat! But that's the kind of risks you take.

Anyhow! I haven't ended up with a million in the bank, but I still reckon I'm a millionaire! If you've got a couple of good mates and you've got your health and your family is healthy, to me that's what being a millionaire is about. Good health and good friends! What more can you want! Everything else can take care of itself.

4

Elaine Cluff

ॐ ॐ ॐ

Introduction

Mrs Laura Edgar with her mother's Memoirs.

The material for this document is extracted from a typed manuscript offered to me by Mrs Laura Edgar of Charters Towers, which had been written by her late mother, Mrs Elaine Cluff. Mrs Cluff had spent her childhood as the daughter of the manager of Cambridge Downs in the early 1900s and remembered the loaded wool wagons straining to cross the Saxby River, on one occasion becoming bogged in the sandy bed and the horse-team having to be replaced by bullocks to get it across.

After finishing her schooling she trained as a nurse in Sydney. She and her husband Frank were married in Townsville and honeymooned on Magnetic Island before beginning the long train journey to their future home on Tralee, an undeveloped block south-west of Winton.

She sketches evocative pictures of her new life; the pleasures of her first little home, 'two front rooms and a kitchen', the bough-shed at the back with 'a bench for wash tubs', the 'beautiful water in the creek' carried up to the house in 'two buckets' and the pleasurable once-weekly ride to neighbouring Franklin for 'supplies and mail'. The lack of fresh food, the loneliness, the difficult living conditions are never complained of but are cheerfully recalled as part of the early years of a successful marriage.

Then came the day of heart-stopping anxiety. Three-year old Tom was missing; lost and alone in the bush. Friends and neighbours rally; one great-hearted neighbour driving a mob of horses forty miles, knowing they 'would be wanted for the search'. Some readers may recall the 1960s song 'Little Boy Lost' with its plaintive refrain, 'Where's my Daddy? Where's my Daddy? cried the Little Boy Lost' as they share the mounting anxiety of the three day search. Certainly all of us can identify with Elaine Cluff's final words that, sixty years later, she 'still gets upset if she hears of a child lost in the bush.'

The Little Lost Boy

Elaine Cluff

'Mummy! Didn't I find a lot of people in the bush!'

My mother came as a bride to the big wild country of Queensland in 1907-8. She was from Hobart so it must have seemed the end of the earth to her. She had no experience of life on the land. They travelled to Townsville by boat, then west to the township of Richmond by train and buggy, then forty miles out to Cambridge Downs, a sheep property where Dad was the Manager.

After I finished my schooling I went nursing and then did my midwifery training at the Royal Hospital for Women at Paddington in Sydney. Then just after Easter in 1934 my husband, Frank Cluff, and I were married in the Church of England at West End in Townsville. It was a very quiet turn-out; after photos at City Studios we had drinks and a spread at home. Then we had a few days' honeymoon at Magnetic Island and at the Hermit Park Hotel so that we could visit the shops to buy a Beacon Light stove for our future bush home, a carbide lamp and a big basin for letting bread rise in. We arranged for kitchen and dining-room furniture to be railed from Carfoots' Furniture Store to Winton. We also bought a poley saddle and a bridle for me. Frank thought that after my years as a town girl in Sydney he had to look after me. Frank's father and his brothers were building our future little home for us at Tralee, nine miles from their place, Franklin, one hundred and twenty miles west of Winton.

Our trip to Winton from Townsville was by steam train, a slow journey of three hundred and sixty-four miles. The train was never crowded with passengers so you could stretch out on one of the long seats for a sleep at night with no disturbances, though Hughenden at about two in the morning was a noisy station where the railway employees called out to each other while unloading the goods from the coast. Usually a cup of tea and scones could be got at small sidings and when Corfield, forty miles from Winton, was reached, you sat down to a knife and fork dinner with sweets to follow, at the hotel, a big sprawling building with wide verandas.

On arriving at Winton we discovered one of the Cluffs had left their car in town for us to drive the hundred and twenty miles to Franklin. There was a dirt road all the way and lots of stoney gullies. Getting near the Diamantina crossing we were met by Mr and Mrs East of Cambeela who Frank had done a lot of fencing for, at £3 or £4 pounds a week, which was considered fair pay.

At Franklin a meal was ready for us, prepared by Frank's Mum, and plenty of conversation took place. We waited several weeks at Franklin for our house at Tralee, nine miles away, to be finished. The windows and steps still had to be done. We were also expecting our stove and my glory-box with all my treasures of linen to arrive with the mailman. One day the Easts arrived with it all. The mailman had left it beside the road so it was very good of the Easts to bring it on or my linen might have been ruined.

In the evenings I played 'Chopsticks' on the piano with my young sister-in-law, Pat. Frank had put a lot of time into breaking in a pony, Tom Thumb, for me to ride. His mother was a station mare and his sire a brumby. He was nice to ride and very quiet.

At last we got settled in our own home, Tralee, or Mount Gideon, as the Lands Department called it. Our home consisted of two front rooms and the kitchen, which was full sized, also a wide front verandah. The bush shed at the back of the kitchen was where, later, our car was kept and there was also a bench for wash-tubs. Our water supply was from a Brighton Down's bore. Half the water used to run five miles down a creek to us. It was beautiful water except in drought time when Brighton cattle would mess it up. In the early days we used to carry water in two buckets from this creek. I was able to ride Tom Thumb weekly to Franklin with my husband to get mail and supplies. The trip was usually an overnight stay.

It wasn't very long till a baby was on the way, so taking a trip to Winton, we bought an old Model T Ford for twenty pounds. It had belonged to one of the Markwells who owned Gallipoli Station. Jacky Stamp drove it to Franklin for us and Frank gave him his old motorbike for his trouble. So then we could go to Franklin in style!

Frank's Father got a second-hand Radiola and we heard the Olympic Games described from Berlin. This wasn't long before the war broke out. I'll never forget the spectacular description of the various competitors from different countries and also of the crowds and the 'Hail Hitler' salutes frequently mentioned. You could see Germany was working up to something.

Our horse-paddock had to be completed so that our steeds wouldn't clear off in the 24,000 acre property. The old Model T would bounce through the scrub with eight or nine big gidyea fencing posts on the back. I would go out bush with Frank and I learned to cook in a camp-oven. This was my first try at camp-oven cooking and we seemed to have enough to eat! While Frank was away cutting posts, by axe of course, I would go for a walk along the creek. One day I thought I'd found a cat, hearing a lot of meows close by, but I discovered it was a bird mimic; a bower bird. Another day there was a big fat porcupine waddling along. This place where we camped was a wild spot; one could have easily become lost unless familiar with the surrounding land marks such as a hill or particular trees or creeks. Frank was very good in the bush and loved it and all the little living things.

He built a yard at Gum Creek and used to gather the sheep up from the bore drain and put them in the yard and he would be at Franklin with them about eleven o'clock the next morning all ready for shearing. He used to do all the mustering for shearing with his dog.

Then while Frank was away on a droving trip I waited in Winton for my baby to be born. Tom was breech birth and afterwards I developed cracked nipples, a terrible condition, but a friend from my nursing days, Sister Moyse, carted me off to her place and looked after me. When Frank got back from his droving trip he came in and collected me and we took Tom down to Franklin to show him off. Frank and his brothers, who were all keen cricketers, made a great fuss of Baby Tom with his little cricket cap on.

When a cricket match was on, we would go from Tralee to Sandhills, Lindsays' property, where we all camped out. You crossed through part of Verdun and Brighton to get to Sandhills. Frank's Mum would cook plates of jam tarts in the camp oven but no sooner would one lot be out than it would be eaten up.

Once we had some rain! Food was running out but the big creek was crossed after the boys worked on it. The Cluff boys were good at making such crossings. As it was dark we made camp, first having a cup of tea made with muddy creek water boiled in a camp oven! There was just a small piece of damper for each of us. When we got to our place next morning I made puftaloons[1] and we ate them with golden syrup and weren't they tasty! The cup of tea without the earlier mud was appreciated.

Little Tom and Laura Cluff playing outside the Tralee homestead

Another time we went to Diamantina Lakes for a cricket match. The McCullochs were the hosts. We camped along the road and dingoes were howling most of the night because it was cattle country. Mr and Mrs Donnellan from Davenport Downs,[2] and the Milsons from Springvale were there. The men had a good day's cricket and the women and children enjoyed one another's company. By now I was expecting another baby. This time it was a little girl, Laura, born at my friend, Sister Moyes, now Mrs Gabbard's, nursing home in Winton.

So now we were settled in our little home, nine miles from Franklin, with our little son and daughter and time marched on. By this time we were on our fourth second-hand car, a Chev IV. Earlier we'd had a Rugby and an Essex. On Thursday mornings we would dress up and take our weekly trip to Franklin for mail and supplies, having most of the day there.

Occasionally we would visit neighbours. A trip to Brighton Downs was a special occasion for Christmas Day because Santa was visiting there. This was a great excitement for the children of the surrounding homesteads as most of them had never seen Santa Claus. In earlier years Brighton Downs homestead had been a collection of iron buildings

---

[1] Puftaloons; Also known as Fried Scones; cooked till golden brown in deep hot fat and eaten with golden syrup. Can also have shredded corned-beef added into mixture, in which case eaten with tomato sauce.

[2] See '*Red Sandhill Country*', From the *Gulf to God Knows Where, Volume One,* for Ethel Donnellan's account of life on Davenport Downs

shimmering in the sun on a stony ridge, but in the Lukes' day it had become a real oasis, with lovely shrubs and flowers and a vegetable garden. Mr and Mrs Luke made us all very welcome for the overnight stay.

At Tralee, Frank was doing the work of three men. To keep the pot boiling until our wool-clip was sold, he was dogging for a group of properties and also shooting kangaroos for their skins. These had to be pegged out with a few inches of wire for nails into the earth and carefully protected until they were dry and later wrapped in hessian. They were then sold for you by a Winton stock agent.

Frank was also an excellent whip-plaiter. Stockmen would write and beg him to make one for them. He used a suitable length of harness leather, then plaited over it with strips of kangaroo hide tanned and weighted with bits of tin foil or lead, usually the lining of a tea-chest. It was then plaited over again with a narrower lace, usually an eight strand plait and completed with a cotton cracker. It was said that if a woman's wedding ring would travel the length of the whip from one end to the other it was a good one. Frank used to get three pounds for a whip and five pounds if attached to a handle. This extra money was a great help as we were getting no money until the first wool cheque came.

By now we had fowls and also a few goats who used to come home every evening, so our living had improved. I had never really got used to the diet of continual corned beef, so as our goat herd grew, one would be butchered and I'd make roasts and stews. At the creek crossing where the bore water flowed over the road Frank made a garden so we had nice vegetables. All had to be watered using buckets.

By now a third baby was due. It was the rainy season and Frank was worried about getting bogged after some rain we'd had, so we set off for Winton via Middleton. At Middleton, Mr Long rushed out of the hotel and said, 'I advise you not to stop! Two children with polio have been taken away today from here by the Flying Doctor!' Then when we got to Cadel Creek the water was rushing over the road. But Mr Banning and his sons from Woodstock came and helped Frank to cover the engine and then pushed us over the stony bottom through the rushing water and we were able to continue on our way. Once we got to Winton, Frank had to go home again to go droving, and about a month later my baby was born, a little girl who we called Margaret. After a few days Frank came in and collected us.

Margaret did well until she was nine months old. Then she became sick and I thought, 'Pneumonia!' Frank's people drove over to Old Cork station and were able to connect to Winton to get the Flying Doctor from Cloncurry[3]. Dr. Alberry and his pilot landed on the claypan a few yards from the house. Frank had marked out the ground with old tins, and I had sheets flapping on the line so he could see which way the wind was. I had to go with the baby and leave Frank and his mother to care for Tom and Laura. This was November and I can still see the horrified look on the sister's face at the hospital when I produced my bottle of muddy boiled water for Margaret to have a drink. She hurriedly boiled some Cloncurry water and stood it on ice to cool it quickly. The little thing's temperature was 106 degrees

[3] The first flight of the Aerial Medical Service, initated by Presbyterian Australian Inland Mission minister, the Reverend John Flynn, and later to become the Royal Flying Doctor Service, was from Cloncurry in 1928.

when we arrived and they put her in a baby bath with a block of ice. No antibiotics in those days! She mostly had Grey's Powders. I stayed at the hospital with her and the doctor used to visit her a couple of times a night, she was so very ill. At last she began to improve and the nurses had her thoroughly spoilt. Matron even gave her a doll.

Actually there were very few toys at Tralee. Our kids mostly played with what we had; chickens, kittens, pups and goats. They also had a pet baby emu which used to peck at the nail tops in the wooden floor boards and another time they had a baby eaglehawk. They frequently had joey kangaroos. Once Frank's Dad had to go to Townsville to see Dr Halberstater and when he came back he brought some little bottles of perfume for the children to play with. They mostly used it to make their pets 'smell nice', and even put the tiny bottles in a 'lady-roo's' pouch.

When Margaret was approximately fifteen months old, we had a nasty experience. Frank used start off in the mornings about 7.00 a.m. after milking the cow and getting his horse from up the horse paddock. Taking his lunch, a lot of times he would be riding all day and get home shortly after dark. He had said to me a couple of times, 'I'm leaving a patch of dry bulrushes in the creek. If you ever want me home, light them. I'll see the smoke and come home as quickly as possible.' But being distressed when I should have done this, it just didn't come to my mind.

One June morning young Tom, then aged three, nearly four, and Laura went out in front of the house to play. Laura had her little dog which we called Dainty, and Tom had a little cart which Frank had made for him out of a box. I told them we would go to the garden after I'd washed up and dressed the baby.

When I looked out I could see Laura running with her dog but I couldn't see Tom. I thought he must have gone along the road to the garden. There was this bank they used to jump down to play in the sand. But when I got to the garden with the two girls there was no sign of Tom.

I took the two girls in the pram along the road a little bit further and I saw where both the children had been pulling around an old bullock's skull and all the white bullock bones. There was all bush around and I couldn't see which way Tom might have gone. I hurried back to the house and put the baby in her cot for a sleep. Then I took Laura by the hand and walked along the edge of the creek. Then I found some tracks where he had dragged his little cart across, so I tied a piece of rag on the tree near them.

We walked up onto the highest ridge but could see no sign of him. By this time Laura was tired and starting to play up and wouldn't walk. I carried her back to the house, and locking both the girls in the house, I went for the pony from the horse paddock. First I left a note in the kitchen and another one tied on the bar of the gate at the crossing to my brother-in-law Lindsay's place. Later he said he came along with horses and missed both notes but heard me calling out when he was opening the gate. He quickly began riding in wide circles to search for Tom, calling out his name. He met Frank coming home to learn of the news of his little son lost in the bush.

Shortly Frank's father and mother and my brother-in-law Pat arrived on their way to Sandhills. When it got dark I said, 'If Tom is anywhere around he may go to a fire.' So that night everyone camped at various points keeping fires going. Later we decided that though it was very cold he would probably be so worn out that he would have gone to sleep and wouldn't see the fires. In the morning Frank's father drove to Old Cork Station and managed to notify the police in Winton on the phone. The Police in Winton put word out from 4LG Radio Station at Longreach. Soon people were arriving from everywhere to help; Ted Brown and his wife who used live at a camp not far from us, and later that day, old Mr Charlie Moore from Mundurin station to the north of us with a mob of horses to help. It was a big ride for this aged man, thirty to forty miles. He said we would need the horses for the search.

People from around Middleton were early on the scene. The two old black men who were working for Moores, old Paddy and Tom, did well with tracking. They followed where Tom had tied a piece of carburetor pipe threaded on a strip of kangaroo-hide lace on his cart. This dragging along behind it turned over stones and marked the ground. Tom was wearing sandshoes that hardly left any tracks. The wheels of his cart had rubber tyres so they hadn't left any clear markings, especially as the ground had hardened after several earlier falls of rain.

Laurie Luke[4], the manager of Brighton Downs, arrived in the pouring rain. He had Johnnie Williams with him. They had cattle on mustering camp but when they heard the news on the wireless they had just let all slide and come at once. An Inland Mission man from Mt Isa came with three or four others, as well as school teachers from Boulia and Kynuna. People came from everywhere to help. But the Winton Police couldn't get through to us, only having a motorbike and side-car in those days, because the Diamantina River was up; no bridges then.

Thursday was the day to dress up and drive to Frankin for ' mail and supplies'.

On the third day of the search, the Sunday, three men on horses went ahead of the trackers and on the top of a ridge they came upon Tom sitting in his little cart which was full of manure. 'Hello' he says. It was Friday morning when he went missing and Sunday afternoon when he was found. Bill Clarke, the drover, brought him home in his vehicle, all the men riding behind. Little Tom stood up well to his ordeal. He still had his little tweed hat on, but only one sandshoe. I think the other might have fallen off during the excitement of getting him to the car to get him home. Strangely enough it was the only

[4] See *Where Inland Rivers Flow* in Volume One for accounts of Laurie Luke as a Prisoner of War on the Burma Railway and brumby shooting on Marion Downs.

morning the children had ever gone out to play without their jackets on.

Tom said he had slept in the green grass and the sand but that must have been the second night. The weather was very cold and all he had on was a cotton vest and home made shirt and pants of cotton caesarene. How the poor little fellow slept at all I don't know. He was only three years old, not quite four. This didn't stop him from boasting the next day that he'd almost hit a kangaroo on the nose with a stick.

Because it was so cold I had been keeping a large tin of hot water on the stove, so as soon as he was bought in I was able to put him in a hot bath. In spite of this it took a good while before he warmed up properly. I had him in a cot with blankets and bottles filled with hot water around him. He said 'What are you putting me to bed for? It's not dark yet!' No doubt he wanted to see what was going on out in the kitchen with so many people around. He said, 'Mummy, didn't I find a lot of people in the bush!' Tom always remembered that the school teacher from Kynuna gave him a big slab of chocolate. That was a rare treat, never ever seen at Tralee!

Tom had actually crossed the road going to Franklin but there were lots of sheep tracks, so his didn't show up. We had a hoppy-legged sheep dog at the time which was almost always with Tom. Unfortunately the day Tom became lost Frank had taken the dog out round his dingo traps to try to entice dingo bitches. If the dog had been with Tom he would have shepherded him home because they were great mates.

By this time rain had set in and people were in a hurry to get home before the creeks rose. Frank's dad had to go to Franklin to do what he could to let people have enough petrol to get them back. For years afterwards people from all over the place would come up to me and say, 'We were all packed ready to leave to come and help and then news came over 4LG that he had been found.'

Mr C. Moore wrote a nice article to the Winton Herald thanking everyone who had helped in the search on our behalf. Thank goodness, as I was trying to compose something to post in on the mail myself. After this experience I wouldn't ever allow the children to wear sandshoes again. It had to be strong leather shoes or bare feet. And I used to tell them, 'If ever you are where you can't see the house, break down bushes and build a cubby house and camp there until we come and find you, and if you walk around in the bush, use a stick like a toy hobby-horse to leave a mark where you go.'

And I always think that to make a big smoke or fire, would give a lost person something to make for. Had I lit the bulrushes, as Frank had said, little Tom may have seen the smoke column and saved a lot of worry. But at the time I was so worried out of my mind that I forgot. To this day I still get upset if I hear of a child, or anyone, being lost in the bush.

5

Dale Appleton

ॐ ॐ ॐ

Introduction

It would be hard to find a more welcoming, unassuming couple than Dale and Kris Appleton, though Dale has, by hard work and shrewd judgment, made himself a millionaire many times over. Starting off as a country boy in small-town Clermont, Dale was determined to break out of the working-class struggle of his parents' generation. He set himself certain goals; to learn to work in with people; to treat every man with respect; to listen to advice from older more experienced men; and never to drink. He now has top-grade cattle properties across Central Queensland, recently selling Strathmore in the Gulf, to buy Craven, near Alpha.

Dale and his wife Kris work as a team. Every statement Dale made during the interview began with 'We' not 'I'. It was his tribute to the quiet lady who agrees that she has always been the book-keeper of the partnership. Dale is the first to admit that he can't handle a computer. Kris laughingly recalls the time when going down to Brisbane to have her babies was her 'holiday' for the year.

Although this interview took place in their luxury unit overlooking the sparkling waters of Townsville's Cleveland Bay, Dale says, 'Kris and I like to see the ocean for a few days now and then, but if you're used to those arid areas, well, that's what suits you best. You're really only happy when you get back there. Clermont's our town. It suits us.' For this reason, Bulliwallah, Dale and Kris's first significant step on the property ladder in the 1980s, will always be home. As he spoke, Dale touched the downy-soft head of Lucy, his little grand-daughter, who had been toddling happily around us as we spoke; 'This is what makes it all worthwhile' he said softly.

ॐ ॐ ॐ

Never Say You Can't Do It

Dale Appleton - Grazier

'Basically, it comes down to common sense and decency'

My family, the Appletons, have been living around the Clermont area for about five generations. I think my grandfather's father was a barber in Clermont. Originally they were Italians. The name could have been Appeltonio, or something like that. The next generation, Tony Appleton, built up a stock and station agency Then he bought a number of properties; Kilcool, Trebarney, Tango and Laglan - one of the pick properties in the Clermont district. But, over the years, due to circumstances, they were all sold.

That's something that I've always been mindful of. You can have it; but you can also lose it.

I grew up at Native Bee, about twenty kilometres from Clermont, with my Mother, Father, sister Cynthia and brother Vic. I was the youngest in the family. My father used to grow vegetables and sell them round the pubs in town. He used to run the sale-yards; and do day work, mainly speying, some years up to 21,000 head.

I used to sneak into the rodeos, or whatever big 'Do's' might be on around the town, and I'd hunt round and collect bottles to get money. Any bottles I spotted I'd cash them in at the catering service just to get a couple of pennies each for them to have some money in my pocket. Or, when I was a bit older, and in the pony club, I'd be riding a clapped out bloody old horse, so hard-mouthed I wouldn't be able to turn it. And there'd be my friends, they'd be riding little ponies that would have been brought up especially from Brisbane for them. I used to I'd think, 'Why can't we have things like them?' So that gave me the ambition to try and achieve something in my life. I was determined to work my way up the ladder.

I always remember one old fellow, Bluey Jensen; he came up to me one day and he said, 'Listen, Young Fellow. It's in you so-and-so Appletons to drink, so you just be careful!' I never forgot that. And as a matter of fact, I haven't had a drink since 1985.

When Kris and I got married, we had a house just outside Clermont, with no lights and no water and a backyard copper. Kris was about seventeen and I was about twenty. I had to borrow money to get married and this is where the hardship sort've hit. Having to borrow money! Eventually we bought a caravan, and lived at Native Bee. All the time I was doing this, I was determined to achieve.

I had an uncle, Charlie Tindale; he was a cattle buyer for Lakes Creek. And as a cattle buyer he could get all the cheap ones. He used to put them in this little paddock, just a few miles out of Clermont. And as a young fellow I used to trot down there on a horse and give him a bit of a hand when he was spraying them. And then trot home again. And doing this, we got a bit of a relationship going. And one day he said to me, 'How would you like to buy this paddock?'

I said to him, 'How much would you want for it?' He said, 'I reckon $13,000.' I said, 'Well, Uncle Charlie, I'd like to but all I've got is $3,000. I had to borrow money to get married.' He said, 'Well, I'll tell you what I'll do. I'll take your $3,000 and we'll leave the rest. Four years. Five percent interest. Two and a half thousand a year plus five percent interest.' And I thought to myself 'I've got nothing to lose here.' So we did the deal.

Many years later when our son Loid and his wife Zabby had their two little daughters, they called them Charlize – Charlie for short – and Izabelle. A bit later, when we got talking about 'Uncle Charlie and Aunty Isabelle', the connection with the Tindales in the naming of our grandchildren struck to us.

But that country of Uncle Charlie's was all rosewood and ironbark and it was freehold. You could get a royalty out of the ironbark, selling it to the Blackwater mines. What you get is an ironbark timber about twenty foot long and a foot through and they run a band-saw through it and they call it a 'half-crown', and it goes into the underground mines. And then they wanted what they call a 'prop'; it's about six inches round and about twelve foot high. Contractors would come in and cut the timber out. They might have a contract to supply *x* amount of timber, and he'd get sub-contractors to come and cut. So we collected the royalties. Trevor Maquire had a contract to supply timber and I cut posts on the weekends to make extra money.

Then we bought a run-down house in Clermont for $17,000. We had two boys by this time. And all the time I was thinking; 'I'm going to build a decent house for Kris and the kids as soon as I get the opportunity!' So, many years later, when the opportunity came, we built quite a nice home at Bulliwallah.

I was on day-wages at the time. Dad was running the sale-yards and I used to work for him. At the time I didn't think much of it as a job, but working at the sale yards turned out to be very valuable experience. Over the years I met lots of agents and graziers and cattle-buyers and you'd meet with all the old drovers. They used to have to take delivery of a mob at a certain time and deliver at a certain time and yet still have the weight on the cattle. And all the time I was meeting these old fellows and listening to them, I was picking up a lot of knowledge about stock without realizing it.

So we got the money we owed to Uncle Charlie paid off, and now I could see that I could double my money, because I could get twenty-six thousand for the block if I sold it. But while Uncle Charlie was still alive, I didn't have the heart to sell it because he had been good to me. But as soon as he passed away – poor old fellow; he got cancer – we sold the paddock and we got $26,000 for it.

That was about the time of the beef slump; about 1974. So we bought cows and calves for nothing much. And there was a property called Boolaroo, north of Clermont. The people who owned it wanted to lease it for twelve months so we shifted out there. Then they wanted to put it on the market and they wanted $250,000 for it. So we sold the house in town and with the money from Uncle Charlie's block and the house, that was $50,000. We could borrow $200,000 from the bank. And back in those days that was a lot of money to borrow, in comparison to today. My Mother and Father went guarantor for us, which was a big risk to them as well. So we bought Boolaroo. I would go to the cattle sales in Clermont and they would say to me, 'You paid too much for it. You're mad. You'll lose on it!' It used to worry me because they were older men and I respected that. That's the way I was brought up. I was always told to respect my elders and no matter what they say, to take notice. And I still do.

After they told me that, I thought to myself, 'Well, there's not much I can do about it. Maybe I shouldn't have bought it.' And things were pretty tight. We had a lighting plant, but sometimes we wouldn't ask the fuel truck to come out. We'd just buy a forty-four gallon drum of fuel at a time, so we didn't have to pay out a bulk amount of money on it. And I was doing day-work still. It was seventy kilometres into town and a fair bit of black-soil road. Or I'd go and do mustering for the neighbours.

There was one old chap, Arthur Lee. We got on well together. He was a farmer and he had some cattle country. We used to run about three hundred head of cattle on his block that he called Pernoise, and we used to fix his fences up, or give him a killer. Just a good relationship that we had going. If ever we got stuck he'd give us a bit of a hand with the work. I knew that if I wanted to get somewhere I had to build up a relationship with people. If you help them, people will give you a hand back.

There was an old homestead on Boolaroo, but it had been let go. An old-style place, set low – if you had to go underneath it, it was a drama, but nice timber floors covered with old lino. The waters were all bores. And two dams. Fifteen thousand acres.

But then the main thing that came out of Boolaroo was that there was a railway line being built from Blair Athol to Goonyella; to the coal-mines which came straight through us. We got compensation out of that of about a hundred thousand dollars; sixty thousand dollars for the loss of land and for inconvenience; forty thousand for common-fill, a bluemetal, and since it had rained, and had filled the excavation they had dug, they also bought the water. When the Railway started the compensation talks, we were asked 'What do you want for your land?' One of the landholders affected by the railway line got a bit too greedy. He said a huge amount of money. He could have got a hundred thousand dollars but what happened was that they went and resumed him and he only got the market value of the land.

So it was a win-win all the time. See, when these people come to you, if you don't want anything to do with them, well, you'll get less out of it. You have to think to yourself, if it's going to happen it's going to happen, so you might as well work in with them. And then Theiss Bros put up a fence that had the wrong alignment. So we pulled it out and put it in the right place and Theiss paid us. So, the railway line went through, and we got money out of it.

Once the railway was operating, grain-silos were built just three kilometres down the road from us. That immediately put value on the property. So with the money we got from the railway we decided to pull all the trees on the property; all chain-pulling, done by contractors. Three-thousand acres of cleared land was put aside for farming, and we put on two share-farmers, Errol Vandersee, and Kris's father, Ted Williams. They grew mostly sorghum, and sun-flowers for cooking-oil, and wheat. The sorghum was for the local market, but the wheat went overseas. All the time, the asset-value of the place was going up.

By then we'd been there four years and we felt we wanted to get into some cattle country. So we put the property on the market. In the meantime we bought a property called Kilcool, between Alpha and Emerald, at Bogantungan; fairly rangey sort of country, but it wouldn't have mattered where it was, we were just keen to get back into cattle. We paid $550,000, off the estate of the Appletons. I was a half-share, my brother Vic, was three-eighths, and my father was an eighth.

I'd put Boolaroo in the hands of an agent, Lloyd Hansen, at Elders, in Clermont. There was a phone-call this night, at Kilcool, and Lloyd said, 'I've got some people from Kurindi, in New South Wales, and they want to have a look at Boolaroo!' I had a caretaker there that could show them around. So they went out, and that evening there was a phone-call to say they wanted to put an option to purchase on it. So this place we had bought for $250,000, we put $1,500,000 on it. There were a lot of negotiations, but we ended up selling that place for one-point two five million. In those days there was no tax on that so we picked up one million. So from my first purchase from Uncle Charlie, we went from $13,000 to $26,000, and then from there on to Boolaroo, and then, after Boolaroo sold, I had a million dollars in the bank. For nineteen days!

But then Bulliwallah was on the market for $875,000, so we signed up for it. But at the stage we signed for it, the sale hadn't gone through on Boolaroo. And I kept thinking, 'I hope to hell we're going to get the money!' But there were a couple of weeks in it, so it worked out OK.

Bulliwallah, and Bingeringo adjoining it, were in two leases; 100,000 acres each block, and I basically knew that property, because getting back to my old friend Bluey Jensen; back in 1969, there was a very bad drought; and Dad and his friend, Feeny Finger, took up country of Bluey Jensen's, Hyde Park, which is inferior country with poison bush on it. And we used to have to dig the poison out and put up fences by way of agistment. So in those days I had about six weeks on the grubbing. You can't cut heartleaf. You've got to dig it out. We camped in a tent on the banks of Tomahawk Creek. That's another thing that probably did me good. And you had to walk the cattle up to Hyde Park. Bully Creek had all sand in it and there was no yard, so we had to build a yard for these old skinny cows. And to get there we'd have to go through the Bulliwallah bullock-paddock, and there were all these fat bullocks, and Dad with these skinny old cows!

So that's what I say to these young fellows; don't say you can't do it! There I was, in 1969, digging heartleaf poison on the banks of Tomahawk Creek. And I go back there in the 1980's and I've bought the place! But I could still remember those three thousand bucks I started off with.

And old Bluey Jensen, we were quite friendly with him. In fact our youngest son, Loid, is named after him. He was a good old man, but he lived rough. He lived on dried meat. If you went to his place he'd make a damper, but there was never any butter. He didn't bath a lot, old Bluey. But once you got him in the bath you couldn't get him out. He'd come over to our place and he'd say, 'I'll have a bath!' He got that way he enjoyed it. He'd come for a few days and stay a fortnight.

We put in the work at Bulliwallah on development. We pulled about eighty five thousand acres of country, mainly gidyea and blackwood and seeded it. A lot of the country down there - at first you could only pull gidyea and blackwood - then when the tree-pulling issues came in they would only let you pull box and ironbark. A lot of that country, the box country – that sandy, loamy country – has turned out to be very good buffel country too. We were probably fortunate because you could put out half a pound to a kilo over an acre and once you can get it established, over a period of years it just looks after itself and spreads. One of the main things, is if you can spell it, over a year or two.

Bulliwallah homestead today.

But now the seasons are getting drier. Waterholes that used to last, they're not lasting now, so you've got to dig them out. And we'll have to put more dams in. And the other day at Mt. Hope, we were putting a bore in and where the water-table used to be at eighty-foot, now you've got to go another fifty foot. The water-table seems to be dropping. With every place I've had I'm always doing more water. And right through the system they had pump-jacks[1]. Bulliwallah had copper tanks and copper pipes. Now we've put in poly tanks. With pump-jacks you've got to have a man on them all the time; or two men, to check that they're running alright and the fuel hasn't cut out. Now we have a counter-balance in the tank, the float cuts in and automatically switches the water off. At Bulliwallah the water was so bad that in about two years all your bore-casing would be shot. That's why they had copper tanks back in the old days. So now we've got all poly tanks and stainless-steel pipes. So that saves us something again. So now we can do with one bore-man instead of two and the same man that does the bores can check the boundaries. In the old times I used to do my own boundary-riding and it took time away from other work.

We had a lot of problems with dingoes. But everybody does. We should trap more. When we first went to Bulliwallah and Bingeringo we had over thirteen hundred brumbies on the place, but we eventually got rid of most of them. There was a chap called Tiger Flohr; he used to break-in horses for us, when we were mostly mustering by horses. He said

[1] A motor-driven device fixed at the top of a bore or well to continue pumping when the wind has dropped and the mill is not turning.

he'd get rid of the brumbies for us. He ran them in with a helicopter and sold them.

Years back we used to spend our days riding a horse but now we use the motor-bike and the helicopter. The horse is still the best way to get cattle into the yard but we can still get one thousand head yarded in a day using bikes. Our yards are designed to make drafting and loading easy. We've got long, skinny yards and we've got a double-decker ramp. When we got to Bulliwallah there was only one trough in the yard, but now I can water nine yards at a time. We just stream-lined a bit. We've got lights in the yards so we can work cattle at night. They're very handy if the cattle come in just on dark and the trucks are broken down. And, say we want to load before daylight, we can start at four o'clock. Or if anyone rings and they say 'When do you want to load?' Well, I can say, 'You can come whenever you like.' We built a shed over the yards so we can work cattle in the heat; also the breeze can still come under it. But, distance is still the problem.

We've all had to cut costs. And with the labour-problems we've got these days I've put a lot of lanes in. Once, when you worked your yards, you'd probably have five or six blokes standing on your drafting gates. If you can have six blokes it is probably going to be better, but if you can't, you have got to cut, and cut and cut your costs. If you sit down and work out another way of doing things it's surprising how you can cut costs.

When old Fred King [2] had Bulliwallah he had Aboriginals working for them. In our time we only had the two old timers. One of them was Arthur Frog. Arthur went to Bogantungan to vote one day. And they said, 'Your name, Sir?' and he said, 'A. Frog.' As far as he was concerned that was his name. They said, 'Beg your pardon?' And he says, 'A. Frog.' And they say, 'Beg your pardon?' And old Arthur gets cranky. He tells them, 'I am f...ingwell A. Frog!' His brother was called Freddy Frog.

Loid and Dale Appleton at Bulliwallah. Dale has improved handling facilities in the yards; a 'double-decker ramp' and 'lights for loading at night'.

We wanted to get Arthur a pension. I said to him, 'How old are you, Arthur?' He didn't have a clue whether he was sixty or eighty. And when he got the pension, all his relatives would be asking for a hand-outs. When we went to town, we'd take Arthur, and he'd hit the drink. Coming home he would be all subdued, and he'd tell you, 'I bin fight, y'know'. And I'd say to him, 'Yes, Arthur, I know you have.' But he was good with the kids. They thought the world of him. And he was a bit of a gardener. He made a bit of a mistake with the cabbages one year. He planted about four hundred of them and had them all coming on at one time. I had another dark fellow working for me; Randolf Powder. And the two of these old fellows used to work together,

[2] See '*Taking Up Bulliwallah*' in *Barefoot Through the Bindies*, Marion Houldsworth, 2002, C.Q.U Press

but then they'd get into an argument and they'd fight. Poor old Arthur has passed away now, but the sad thing was, that for all the years that he lived in Clermont, at his funeral there were only fourteen of us. I was a pall-bearer. I caught up with Randolf in Dingo last year, 2006, and had a good old talk about the early days at Bulliwallah.

Kris and I have three sons, William born in 1976, Richard in 1977, and Loid in 1978. Kris used to reckon it was her yearly holiday going down to Brisbane to have them. Our first son, Ray, was stillborn. That was one of the downturns in life. Life seems to give you the good and the bad and you have to use the bad to strengthen you.

With the tax system now, once you have built up a certain level of assets, you get faced with a tremendous tax-bill. But until you reach that threshold you can still do it. I've got a fencer whose been working for me for ten years and he wouldn't buy a house. And his kids were getting to school age, and I said to him, 'You've got to buy a house. Your children have got to go to school.' And he saw a house in Charters Towers for $35,000. He debated over it. I said to him, 'You go and buy that house.' So he bought the house, and now it's worth double.' And every now and then when I see him on the fence-line, I say to him 'That $35,000 house. It's a $70,000 house now, isn't it!' And he reckons, 'Yair! Not too bad, eh!'

That's what I mean. You've got to be prepared to take the initial risk. It's no use saying, 'It's difficult!' Everything's difficult! I've got a few basic rules for myself; respect your elders and learn from what they have got to say. They've had a lot of experience. And talk to everyone on an equal footing. Even if a man is in the gutter, still give him some respect. You have to learn to work with all levels of people and to work in with them. And then keep your eye open for opportunities.

When we first bought Bulliwallah I was fairly terrified to go and do a deal with the owner, Malcolm Dixon. He was a businessman. I had a friend called Paul Walker; he was with Dalgety's, in merchandizing. I said to Paul, 'Look. You go in! You go and do the deal with him!' I didn't have the confidence to do it. But now, after the deals we have put together, I feel quite confident to walk into a room with anyone, because I have found most businessmen are down-to-earth, decent people. Probably some of those Department of Primary Industries outfits we went overseas with, helped in this respect. Tom Byrnes was on one of them. And the Macdonald family, from Chatsworth, out round Cloncurry way; they are really great down-to-earth people. If I'd had to deal with these kinds of people, when I was young, I would have thought I wouldn't be able to do it. But really, when it comes down to it, it's all about having some common-sense and basic decency. People running those big companies seem to have a lot of it.

Kris and I, we're not social people. We're quite happy just by ourselves at home, or with the family. We don't drink and we don't smoke. We have been very lucky to have travelled overseas as well as in Australia. And that has helped broaden our minds. And, although I like to see the ocean at Townsville for a couple of days now and then, if you're used to the arid places, then that's what suits you best. And I think, being brought up in Clermont, well, that's our type of town. Same goes for Georgetown. It's only a little place; just over four hundred people; but some of the nicest people you could come across; very genuine. They'd do anything to help you.

Some of the overseas trips I went on with the DPI – to Indonesia, Brunei, the Philippines, China; they would say to me, 'How big is your city?' or 'How big is your farm?' I would say to them, 'Our town has four hundred people.' or 'Our farm has two million, two hundred and twenty-six thousand acres.' We had Strathmore then. So there was a sense of disbelief. They are living in towns that have got seven to ten million people. And Georgetown had four hundred!

Dale and Chris Appleton with their little grand-daughter, Lucy, and their daughter-in-law, Susan.

Uncle Roy Tindale, who was Dad's uncle; was a pastoral inspector for Corena Pastoral Company, which Stanbrokes bought out. In those days Corena owned Mirtna, Peakvale, Craven, Pasha, Beaufort and Frankfield, and Uncle Roy was the travelling manager for them. And now it's ended up we've bought Craven, and now Islay Plains. And there's a paddock there called Tindale's. So it's all pretty-well makes a sort of pattern; as though some things are meant to be.

The thing about Craven was that it was sixteen million, and Weetalibah, down near Collinsville, that I'd had my eye on, was only fourteen million. So that's another two million you've got to find! I was at the Brisbane Exhibition; and one of the Agents, Mick Goodwin, mentioned that three different lots of people had looked at Craven and nothing had happened. He asked me if I wanted to have a look. So that's how we finished up buying it. We also had first option on Islay Plains which was run in conjuction with Craven. Twelve months later, we were able to purchase Islay Plains. We purchased another lease, Beelarong, in partnership with Richard and his wife Anna and Loid and his wife Zabby. So with the three leases that gave us 200,000 acres in the one area.

The Gulf has been a good opportunity but there is never any weight in the Gulf. Costs are horrendous up there. And when I say 'the Gulf' that includes Strathmore, two and a quarter million acres. We've since sold Strathmore. There were a lot of horses on Strathmore when we bought it; sixty work-horses. And quite a few brumbies on the Red River; one and a quarter million acres. It joins the State National Park. There could be a couple of million acres up there untouched. Harris's from Yandala at Tamworth bought Strathmore. They also had Go Go up in the Kimberleys.

To have got where we are today, we have had to do a fair bit of trading in properties. Looking at the list of what we have bought and sold we have covered some country; Barracloughs, Boolaroo, Barrylar, Mallawah; all in the Clermont area. Then, Bingeringo, Dawsonvale, Mt. Hope out from Charters Towers; Lava Plains outside Mt.Garnet, Kilcool at Alpha, North Delta and Newhaven at Barcaldine and Strathmore up at Georgetown, Craven and Islay Plains at Alpha, and, in with Richard and Anna, and Loid and Zabby, there's Beelarong at Alpha. Loid, Zabby and their two girls, Charlize and Izabelle, live at Bulliwallah, and Richard and Anna and their little girl, Alexandria, at Islay Plains with us. One of the bonuses of Islay Plains and Craven is that at the local school, Mistake Creek, five of the ten pupils come from our places. We have a school bus based at Islay, and every day Julie Donald does the school run. Our other son, Will, and his wife Susan and their girls, Lucy and Emily, have a seven hundred acre place outside Clermont.

So that is about how we got to where we are today. I was talking to some young people the other day, and they told me, 'We can't do what you did.' I told them, 'Look! You've got to be willing to give things a go. Never say you can't do it.

6

Lennie Forman

ॐ ॐ ॐ

Introduction

Lennie Forman's name is well-known among cattlemen of the north. I had heard tell of Lennie as a lively ninety-year old, with a great sense of humour, who spent his days sitting under the mango trees in Georgetown, always ready to swap yarns of his life as a horse-breaker and head stockman on Strathmore, one of the biggest cattle properties in the Gulf. I was looking forward immensely to the trip to Georgetown to meet this remarkable old man.

So it was a sad blow when, late one afternoon, returning from a trip out west, we called in at Tiddly Triffit's place in Charters Towers, to be greeted by Tiddley with, 'Did you hear about Old Lennie? He died yesterday. The funeral is on Friday.' I was shattered to think I had missed meeting this marvellous old man and recording his life-story.

Then it occurred to me; perhaps the National Library in Canberra might have some record of Lennie in the Australian Drovers' Archive, the material collected by Professor Bill Gammage and ex-drover Bruce Simpson in 2002. I phoned; and Yes! They had! They agreed to forward Lennie's life-story as soon as possible.

The transcript of the recorded interview arrived by special delivery at the very hour of Lennie's funeral in distant Georgetown in the Gulf. Deeply moved, 'I thought 'Never fear, Old Man! We'll give you a bit of a show yet! Rest in Peace!' The story below is a summary of the material recorded by Bill and Bruce and I am grateful to them and to the Australian National Library for allowing me to make use of it.

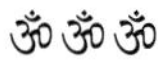

The Breaker

Lennie Forman

'I'd take them into the long yard'

I learned myself to read from the *Register*. I only went to school for eighteen months and that's the only education I ever had. And I was pretty dud, too, I might tell you! But when I was twelve year old I started work on Emu Valley for Fred Trembath for five shillings a week. He had about as much education as I did but he used to get the *Register* – the *'North Queensland Register'*– every week. I'd get a word I couldn't understand and I'd ask him. He'd have to think about it, but he'd work it out, and tell me and I learned myself to read like that.

I was doing station work; horse work. They bred a lot of horses; horses that'd root a bit, but being a kid, if they wasn't pig-rooting along it was no good to me. I put seven years in there and then I went to attend a muster on Fletchervale for old John Halligan[1]. And I was there three years. It was all Devon Shorthorns on all them places in them days; good quiet cattle.

After that I went to Lyndhurst and I was only there three weeks and they gave me the third camp to run. They reckoned, 'You're too good with cattle to leave you doing just nothing, y'know.' I put in three years on Lyndhurst and then I shifted back to Fletchervale and started breaking-in. I'd do four a week. But if they were reasonably quiet you could squeeze five in. And if there was one that wasn't up to scratch I'd keep him the extra time. I was on contract and wages. I'd get a pound a horse. And for that they had to be shod. You had to be able to crack a whip on them and shoe them. I earned my quid.

I had a very good breaking-in horse. She was educated before she ever went to school, sort've. You could put her in the yard with the young colt, and jump on her with no saddle or bridle or anything, and she would straight over[2] and push the colt on the rails. You could put a halter on him and slip off her anywhere. I'd always catch the colt off her like that. I

[1] To 'attend a muster' is to be present at a muster on a neighbouring property in order to reclaim cattle belonging to ones own herd, that have strayed across the boundary

[2] This is accepted colloquial usage, to employ a non-verb such as a preposition in a verbal sense; e.g. 'and I up him' meaning 'went at' or 'I into him' meaning 'fought'. Here 'she straight over' implies 'headed purpose-fully'.

wouldn't go trying to lasso him or anything like that; that way he might hit the rails and bung his eyes up or hurt himself and he'd be out of action and you'd have to start with another one. So that mare was the easy way to do it. Easy on the colt.

Then I'd put the halter on him and take the old mare out of the yard and just poke him around with a flip and a bag until he's settled down. And I'd give him a break every now and then just to think over what he's been doing. And then I'd lunge him, both sides. I'd get him going round one way and coming back the other. I'd get him going and then pull him in towards me. Then I'd get him going the other way and pull him in towards me again. I was never rough on them. A lot of people manhandle their horses. But you don't do that. You go about them quiet; bag 'em all over; rub them over with an old bag. Then after a while when you're lunging them, when you step that way, he'll step that way. You go back; he'll go back. And then the last thing is learning to lead, and liking to lead.

And then I'd put the tackling on him and mouthing gear. I'd leave them for a while and then have a look at their mouths, to see if both lip sides didn't pinch and get swelled up.

And then I'd start driving them in reins. Both ways. I'd have the reins tied back to the breaking-in gear and I'd drive them in reins.

I'd take them into the big long yard and start driving them both ways. I always drive a lot in reins and I never had a bad-mouthed horse. Only them bloody mules. The mule is a bad-mouthed animal. Then I'd bring him back into the round yard. I would never leave a horse where he could stand on the reins because it jerks his mouth and that's it.

And then I'd put the saddle on him, drive him in reins again and then step on to him That'd be about the third day. I'd lead him outside; both sides. And then I'd give him a ride around the yard and out to a bigger yard.

And the next time you get him, you'd saddle him up again, drive him in reins round the yard, then get on him and away you'd go. If I could get someone else to take him out for a ride, I would, but you couldn't always get anyone. Women were the best. Women are good off-siders[3]. If I could get a good off-sider that could do half the breaking-in I'd give them half of what I made. I had some very good fellas at times that went on after to be horse-breakers themselves. Kevin Norton was one of them. Arthur Carlson. And Lancey

Snow Edmunds, who often off-sided for Lennie on Lyndhurst. Lennie said Snow and her sister Anne were 'good off-siders'.

[3] This is a reference to the Edmunds girls on Lyndhurst, (See '*The Lady Drover*' in Volume One) in which Ann Brunner refers to her sister Snow and herself working with Lennie Forman.

Owens. He was unthrowable; the best man I ever seen on a bad horse. Ray Davidson, on Dotswood; he was another good man. But a lot of breakers used to be terrible drinkers. It goes with the job.

On the first day I'd only do as much as the horse could take; what he wanted. He'd tell me. As soon as he'd had enough I'd give him a little bit of a blow[4]. But some horses would catch on real quick. Chudleigh horses, you could do six or eight a week. They were the most intelligent horses I ever handled.

I never broke in harness horses. I'd break them in to ride first and when I'd finished with them then they could do whatever they liked with them. A bronco horse, well, you can generally just get one out of the mustering horses, long as he's got a bit of weight on him; a clumper[5] sort of fella.

Abandoned Jackaroo Quarters at Dotswood station. Dotswood is now an Army Training Reserve

I broke in at Hillgrove, Allensleigh, Dotswood, Gainsford, then to Toonba, Black Downs. Old Waite, there, he was a hard man. It had to be right. Once I got the name as a breaker they wanted me every year. I didn't just hand them over after the two rides. I used to keep them until I reckoned they were right; five or six rides outside the yard. The last thing I would do with them is shoe them. They used to say I was a crackerjack shoer. You had to learn pretty quick out there. It was hard country and you had to have your horses shod. Altogether I must have broke in just on two thousand horses.

I never got hurt off a horse, breaking-in. Never been thrown. But I've bit Mother Earth a couple of times when the horse fell with me out mustering. We were out once in wet weather and I was riding this big clumper mare, a very good mare she was. But she couldn't see this hole; and neither could I. It was full of water and grass. I went to block this bloody bullock and we landed in the hole. She landed on top of me. I got up and shook myself and I couldn't move m'arm. I sang out to the other fellow and he come over. He said, 'Your bloody arm is broke; your collarbone!'

So I led the old mare over to an ant bed and got on her and carried on the day. Just kep' going. Next day I stopped in bed. I couldn't get m'tail up; couldn't get rolled over. The other bloke that was with me – he was a hard case – he said, 'You'll get over it. It'll heal.' I've never seen a doctor about anything. I didn't know what a hospital looked like.

And then I gave the breaking away and went back to running mustering camps. I was on Dotswood, as head stockman. Each man in the camp – say there were nine or ten men – you'd give him four or five horses. That's his horses for work. They'd ride them alternate days. We'd muster in to the waters.

[4] bit of a blow; a spell or a rest

[5] clumper; horse of heavier build

And then they shifted me from Dotswood to the Gulf, to Strathmore. It was a big place, over four thousand square miles. Hardly a road; hardly a fence. Early in the year when the buffalo flies are bad, well, it pulls a lot of cattle together; and wet weather, when the rivers are up high, that'll hunt the cattle out of the islands. All you've got to do is go down the bank of the river and pick them up. But you have a bit of a job with them tough old bullocks. They'll dive in the river and be swimming around. They get cunning.

Yarding horses to have their tails and manes 'pulled' free of burrs and grass seeds.

And in the Dry, we'd fire certain parts to get the green pick coming. You'd always carry a box of wax matches and on them sand ridges and them big flats you'd think the whole country was going up. But it would only go till dark and then the dew would knock it off, because early in the Dry there's still a lot of damp in the air. If you leave it too late in the year the whole bloody country goes up. We'd burn way back from the water first. And as soon as you've burnt it the cattle will come in on that burnt feed and you can get a pretty good muster. We'd leave the hilly, stony country till later in the Dry, just before the storms. And the storms bring on the green pick again.

On Strathmore we moved the camp around by pack-horse. You'd have ten or twelve of them. The main benefit of packs is that you can go just wherever you like. Say there's a camp twenty miles over to the west, you can go there whether there's a road or not. Your instinct will tell you. Though you'd nearly always have a black boy who was born and bred on the place that'd know. Later on they got an old Blitz. It was bogged more often than not. One blackfella said to me, 'We oughta burn that thing!'

Up there we'd do a lot of open broncoing, all out of the forest country. You'd pick a camp and you cut a tree, a tree that's forked – you leave it standing but you cut it off at the fork, and when you rope a calf you'd drag him up and the rope slides in the fork. And then you get leg ropes on to him and pull him down and brand him and castrate him. Some of them black-boys was terribly good. The work seemed to come natural to them. We'd reckon on doing a calf every two minutes. Having good catchers was the thing. We'd do three hundred calves in a morning. And once you've got a team that's used to broncoing, by geez, they're hard to beat. You would have two men on the catching and dragging them up and about six on the ground do the cutting and branding and they'd be kept busy. You needed plenty of men because you had to have men holding the cattle too. No yards up there. The cattle got used to it, though. As soon as you rode on to a camp you could see the cattle were quiet.

And y'know, there wasn't a lot of fresh meat out in the camps; mostly corned beef, and there was a bit of a delicacy some blokes would eat in the branding. You'd always take a billy-can with three parts full of water and a bit of salt in it. And when you cut a calf you'd chuck his stones into it. Then you'd take them back to camp and either make a curry of them or stew them or put them on the coals and roast them. Good tucker! Or you could chuck them in the branding fire and eat them. Bloody beautiful! And I'm ninety-one now, and they give me two new knees not long back and I'm that fit I could get up and dance around. I put it down to eating them calf balls! Calf balls and brisket with plenty of fat on it. That and plenty of hard work.

7

Toby Rogers

ॐॐॐ

Introduction

We arrived at Sutton Downs, the property of Toby and Bernice Rogers, on the Muttaburra road south of Hughenden, on a day of forty-degrees-in-the water-bag heat, to be greeted with a cheerful, 'Come on in! We've got the cooler going for you!' And so they had. The air-conditioning in the main lounge blasted coolness through the French windows on to the back verandah where a long table was set for a lunch of roast lamb, baked vegetables and garden greens. Toby had killed especially for our arrival. Sweet, tender and flavoursome, the lamb was straight off Mitchell grass country and 'had never seen the inside of a freezer'. We all backed up, unabashedly, for hearty seconds.

Lunch cleared away, we sat around the same large table and the recording session began, the clinking of tea-cups helping to maintain an almost party atmosphere. Boxes of old photographs and papers were brought out. Toby, a fine-looking man in his mid-sixties, is well known, not only for his feats of camp-cooking for community gatherings right across the north; (he says, 'I found I enjoyed it!') but also for his dry sense of humour. A long-forgotten School Report from the Correspondence School came to light. Corrections had been written in the meticulous copperplate of a patient, long-ago teacher; 'Toby; Four tens are forty. You wrote four hundred and forty four.' Toby conceded he was probably thinking of cattle numbers at the time. He would have been seven years old. Across the bottom of the page had been added, 'Toby, Congratulations on your promotion.' Toby laughed, 'Yeah!

That's probably the only bloody promotion I ever got in my life, too!'

Toby will tell the tallest story with a perfectly straight face. Any conversation with him is punctuated by shouts of laughter. But the snake-anecdote of fishing on the Einasleigh with his son Shane, arose from the fact that Bernice, who had gone downstairs to bring up the washing in the teeth of a rising wind bringing dust, returned with a loaded basket and a laconic, 'There was a snake under the washing-line. I killed it.' Asked what she had done with it, she replied, 'Oh! Just chucked it over the fence.' Later I asked to see it, by which time, the remains, neatly chopped in half, pale, yellowish brown, with a mean, arrowed head, possibly a downs tiger,[1] *were swarming with black ants. But Bernice was unconcerned. She wanted to show us the beautiful garden she is creating at the front of the homestead, an oasis of coolness in the horizon-wide, drought-bleached plains of the Hughenden to Muttaburra downs.*

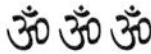

Live Like It's Gonna Rain

Toby Rogers – Grazier

'a bit of a reputation as a camp cook'

The worst fall I ever had from a horse was at Redcliffe. We were clearing horses out and my horse, a beautiful big black gelding, Scamp, fell with me. When we went down I hit a rock and punctured my lung. That was the biggest bloody drama I was ever in. I was on a drip in the hospital and they had to keep draining the lung. I tell you what! I've never smoked since!

I grew up at Redcliffe, fifteen miles south of Hughenden, on the Muttaburra road; timbered, black-soil downs country on the head of Walker's Creek and I've been involved with the pastoral industry most of my life.

My father bought Redcliffe in 1932 for £12,000. I have the diary he kept from the day he first took over; 'Mustered the back country as far as the ridge.' Redcliffe had plenty of bores but the water was full of soda. You couldn't drink it. If you washed your clothes in it, it would take all the colour out. But OK for cattle. We had rain-water tanks for the house. We never had much of a garden because of the water, but in after-years, when they had a dam, they could grow anything there, grapes and all. Redcliffe never flooded. It was too high on the watershed.

[1] *pseudechis colletti*, found in dry areas of western Queensland, including Nonda, Aramac, Julia Creek, Winton and Hughenden, in deep cracks in the black soil. Listed as the nineteenth most venomous snake in the world by Sutherland, 1990

My Dad's family came from Longreach. They owned Toobrach station. Old Man Rogers, Dad's father, was originally from England. He came up overland from New South Wales in the late 1800s, and bought up a lot of little blocks and formed them into Toobrach. His first wife died and he married again, an Irish girl, and they had four boys and two girls.

Mum's family, the Rutherfords, came from Rockhampton. Her father was a chemist. At one stage of the game he owned nine shops in the main street of Rocky. I was born, fourteen pounds, in Rockhampton in 1938. There were six of us kids; Peter, Hazel, myself, Mary, Billy and Charlie. Nobody knows me as anything but Toby but my real name is Hamilton Healey. There was an old ringer at Redcliffe by the name of Lynch that was very fond of me. I think he used to call me 'Toby Tiger' and it more or less stuck.

They would take us kids to town in Hughenden about twice a year. And of course, the day you came to go to town and the boots wouldn't fit and be pinching. Before you got to town we'd all be up bawling, 'Me boots are hurting!' And the little kids would be car-sick. You'd get to town and we'd maybe see an old drunk staggering along and we'd be that frightened we'd all stack back into the car and wouldn't budge. And that would be the big trip to town! And it might be another twelve months before we'd go.

Dad was pretty strict. We always had to look lively if he spoke to us. He had too much to do. We weren't game to step out of line. He had us bluffed from the word go. But we made our own fun. We all had our stick-horses; and we'd play pretend-rodeos. Most of our fun seemed to be involved in the work going on. Sometimes we would have picnics up at the rocky dam, with the Nimmos from Railview, fifteen miles away. Bert Nimmo was just fresh back from the war, an ex-P.O.W. on the Burma railway.

We arrived to lunch of freshly roasted lamb, 'straight off Mitchell Grass'. Toby & Bernice Rogers and friends.

Every year we would go down on the old steam train to Emu Park outside Rocky for holidays. And one thing they would tell you was, 'Whatever you do, don't put your head out of the window! You will get soot in your eye.' And the next thing, you're bawling. They'd say, 'What's wrong with you!' 'I got somethin' in me eye!' 'Did you put your head out the window!' 'No! No! I never put me head out!' Strewth! You'd get into trouble!

One year, the Muston boys, Geoff and Dick Muston from Prairie, were going to look after the place while we were away. They carted all our ports[2] into Hughenden on the old Chev truck and piled us all on top. And we get to Hughenden but the train was late in. We're hanging around for hours and then when it gets in, the guard was drunk, and of course the train's not going anywhere

[2] Colloquial 'Queensland' for 'suit-cases'.

until the guard says so. Us kids are fed up. They buy us pies to keep us quiet and they must have been a bit off because next thing we're spewing them up. But eventually they talked the guard into coming out of the boozer to get the train going and they get him on board and he throws the green flag up. And just as we're going to take off, they let the brakes go and the steam goes, 'Sssssshhhhcccchhh!' and Charlie, the little brother, goes, 'Aw! Now we got a flat tyre!'

One year, when we were coming home on the old Sunshine Express up the coast railway to Townsville, we got as far as the Burdekin, and it was in flood. That was before the high level bridge was built. The engine shunts around and next thing we're heading back to Rocky! And then out west around Barcaldine, Longreach, Winton. Right the way round! Took days! God Almighty! You were thinking you were never going to get home!

Redcliffe homestead was a big old low-set place with a verandah along the northern side. It was built on and extended from 1918 and Dad put in a lot of improvements over the years. Mum always had a cook and a housekeeper and for us kids, a governess. We did Correspondence lessons. Not many of the governesses stayed long, but! We did most of our school-work on the verandah outside the kitchen where Mum could keep an eye on what was going on. Sometimes we would ask her if she wanted anything and she would say, 'Yes! Just a bit of peace and quiet!'

Redcliffe, fifteen miles south of Hughenden.

All of us boys went to Rockhampton Grammar. We used to fly down in the old Douglas from Hughenden. I always got air-sick; ended up spewing every time. I absolutely hated boarding school. I'd never been away from home on my own and to get thrown into there! The first day I was there this master said to me, 'What is your address?' I just stared at him. Had no idea what he was talking about! I thought, 'This is a tricky one! This is one of the ones they told me to watch!' It's a big change in your life when you are straight out of the scrub. But I battled on for four years. One year Dad said to me. 'Where's your report?' I said, 'It blew out of the window of the plane coming home.'

Charlie was still at the Grammar when that Fokker Friendship disappeared somewhere off the coast out of Mackay, in 1960. There were nine kids from the Grammar School going home for the May long week-end on board. They never found any of them. Two of Charlie's mates were on that. It took him a long time to get over it.

Whenever we came home from school the first thing we did was to climb on a horse. Dad would plan it that we were home for the mustering. Dad was very proud of his show horses and sometimes he would fly me home early so I could ride in the Hughenden Show; the jumps and hacks and Best Boy Rider, that sort of thing. I used to pull off a few blue ribbons. We were big in the Show. Dad always put fat steers in the Salatina section[3]. We

[3] Named for Joe Salatina, grazier, for many years Patron of the Townsville Pastoral and Agricultural Show and of the Hughenden Show.

always had Herefords. To transport them in we'd chuck all the gates out of the cattle-yard on to the back of the truck and Cobb & Co[4] them together and that was the crate! But for rodeos we would walk them in.

We had thirty-two hundred Herefords on Redcliffe. One year, 1956, we branded nine hundred calves. In the early 'sixties bull-riding was just starting to come in. Before that it was just bullock-riding. We had our own rodeo-ground at home and from when we were young we used to muck around riding poddies and cows and weaners. Then we started travelling around to various rodeos at the week-ends. One time, at Herveys Range, there was this big black bull and he was playing-up bad. Tiger Nelson was the judge. The announcer said, 'The bloke who gets this bull is going to have the ride of his life!' And guess who drew him! They put him in the crush and I get on and out we come! But, he took fright and just galloped! Straight down the ring. Never bucked once! It was a long narrow ring and the whistle blew and I went to jump off him. But the bastard saw my leg and he ducked straight back under me. Threw me fair up! And down I came! I thought I'd busted my leg but I was alright.

After that I started competing at Mount Isa and Winton and Longreach and Townsville. I just loved it! One time – we'd been mustering all day – I got on this big horse we had called Lava – and cantered him all the way home to Redcliffe, eighteen miles. Was home at eleven o'clock that night, rode in the Hughenden rodeo next day, won the bullock ride and collected two quid! Thought I was a millionaire!

I also did a bit of camp-drafting. Mostly in Hughenden. I lived on horses in those days. Good horses that could get over the ground. We had Gundagai, a stallion from Wandovale. Bert Nimmo got on to[5] him and we shared him amongst the four places, Redcliffe, Woodbine, Railview and Launceston. They each put in a hundred guineas. He was an older horse, but well-bred. Stall-fed all the time. You couldn't let him out because he would have galloped through any fence. We had forty-odd beautiful big mares there on Redcliffe. Beautiful horses.

After I left school I went out contracting with a bloke named Alex Schaffer; cutting posts and building yards. We'd do a bit of 'roo shooting and pig shooting as well. That would have been the early 'sixties. We were working on a place called Marionvale when decimal currency came in. Went to town and came back with all this funny-looking money we had never seen before.

Dad died in '56. He was only forty-two years of age. My mother had a very lonely life after that because she never really went anywhere or made very many friends outside of the family. And when she died she was virtually on her own. Young Charlie was the only one at home at the time and he phoned us up and said he couldn't wake Mum up. She had died in her sleep. She is buried in Hughenden. So then the six of us kids were hit with heavy death duties on Redcliffe. We didn't have much option but to sell the place up and all go our own separate ways.

Bernice and I were married by then and I had two places, Mokana and Loana. Mokana

[4] Colloquial; join together roughly; possibly a word-play on 'cobble together'

[5] get on to: to find out about something.

was a block resumed off Redcliffe. I bought it in 1979, after I sold cattle I had out west. It was all spinifex and gidyea with black soil strips. There wasn't anything on Loana, an adjoining property on the south-west of Mokana, just a shed and a set of yards, so we worked it from Mokana. Then in 1983 Evandale came up for public action in Hughenden. We sold Mokana and Loana and bought Evandale. We moved six hundred head of breeders from Mokana to Evandale on the day that Australia took the America's Cup off the Yanks.

Evandale was thirty-five miles south of Hughenden on the Muttaburra road. It was 20,000 acres of open downs country. Mostly sheep. I had a lot of cattle there at one time but I sold them and went over to sheep. I had eighteen thousand head until the price went out of wool. Evandale homestead was a big old rambling place, all weatherboard, about twelve rooms to it; men's dining-room; big old kitchen; verandah right across the front and down two sides. I spent a fair wad of money on the place over the years to bring it up to standard. Those old homesteads take a lot of maintenance. Bernice had a tennis court and a lovely garden there. She always has to have a garden. And animals and pets.

I like sheep. I enjoy working wethers with my kelpies though the ewes just about drive you mad at times. But with good dogs they bring the tail along and when I get within about four or five hundred yards of a gate I clear off up ahead on the bike and open it and let the dogs bring them to me. They run around to see where I am and I say, 'Go back! Go back!' and they get in behind them again. I keep the bike's motor going so they know where to come to. They bring them to the noise of the bike.

But talking of good dogs. Once out at Kynuna I had a thousand ewes and I had to take them in to the siding to load on the train. I couldn't get any men but I had a good dog, a very clever little kelpie bitch. We'd been on the road a couple of days and she was heavy in pup, poor bugger. And on the tail of the mob were five ewes heavily in lamb. So I'm keeping a bit of an eye on them, and I'm poking them up to the brake this night, and here's a go, the five ewes aren't there. So I say to my dog, 'Go back! Go back and fetch 'em up!' and away she goes. But, anyhow, she doesn't turn up that night. So in the morning I left the sheep in the brake and I go back looking for her. And when I find her she's bringing the five ewes along and the ewes had dropped their lambs. And I can see she's had her pups. But no sign of any of them. So I think to myself, 'Bloody hell! This is a nice mess! I'd better go back and see where the pups are.' So I go back over the ridge, and bugger me, here's her five little pups and they're bringing the five little lambs along! Yeah! That's kelpies for you! You can't beat 'em! They're clever, alright! And they are just as good working with cattle. You don't need heelers in this open country.

Bernice and I have three kids; Jackie, then Carrie and Shane. They all went to boarding school, to Blackheath and Thornburgh in Charters Towers, and loved it. Shane and I went fishing the other day with Jimmy Edwards up on Lyndhurst on the Einasleigh. And I'm sitting on the bank up against a big old oak tree and Shane comes down and he says, 'Listen Dad; right behind you, wrapped around that tree, there's a bloody great snake and he's sort've looking at you and you're going to be his next move. The best thing you can do is go straight ahead.' Well, there's a four foot drop in front of me into ten foot of water! So I just started edging quietly away to my left. And here was this bloody great tree-snake and he's hanging on the side of this she-oak. They don't seem to have to wrap around. They seem to be able to just clamp on. God! He was a big fellow! But pretty, eh!

In the floods of '55 Evandale had big stock losses; lost over three thousand head. The Wet come and then another one come in behind it. The channels couldn't handle the run-off. There were a hundred thousand sheep lost between here and Longreach on the Sunday night. We're part of the Lake Eyre Basin here. Any water in that creek out the front goes down to Lake Eyre. Those hills way over to the north are the catchment area. You get up in the morning and see big storms up there. The water takes two days to get here. Generally you don't have to move your stock back. Or only for really big storms. Then you might have to swim them out.

In 2000, the first year we were here at Sutton, we had a flood when the creek backed up right up over the flat. There were a lot of cattle trapped down beyond the fence. And the creek was getting pretty bloody big. I said to Mum, 'We'll have to get the helicopter out and cut the fence to let them go.' I couldn't get down there. It was too strong. We were out the front watching it and there was this one cow over on the high ground and she's calling and calling. And she come up the fence and she went across way out on to the high ridge, and she started calling. I thought to myself, 'She's got a calf.' But, no. She went back, swam across, got the whole mob and took 'em back after her, calling them all the way! Took them to safety! And when they swam they had the calves in between them. But that cow never had a calf herself! She just went and found a good high spot and then went back and called all the others after her. A wonderful thing, eh! I couldn't get over it. We were out the front there, watching!

Toby and friends after a nights' fishing on the Einasleigh. It was on the Einasleigh that Toby's son, Shane, told him 'There's a bloody big snake looking at you and you're going to be his next move.'

I've never seen anything like that before. But I've heard about it. Over at Peter Browning's place, one big Wet, they had a mob of bailer cows and baby calves trapped. And they were watching them from the house. And they said, 'Well, they've got to go directly. And all those calves will drown.' But when it was time to go the cows got all the calves together on the outside and they swam with them. Bunched the calves together and swam them right across the river! Animal intelligence!

I don't have horses any more. Only the old pensioner-fellows that are left, the poor old beggars. I found that by the time I got the horses in I could be on the four-wheeler and have the job done. But I had a piebald mare once. She was one of those that just didn't want to be interfered with. She would do her work and do it perfectly. But when you let her go she didn't want a pat. She just took off. She would never come near. You had to bail her up to catch her but she was a good mare. And one day, I was there at the house and she came walking up to me, snorting, snorting. And I thought to myself, 'There's something wrong with this mare! I stroked her down but I couldn't see anything wrong with her. Nothing broken. No wire.' But when I came back in the afternoon she was dead; puffed up, down the flat. A snake must have got her. I felt bad about that. She'd come to me for help; tried to tell me she was in a bad way but I didn't understand.

I've got myself a bit of a reputation now as a camp cook for all these big turn-outs. It started as a bit of a joke. I always liked cooking at home and there were races being held at Koorinya over near Winton and they asked me if I'd go over and look after the cooking side of things. And I found I enjoyed it. And I've been doing it ever since. Every year I cook for the Hughenden Show. They make a fair bit of money out of it. It's no problem if everyone bucks in and pulls their weight. The team-work makes it enjoyable. I always take a load of gidgea because you can't beat a gidgea fire for the slow steady heat you need for cooking with camp ovens.

But, God! Some funny things have happened over the years. One time when we were fencing at Marionvale the insects were that bad that the bloke that was doing the cooking, when we come back to camp at the end of the day, he wouldn't put a light on or you'd have insects crawling all over you all night. So he goes to the old kero fridge and gets out a leg of mutton and chops it up and throws in a few vegetables and puts this stew on. And after a while he serves it up, still no light. I ate mine and I said, 'That was that good! I'll have some more of that!' I went back with a torch, for the second go, and I said, 'That was bloody nice, that! Where did you get the rice from?' He said, 'Ain't no rice in it. No bloody rice in the camp.' I said, 'Well, there's some in it now!' But all those little white things weren't rice! But too late to worry about it!

Then there's 'prairie oysters', the gonads when you're castrating weaners. The young ones are alright with salt and pepper. Barbecue them on the branding-irons! If you wanted to be flash, of course, you could marinade them!

I don't do puddings. Too messy. Though I did make a pudding one night, a big custardy thing. It turned out with this big design right across the middle. The boys said 'How did you put that design on? It looks real good!' I said, 'Oh! Just a bit of a trick I picked up.' I didn't tell them about the big moth that landed fair in the middle and went flop! flop! flop! around in a circle. I fished him out when he got to the other side and chucked him away. He'd done his job! Put a beautiful pattern on it!

And at Redcliffe, one time when we were kids – we used to get some rough-looking old sheilas as cooks there at times – most of them didn't have any teeth. But one old bloke we had used to make good pies. We used to wonder how he put the design around the edge of the pie-crust. So us kids are having a squinny in at the kitchen window one time, and here he is, he's got his false teeth out and he's going squidge, squidge, squidge around the edge of the pie-dish with them! Us kids were horrified! We said, 'Cripes! Wonder how he makes the holes in the doughnuts!'

We had some funny old shearers-cooks drift in and out at Redcliffe over the years; 'The Dutchman' and 'Old Busted-Oven' and 'I-Am-The-Cook' and old 'Jimmy-the-Juice.' Jimmy-the-Juice used to get shickered on essence of lemon and one time Dad happened to go up to see how things were going. He said the only thing that was on for dinner was the wireless!

And another old fellow still fancied himself as a bit of a gun with the blades and was trying to get his tally up down the shed. His eyesight wasn't real good, eh! And there's a hole in the back wall from the pen and Dad had hung a potato-sack over it. And they reckon this old bloke raced in and took the belly-wool off the potato-sack before he discovered it wasn't a sheep!

Bernice and I were at Evandale eighteen years and then Sutton, which was better country, came on the market. So we sold Evandale and bought Sutton. It is open downs country, with gum and coolabah channels. Very easy country to run. Wonderful country to muster and work. It only needs two to muster. Two and the dogs. I've gone out of sheep now and gone back to cattle but I keep a couple of hundred sheep on the place for mutton. I like my meat three times a day.

Sutton Downs homestead, south of Hughenden.

I'd like to clean out the creek in the front of the house, Landsborough Creek it is; named by the explorer Landsborough when he was out looking for Leichhardt. I'd like to make a bit of a lagoon; make a feature of it; bring the wild ducks and water-birds around. Mum loves all her animals and pets and birds and ducks. I'd like to take about four foot of gravel out of the bed of the hole while it's dry. Over on the other side there's plenty of shale. There's a lot of stone in this country; a lot of fossils. It's all the bed of the old inland sea. Out at Richmond you see beaches and beaches of fossils. Just like someone has stacked them. I'd like to cart some stone and throw up a bit of a dam wall and make a permanent waterhole out in front of the house. Feed the overflow of the bore into it. But you're not allowed to dig down below the natural bed of the creek. The DPI[6] determines it. Someone would have to come out and give it the OK.

[6] Department of Primary Industries

I can't understand their thinking because the water all drains away to Lake Eyre and evaporates. And, God! That Lake Eyre! It's a dreadful place! There's nothing there! Absolutely nothing. My brother, Bill, and I and two mates from the Grammar School, Harley and Peter McKenzie from Duaringa, went down there last year. I always had the idea that I would like to do that trip. You can drive down in a couple of days, five hundred and sixty ks, down the Birdsville Track. But there's nothing when you get there. Just miles of mud.

And you pull up at the roadhouse at Mullumata. I thought, 'Well! What a place! You haven't seen a thing for hours and bloody hours! When you get there you're still no-where! When you left there was no-where to go! But this pub was full of young people and they're all happy! Really pleased to be there!

The competion for diminishing grass in drought time means kangaroos are culled.

We had a couple of beers and went on a couple of hours to Coopers Creek and camped the night. You don't even know you're at Coopers Creek. There's just this area where a few gum-trees are growing and a bit of a stony crossing. Then you get to William Creek. 'Population 7 and a blue heeler!' They've got all these rocket heads from Maralinga parked in the yard out the back of the pub. I can say I've seen Lake Eyre but I never want to see it again!

Being on the land is pretty stressful today. For instance, if we don't get any rain from now, in October, through to February. A lot of young people can't seem to hack it. But I've learned how to turn my back on it. You've got to live like it's gonna rain tomorrow, not next year. That's the only way to go. You can't worry about what you're going to spend on the drought. With modern-day prices you can spend $100,000 on feed for your stock but that's nothing because you can't buy many cattle for $100,000 to replace them when the time comes. One drought there, it was costing me $240 a day to feed stock. You can't worry about that otherwise you'd go off your rocker. Stress tablets! It makes me laugh. Down south there's plenty of young blokes walking round the streets that haven't got a responsibility in the world and they're living on stress tablets!

You've got to be a special sort of a person today to stick to the land, even though they've got a lot of bloody handouts that we never had when we young fellows. In those days if you got trapped in the drought, well, you just had to go and cut scrub for your stock. You couldn't truck them out. There were no road-trains. If you got trapped in, well, that was it. You were Irene Goodnight. And go and start again. Plenty of times that happened. The bank closed on lots of people. That's when it's nice and stressful! When you've got to walk away from it all and leave it behind you. After the years you might have spent there, trying hard. It's just the luck of the game.

But for my money, being on the land is a good life. There's been some great changes come in over the years. Among of the best would be poly-piping. It can double your carrying capacity. You can run water miles out where stock couldn't walk to. In the old times cattle might walk for eight miles to get a drink. They'd wait till night time when it was cool and then start coming in.

But, all round, the best advance in the bush would be the helicopter. Any emergency on the property; someone gets hurt or a kid gets bitten by a snake, well, you just ring up the chopper and down he comes and away you go! And if I'm in trouble with stock, say in a flood, I'd be down trying to save the cattle and maybe get drowned myself. Nowadays you just ring up and down comes the chopper and pushes them out. What's four or five hundred dollars!

Like, old Johnny Vincent, my old mate, once he was down at Zara in the big mud. The chopper took me home, and I said to the pilot, 'When you're going back up, grab old Johnny and take him home. He won't want to get in, because he's never been in a chopper, but don't argue with him. Just grab him and put him on board.' So they take old Johnno back up to Hughenden and I ring him up. I said, 'Hey! Johnny! How'd you get on with the chopper?' And d'you know what he said? He said, 'That's the best bloody thing I ever been on! It never spun round once!' He reckoned he was going to trade his old truck in on one!

8

Helen Clark

Introduction

Helen Clark's life is illuminated by the immense admiration she has for her pioneering mother, Phoebe Atkinson of Camel Creek.[1] *Helen took me to meet this wonderful lady at the Good Shepherd Retirement Home in Townsville.*

When, after a morning's recording, our feisty raconteur was summoned to Lunch and Rest Time, Helen and I made our way to a charming Federation tea room in the nearby Palmetum. As we chatted over salad and quiche, quiet, unassuming Helen reminisced about her childhood growing up on Camel Creek station, where 'all the kids had their jobs', adding that as a sixteen-year-old she had become a governess on Mellish Park station in the Gulf. Sensing the beginning of a story, I said, 'Wait a moment, Helen!' and fished hastily in my shoulder bag for my Sony micro-cassette. I was soon glad that I had. Helen had a great story to tell, a flood story. Her down-to-earth childhood experiences on Camel Creek station would have been a source of reassurance to the distressed young mother on isolated Mellish Park, as the flood waters rose around the homestead.

Helen then revealed that having inherited an ardent love of bush poetry from her mother, she and a friend, Denise Farr, had organized a hugely successful Bush Ballads and Bulldust event at Woodstock to which people had come from near and far. It is their hope to repeat the event annually. Daughter of a truly remarkable woman, the same could be said of Helen Clark herself, but she would be no little surprised to find herself thought so.

ॐ ॐ ॐ

[1] See Chapter 20, '*Bred by a Bloody Woman*!' for the story of Phoebe Atkinson.

The Practical Governess

Helen Clark

'We put the calf in the top of the linen cupboard.'

I grew up on Camel Creek station. My father died when I was seventeen months old and my mother ran Camel Creek from then on. Actually, she had been in charge from before then because he was very ill for a long time.

At Camel Creek the main house and yard and garden were on one side of a square known as 'the flat' and in the1950's, the horse yards, cow yard and bail, feed shed, machinery and saddlery shed with forge, vehicle sheds and butcher's shop were on the other two sides. On the far side was the original hut and the big lagoon where we used to swim and collect waterlilies for Mum. The cattle yards were beyond the lagoon, about a quarter of a mile from the house.

Before their marriage, Dad had owned Camel Creek and lived in the original hut during the mustering season. By the time Mum came to Camel Creek a two bedroom cottage had been built, but there were hardly any other internal structures apart from a set of yards. They started from scratch and built the place up. Dad put in a lot of fences and dams. After Dad died, Toby, my eldest brother, continued with the work he'd learnt at Dad's knee. He maintained the machinery and lighting plant and serviced and repaired the vehicles. My second eldest brother, Keith, was interested in everything mechanical and liked to build things. Us kids, Lindy, my elder sister, Donny, my youngest brother, and I used to help with the cattle work; the mustering, branding and the drafting. Lindy learnt to ride at an early age and was as good as any man in the stock camp. Donny was also an excellent rider and had a natural ability for working cattle.

Toby, Keith, Lindy, Donny and I, as well as the stockmen's children, Maureen, Kenny, and Alan Grant and Mum's cousin, Beryl Wilson's three youngest children, Diana, David, and Stanley, were all taught at Camel Creek by Correspondence. The lessons came by the mail-man once every week. We began with the Preps: One, Two, Three and Four, then on to Grade One. Mr.Laffey was employed to teach in 1946, then a succession of governesses but then Mum took over. The schoolroom was the side verandah with proper desks and blackboards.

Mum was strict. One time Donny and I came into school with cheeks bulging with mouthfuls of watcr. But I didn't rcalizc Donny had swallowed his and was just puffing his cheeks out. Mum asked me a question and I couldn't answer. I couldn't swallow the water. I started to laugh and I sprayed water everywhere! I got a fair sort of a switching round the legs for that.

Mum was also very strict with spelling and reading. We read aloud to her. And we were not allowed to slump in our seats. At the dining table we were not allowed to slump either. Mum would walk along behind us and poke us in the back to make us sit up.

All the children on the place had jobs; sweeping the smoko-shed between the kitchen and the house; bringing in the wood for the fire, feeding the chooks, watering the garden, weeding. There were house cows that were brought in for milking. 'Kingie – Mrs. King, the lady that helped Mum run the house – used to do the milking and so that she would know where I was as a toddler, she used to take me down to the bails with her and sit me on the cow's back until she was finished. Later on the milking became Lindy's job.

Camel Creek was home away from home to many children.
Helen, front row, dark hair.

But we had a lot of fun. There was a tree down near the creek where the big boys built a tree-house. Actually it wasn't much more than a platform but we thought it was marvellous. There was a plank for walking from the branches. During the construction us little ones were the 'go-fers'. It would be, 'Oh! Helen! Just slip up to the shed and see if you can find a such-and-such.' We would just get back and it would be, 'Just slip up to the house and bring a - ' whatever it was they thought they couldn't do without. But we thought it was wonderful, helping these master-builders.

At Christmas we always had Christmas presents. Mum always gave books. Every child was given one. And she might buy a compendium of games. Correspondence School was a good grounding to go to boarding school. When I was nine years old I went to Blackheath College in Charters Towers. I was there from 1957 to 1960. My education was as good as anybody else's in my class. I was dux of the class for the four years. Then I had three years down at Moreton Bay College in Brisbane.

When I was sixteen I felt I had finished my formal education and I applied for nursing. But I had to wait eight months before I could start so I decided to go governessing. I found a job with people named Patterson, on a station named Mellish Park about thirty miles from Gregory Downs in the Gulf. To get there I took the train to Cloncurry and then went by the mail-man, Kevin Hansen, out to Gregory Downs. I remember that on the steering wheel was this strange name that I had never seen before. 'Toyota'. That was 1964.

The day before this, there had been flooding, so we only got as far as Nardoo Station. The river there was in flood, and they had to put me in a boat to take me across. So that was an adventure for a start! But I knew the people, Fay and Ken Webber, so I spent the night at Nardoo. The Pattersons, Beryl and Dave, came from Mellish Park to pick me up the next day.

The Pattersons were very nice people to work for. I was teaching two children, Frankie and Susan. The Aboriginal children on the place used to come and check me out during lesson time. One day this big goanna came running past with about five or six piccaninies chasing after it. Of course, this was an excuse for Frankie and Sue to go chasing after it too. The poor old goanna ran up this tree that was about eight feet high. With his weight the tree bent over until it was almost touching the ground. Those Aboriginal kids pounced. They grabbed him and went marching off with him down to their camp. Later they came back and invited me down to the corroboree they were going to have to eat him. I had to say, 'Thank you very much, but I don't think I could possibly eat any goanna.'

I had only been there a little while when there was a cyclone in the Gulf. The creeks started coming down. It was strange where they had built the homestead. It was on a flood-plain between two creeks, Plum Tree Creek and Firey Creek. Firey Creek was only a couple of hundred yards from the homestead. Most of the time it was dry. It was only because of the cyclone that it came down. When they bought the place the Pattersons had been told that the ridge never flooded.

But that afternoon as the waters started to rise, the Aboriginals just went. One of the men came over and told us, 'We're all taking off for the hills! We'll be back after.' But at least he came to tell us! And it was already very deep by then! They took off for the funny little flat top hills that you see out west. But we were busy trying to pick things up and get them out of the water. The shed had a lot of bags of cement stored in it. 'Save the cement!' was the order of the day. We had to carry it to the house and stack it into the spare bedroom. I only managed about two bags.

The kitchen, school-room, the radio-room and the laundry were all on the ground. Upstairs, three or four steps up, separated by a breezeway, were the bedrooms and lounge and the verandah. That afternoon the water got higher and higher and when it started bubbling up through the floor of the kitchen we really had to move. Only half of the building, the part above the kitchen, was sealed. So we put mattresses up into the unsealed part and some bedding for the kids. The water was moving pretty fast by then and we were all grabbing chooks and throwing them up onto the rafters.

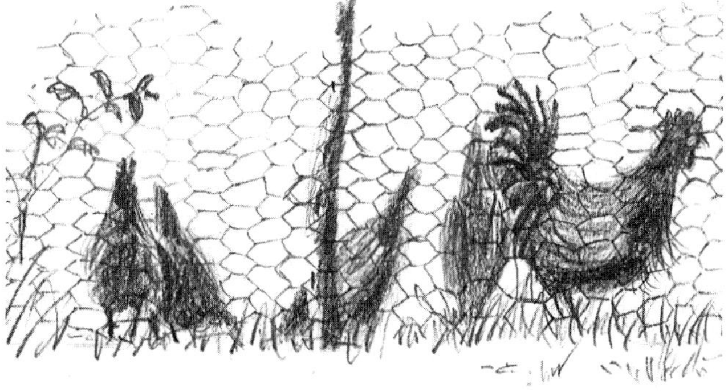

Beryl had this nice china cabinet, a modern one with sliding glass doors. She asked me what I thought she ought to do with it. She was pretty upset. I said we ought to try to get it up on to the kitchen table. So we emptied all the china out and she and I picked the cabinet up and lifted it on to the table and then put all the china back into it. We also put the flour and other stores up as high as we could. By then it was starting to get dark. Beryl gave us all a meal because we didn't know what might happen during the night.

When the water got too high Dave made the kids get up into the ceiling. And then he remembered the pet calf. It had been shut in the laundry. So Dave and I got the torch and waded round to the laundry. (Beryl did all her own laundry herself. She used the copper and a petrol-driven washing machine that you had to kick over like a motor-bike to get started.) By this time the water was rushing into the laundry and all that you could see by the light of the torch was the nose of the calf with his little nostrils sticking out above water. Dave picked him up in his arms and I had the torch to guide him back. It was pitch dark. The dog, a boxer, had floated away in the flood.

When we had rescued the calf – and he was very strong and very indignant – the next problem was what were we going to do with him! There was already three feet of water through the house and so where were we going to put a very cold wet calf! But Beryl had a linen cupboard that was open at the top so that the top shelf was like a calf-sized pen. So we put him into the top of this linen-cupboard. He could just put his head over the side and all night he went 'Blah!' But he was lucky to be alive because Dave had only just remembered him in time. And as the chooks dropped down from the rafters we kept chucking them up again.

When there wasn't anything else we could do, us adults got up into the ceiling too. And Dave took an axe up in case he had to knock a hole in the roof for us to escape through on to the roof-top if the water came up too high.

In the morning when we came down, well, you couldn't believe the mud! We spent days shovelling it out of the house; hosing it out; washing the bed spreads; washing everything! A lot of the cement was ruined because the water had got into the layers of bags at the bottom. So for all our efforts, a lot of this precious cement was had it.

The china cabinet survived the night. The water had just covered the top of the kitchen table but didn't get into the cabinet. And we had saved the flour so Beryl could still make bread. When we went walking around outside there was this white chook sitting on the fence just staring. I thought it was dead because I felt its comb and its feet and they were like ice. I thought, 'Oh! You poor thing!' and then it went, 'Brahk!' and blinked. So I picked it up. By then Beryl had got the cast-iron stove going so I put this chook in the wood-box beside the stove to warm it up. That poor old chook! It wasn't very long before she laid an egg and she didn't even have time to put a shell on it! She was so shocked!

When the water went down two days later, the men went down the river in the boat to see if they could find any cattle to save but all they saw was a lot of drowned cattle. But there was the dog! He'd got himself on to a bit of an island.

The cattle losses were very heavy. The Pattersons lost so much stock that they told me they just couldn't afford to employ a governess any more. But they found me another position, with the Clarkes on Almora, teaching their two children Leslie and Carmel. In August I left to begin my nursing course at Townsville General, a four year course.

But after two years I met my future husband Bob at an old-time dance. As I was leaving with my girlfriend we heard a loud 'Oi!' Ignoring it, we got into our taxi. Next thing Bob rushed over from where he had been standing with his mates. 'Didn't you hear me yell 'Oi!' he demanded. I firmly told him, 'I don't answer blokes that yell 'Oi!' at me!' He said, more calmly, 'Well, will you go to go to the dance at Woodstock with me tomorrow night?' As the taxi moved away, I told him where I lived. We still hadn't exchanged names. The next night he came and met my mother and my brother before we went off to the dance. He told me later, that he was very relieved I was the same girl he had met the night before! We were married on January 14th, 1967, at St James Cathedral, Townsville.

In 1990, thirty years and six children later, I still hadn't forgotten my desire to do nursing. In 1991 I enrolled at the TAFE[2] College in Townsville and did a Nursing Bridging Course with the idea of going to University and doing a Bachelor of Nursing Science. I started studies at James Cook University of North Queensland in 1992 and after a lot of hard work graduated at the end of 1995 with my Nursing Degree, a Registered Nurse at last.

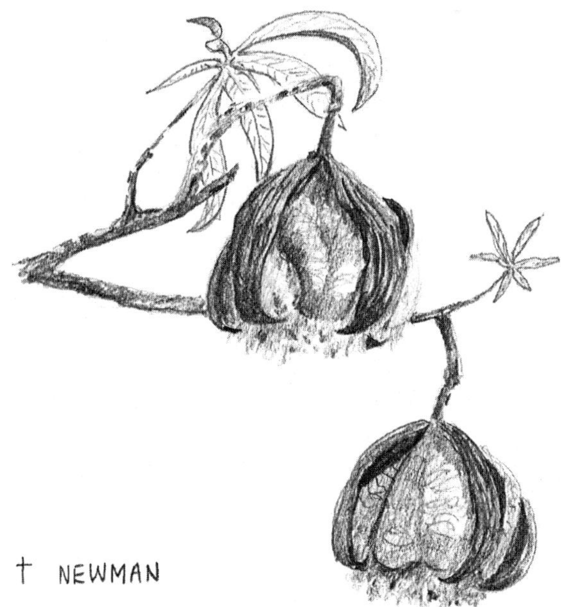

[2] TAFE: College of Technical and Further Education

9

Kerry Kendall

ॐॐॐ

Introduction

You would never guess that Kerry Kendall, immaculately dressed and face alight with enthusiasm, suffers chronic pain from a serious back injury sustained as a very young ringer on historic Dotswood station. 'It only hurts if I think about it,' he laughs.

Dotswood Station, one of the earliest properties in the north to be taken up, was selected in 1863 by Philip Somer and his partner John Hervey. This was two years earlier than the first buildings were erected at the new settlement of Townsville on the coast. At that time Dotswood would have been regarded as a remote run, Bowen being the administrative centre for the north. When a boiling-down works was established at Townsville in 1866, the first cattle treated for 'tallow and hides' was a mob of five hundred from Dotswood, at £2/6/- per head. The property changed hands seven times until 1930 when it was taken over by the Queensland State Government and run for fifty-eight years as part of Queensland Stations Pty Ltd, who also held, among others, Lyndhurst, Wando Vale, Vanrook and Strathmore in the Gulf and Keeroongooloo in the Channel Country. During Australia's involvement in the Vietnam War, Dotswood was taken over by the Commonwealth Government for army training purposes.

Kerry gives a good account of life on Dotswood. One highlight was of Wombinto, a 'wild blackfellow', on the Little Star River behind the Paluma Range. Readers should not be offended by the term 'blackfellow'. In the time of which Kerry speaks it was still an acceptable term in everyday use, in no way intended to offend. Kerry has been on good terms with people of Aboriginal and mixed-race origin all his life and held by them in equally high regard.

Kerry introduces us to some memorable men he was 'proud to have worked with'; Fred Kreidemann, Ray Davidson and Mick Paerks, who could plait number-eight wire. We can enjoy, through Kerry's keen powers of observation, the wild-life on Rutland Plains on Cape York Peninsula, one of Australia's remotest cattle stations; crocodiles, magpie-geese, barramundi, 'big muddies waving their nippers' and the rare golden-shouldered parrot flashing through the bush. The account of the overturned boat and the struggle to save the two children is told simply and movingly and exemplifies the extraordinary nobility of the human spirit when called upon to protect the young.

After some years of working in the Territory, Kerry was forced by ill-health to retire. He now lives in Mackay and takes pleasure in his fine collection of rare Australiana and his wide circle of appreciative friends in the cattle industry.

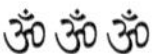

The Young Ringer

Kerry Kendall

'I worked with some good men in the bush.'

I was always destined to go ringing. When I was a kid in the mid-fifties the drovers used to come down over the range on their way to the meat-works in Townsville. Riding about up the top of Ross River, I got to know them, old Harold Lavery and old Clyde Quinn. One time they had this big mob of bally bullocks[1] on dinner camp. The bullocks never moved as I rode up. They were a perfectly uniform mob from Dotswood, thirty miles north of Mingela, with the 'D O T' brand.

When I turned fifteen I got a job on Dotswood. The homestead was a big old historic place with nice gardens, out-buildings and good ringers' quarters and they fed their men properly. The manager, Bob Morrison, knew how to work men to get the best out of them. The tucker was as good, which meant he got men who stayed on. Dotswood had good horses which in turn meant good cattle. Dotswood was about nine hundred square mile then, but in the early 'sixties, four blocks were resumed off it; Mirrambeena, which had been the Dotswood bullock paddock, Payne's Lagoon[2], Lancewood and Kirkland Downs.

The herd was predominately Hereford but they were starting to introduce Brahmans, using 1XL bulls from Glen Prairie outside Rockhampton. The station camp was the bullock depot to fatten stores from Strathmore and Vanrook in the Gulf that were walked down by an old drover, 'Seventy' Priestly. There were seven or eight of us in the Dotswood station camp with Boz Bancroft as the head stockman. Boz was a top cattleman and horseman and

[1] Bally bullocks; white-faced Herefords

[2] See Chapter 4, Volume One; John Nicholas, *With Persistence and Determination*

understood bullocks. It was an era when one or two pounds weight on a beast meant a lot. Nothing was ever galloped as it is today with motor-bikes and helicopters.

Not long after I started there, two contract musterers, Gordon Davidson and Alex Corbett, were down on Mirrambeena, and Gordon Davidson, a hell of a good man, got crook. Mirrumbeena was down towards the Burdekin on the northern side of Keelbottom creek. It was the wet season and the creeks were up. Alex knew enough to realize Gordon was in a pretty bad way and needed medical help. He got him on to the tractor to drive through up to Dotswood but they didn't get far before the tractor bogged. So Alex walked back to Mirrambeena and caught two horses. He got Gordon into the saddle and set off for Dotswood again. By this time Gordon was really in a bad way. Eventually Alex gets him up to Dotswood but the homestead was on the far side of the creek and it was running a banker.

He yelled out and the house-girls at the homestead heard him and we all went down. One of the ringers, Bernie Mossman, only a young fellow, about eighteen or nineteen, but pretty athletic, said, 'I'll swim over and give Alex a hand to tow Gordon across.' He pulled off all his gear off and swum over. Then he and Alex stripped off Gordon's boots and gear and Alex strapped his stirrup leathers around his chest and pulled Gordon's arm through and swam supporting him. The current washed them downstream but big Alex Corbett just powered across. We got Gordon up on the bank and carried him up to the homestead and the Flying Doctor was called. It turned out that what Gordon had was appendicitis. Without Alex's help he wouldn't have made it.

The outstation on Dotswood was called The Star. It had a top homestead with gardens and outbuildings right on the bank of the Little Star River. Fred Kreidemann, a very capable man, was the head stockman. He was very good with young fellows. He wouldn't put you on anything he thought was going to be too good for you and any beast that had to be thrown he would be there to keep an eye on things.

The Star was where most of the Dotswood breeding was done. A lot of the country ran right up into the mountains behind Paluma and Herveys Range, with a lot of water coming down from the heads of the Big Star River and the Little Star and Keelbottom Creek, all good waters, but wild country. There was a lot of tropical rain forest which meant there were problems with the stock because with so much water and so much forest you got a lot of cleanskins. But it was good experience for a young fellow.

One time I was riding a colt, chasing a beast and this colt got his feet tangled up in the flannel weed[3], wiry tough stuff, growing on the edge of the airstrip. When he fell he came over on top of me and knocked me out. The ringers took me in as far as they could to meet the ambulance and I finished up in the Charters Towers hospital. I had a sore head but mostly a very bad back and neck. I might have been pretty lucky.

I loved working on The Star. Every day there was something new to be learned. Or to be found. Jimmy Mossman, another young ringer, the same age as me, found a blackfellow cave when we were mustering up along the Big Star River. He was riding along up in the

[3] *sida cordifolia*

top of these gullies when he came across it in the side of the hill, very well camouflaged. He called me to come up and have a look. Inside there was a bit of bark and an old axe; not a blackfellow axe, a little steel axe, three-quarter size, but with a bush handle in it, and a flour drum and two magazines, a *Man Junior* and a *London Opinion*. Jim took the axe back to our camp at The Basin where Fred Kreidemann told us 'Thanks!' and that he'd have it.

It seems that in the 'thirties, there'd been a blackfellow called Bobby Wombinto, living in the wild country on Dotswood. He'd been brought up by the Moore family of Ravenswood. He arrived down at Dotswood with his own plant of horses, which was very unusual for a blackfellow, in those days. One day the book-keeper came up to him and said, 'Bobbie, there's a policeman comin' to get you today. He's gunna take you back to Palm Island to live.' Palm Island had been established as a re-settlement centre for Aboriginals from across North Queensland. Bobbie didn't want to be taken away so he left his horses, his swag and his clothes and went bush. He just disappeared and after a while he was forgotten.

Quite a few years later, men out mustering started seeing bits of signs like a hole cut in an ironbark where a possum had been chopped out or places where little cooking fires had been lit. People became aware that there was a 'wild blackfellow' up there. No-one knew who he was. They'd all forgotten about Bobby Wombinto.

Then one time, Fred Fryer was riding along and he came across a log with the name 'Wombinto' chopped into it with an axe. Or ringers mustering up there would come across holes in the bottom of a tree with a piece of bark or a branch across where this blackfellow would have chopped a possum out and blocked it up with a piece of bark so that he could come back there in three or four months time and tap the side of the tree and know how far down the hollow came and if there was another possum in it.

And one day there was a fellow up there riding round - probably pinching cleanskins; which was what happened in those days - and he heard this chopping noise in the distance. He sneaked up and he saw this little blackfellow cutting a hole in a tree. So this bloke took out his tobacco tin and just handed it to him. This eased the tension and they had a bit of a yarn and he found out that it was Bobby Wombinto.

They had a yarn and then Wombinto disappeared again and wasn't seen for some time. A few years later Charlie Freeston was riding up in a little pocket at the head of the Keelbottom and he come across a little tiny fire and he looked about but couldn't see anyone. What used to warn Bobbie was the birds. A butcher bird, when it's startled, will make a certain call. So Bobbie might hear a butcher bird's warning and he would take off and hide.

And over the years the ringers got to know this old blackfellow was up there and if they had any old clothes or a spare tin of tobacco or a bit of tea or sugar they'd hang it in a bag in a tree for him to find. And when they'd come back the bag'd be gone and there might be a pair of hobbles or a horse-bell that had been lost, hanging there. In that country there were these little block-fences; not a proper paddock fence, just a three-wire fence maybe from the top of a ridge down to the river, to block the cattle from getting up into the mountains. And sometimes the ringers would come across a place where the wire might have fallen down and been tied up again and they would know it had been done by Wombinto.

Gradually, Wombinto started to show himself a bit more. One time, an old drover, Bob Masso, was on his way down to Townsville with bullocks and late one afternoon old Wombinto walked into his camp, stark naked. Bob said he smelled like hell. He'd rubbed possum fat on himself to keep the mosquitoes off. It kept the mosquitoes off alright. But that's what the blacks used to do when the mossies were bad.

And as Bobby started to get on a bit in years he got friendly with an old couple, old Annie and Jack Bamford, who had a little bit of a place right up at the top of the Keelbottom. And every now and then Bobbie'd just come up to their place and to let them know he was there he would tap on a tobacco tin lid. And old Mr. Bamford would hear this and would take him out some old clothes to put on. And he'd stay a while at the Bamfords and they'd fatten him up a bit and he'd chop a bit of wood for them and after a bit he would poke off again.

And then one time the Bamfords were going down to the Townsville Show and Wombinto said he wanted to go with them. He must have bumped into a couple of his relations at the Show. He told Mr. Bamford he was going to go back to Palm Island with these 'lations' to have a bit of a look at the place and if he didn't like it he would come back with them to the Keelbottom. So he went. But he mustn't have been able to handle being cooped up on Palm Island. He was only over there a very short while and he died.

On Dotswood I was privileged to work with some of the best men in the country. Ray Davidson, now he could ride! He was nearly unthrowable. And his brother, Gordon, could do anything with horses and cattle. Their father was an old bushman and drover, Long Tom Davidson. Then there was old Mick Paerks. Mick could plait wire! The average bloke could plait a bit of leather but Mick plaited Number 8 wire! The wire wasn't heated; he plaited it cold. A lot of people have seen toasting forks, just a twist of wire with prongs at the end. But Mick used to do these beautiful plaited fork-handles and the work was immaculate. Not a plait out of place. He made me a fork with my initials in the top and eighteen inches of this incredible plaited handle down to the prongs; a work of art.

His brother Kevin used to make beautiful knives. He'd make them out of cross-cut saw blades and put beautiful inlaid handles on, out of cow horn or deer horn. His pocket knives were spring-loaded just like a Henry Boker or a Joseph Rogers. He'd pick up a bit of old brass from around a windmill that no-one would give two bob for and he'd just wear it away with the file and inlay this into the handle.

The head stockman on The Star, Fred Kreidemann, used to tell me about a place up on the Peninsula, Rutland Plains, that his son Robert was managing. Fred had managed it himself at one time. I thought to myself, 'Gee, I'd like to have a look at that country; the blackfellows and the wild life and the crocodiles.' So I went up. Rutland was an Angliss place on the western side of Cape York about two hundred and fifty miles north of Normanton and two hundred and thirty mile west of Chillagoe. The homestead was a very old historical place with big mango trees. The blacks had good quarters down on the side of a big lagoon, a beautiful spot.

Rutland was taken up in the early 1900s by Frank Bowman. The blacks speared him and he is buried beside the horse-yards. I helped put a fence around the grave. Two Murries[4] that worked with me, Matt Gilbert and Wilson Horace, told me that there was always a lot of conflict between Bowman and the blacks. It was before their time but they knew the story.

Grave on Rutland station of Frank Bowman, speared by tribal Aborigines in 1910 in retaliation for his harsh attitude.

Rutland was completely different country to Dotswood; no hills or mountains. When I first got there I thought, 'How the hell am I going to find my way around here!' The first muster I had big trouble. We got together a mob of cattle, some quiet and some cleanskin wild things. I thought, 'Hell! Now how am I going to find my way back?' But I had good blackfellows working with me and they helped me. There was always something to see or do; different creeks and waterholes. There was a rare parrot that's on the endangered species list, the golden shouldered parrot.

The blacks on Rutland came from Mitchell River Mission, later called Kowanyama, and there was no alcohol there so they were good men to work with. You might have six blackfellows in your camp or for a bullock muster, as many as ten. We mustered all the year round, using pack-horses in the Wet and an old Blitz in the Dry. We had good horses on Rutland. Angliss always bought good thoroughbred stallions.

By the second round of mustering I'd got to know the country. You could go by the water courses which all ran one way, east to west into the Gulf. The sand ridges were nothing like the sand ridges out at Birdsville. These would have been just a couple of feet high, covered with tea tree and bloodwood. There are only two seasons in the Peninsula, the Wet and the Dry. In the Wet there was water lying about everywhere.

Rutland was a breeding property, mainly Shorthorn and then they started introducing

[4] Colloquial usage for 'Aborigine'. The term has become widely accepted as preferred

Droughtmaster bulls from Kirkne station on the Burdekin. We used to send steers away at about eighteen months down to Iffley on the downs country to fatten on the good Mitchell grass.

There were areas of Rutland that were pretty wild. All the coast country had the beach. In behind the beach there was scrub half a mile through and then it would run out into open plains and gilgai flats. That scrub wouldn't feed a bandicoot and in places you were flat out riding through it. The cattle used to camp in the scrub during the day and come out late afternoon to feed on the big open flats covered with coastal couch.

We had a mustering camp called Coastal Springs with a good holding paddock. We would leave early in the morning with coachers and try to get the cattle before they made it back into the scrub. Coastal Springs was a beautiful camp under big shady Leichhardt trees. Most of the day was spent around the camp, or sometimes I might go with the blackfellows spearing fish or catching crabs if the tide was out. When you walked out at low tide there might be, say, a foot of water on the flats. And when you got close to the crabs, those big muddies would sit up and wave their nippers up at you. But the Murries would just put a spear through their shell, chuck them in a potato-bag and sling it over their shoulder.

And then about four o'clock in the afternoon we would leave camp with a mob of coachers and poke along the edge of the scrub. By late afternoon there'd be cleanskins and micky bulls starting to come out to get out on to the good grass. And we would get round them and run them into the coachers. Sometimes there'd be a bit of throwing to be done. Then we'd take them back in the dark to this big holding paddock at Coastal Springs. You'd hear the waves on the beach and we'd be yarding them in the dark. We'd leave again early the next morning and do the same thing.

Once we'd got a mob together we'd move them back to another camp called The Lakes, right out in the middle of a big open flat on a dam and we'd bronco them there. The calves would be branded and any males taken to the bullock paddock. Old bullocks, cleanskin cows and culled cows were moved to the outstation, Lochnegar, where they were kept until the arrival of the *Ida Clausen* to be sent to Queerah meat-works in Cairns. We might put two hundred head on it.

One of the main camps for the bullock muster was Swan Hole. We would walk all these old culled cows and piker bullocks down to what was called The Landing on the Nassau River, which was the southern boundary of Rutland with Inkerman station; a big murky river, a couple of hundred yards across. I'll never forget the first time! We were bringing the cattle in from the watering point to The Landing and I looked up and here was this huge boat beyond the tree line! You think you are a million miles from anywhere and suddenly there's this boat! It was so unexpected! That boat used to come right up nearly to the bank and then they used to winch out a pontoon. It would have been thirty feet across. And then they would put a ramp down with a portable race, bolted together. Then there was a loading ramp right to the very edge of the river. Because of the tidal rise and fall you had to wait for the tide and then everything would come up level. It was a big occasion and everyone, house-girls and all, would come down from the station, probably thirty mile, to watch. The crew were all Scandinavian; Swedes or Norwegians, all blond-headed fellows and they'd invite the whites on board for a big meal. They had a proper chef, and us, we'd been living pretty rough!

Every fresh water lagoon on Rutland was full of barramundi that would get stuck there after the wet season. The floods'd come and when the water dropped the barra would be left. We never had any fancy rods or lures like they have today. The old camp cook, Norm Smith, used to make lures for us out of old pudding spoons. He'd cut the handle off a spoon about half an inch up and drill a hole with a hand-drill and put a couple of copper rivets in with a ring-piece of wire. He'd rivet one big hook in with a bit of baling twine hanging off it and we'd throw these in. We'd always get a barra.

Those old Murries on Rutland always carried their fish spears. We had an old Blitz to carry all the camp gear and we'd be putting all our gear up on top and these old Murries, all they would have would be their fish spears to put on. And when we'd get sick of eating beef we'd tell old Matt Gilbert – he was a terrific old Murrie – and he'd go down and spear a barra for us whites and one for their own camp. We ate separately. And if you went down with them to the lagoon you wouldn't be able to see the barramundi. All you would see would be a tiny little movement in the water. But they would just lean back with their spear and, whisht! It'd be a head-shot every time! Fifteen or twenty pounders. They never missed.

The '*Ida Clausen*' preparing to load Rutland cattle in the Nassau River, using a portable race and pontoon.

Those fish spears, they'd be about nine feet long. They would use custard apple tree for making them but there were a few other different trees they used. They'd use smoke and steam and the heat off the fire to straighten them out and number-eight fencing wire for the prongs. They always used a woomera. I tried throwing a spear with a woomera once. It went thirty feet in the opposite direction. The Murries thought it was a real joke.

All the Murries liked their bush tucker. You could dish them up a nice piece of roast top-side and later you'd go past their camp and they'd be eating a goanna! And they preferred catfish to barra! Slimy things but the Murries would throw them straight in the fire, guts and everything! Same as goanna and geese. Straight on the fire!

In the Wet the magpie geese bred in the big open swamps, maybe two or three mile across, all open water-grass, about two foot deep. All the geese bred together; hundreds and hundreds of nests about four foot apart. Each nest would be maybe three foot across and to make it the geese would just fold the water-grass over to make a platform and gradually build it up, seven or eight inches. They'd chop off the tops of the grass and line the nest with the tops. I've seen nine or ten eggs in some nests, each a bit bigger than a chook-egg; a dirty sort of creamy colour. We would wade out and collect some and scramble them; the geese would just flutter away a couple of feet. We didn't worry too much about crocs. The water was only a couple of feet deep and if there'd been a croc you would have seen it. The blackfellows used to go with bags and get eggs by the hundreds. They'd put grass in the bottom of a potato bag and then a big mob of eggs, and then another layer of grass until they ended up with a bag so full they'd be barely able to lift it. They used to prefer eggs with babies in! They'd just throw them in the hot ashes to cook and eat them by the dozen. They loved 'em!

There were crocodiles about but not as many as you would see today. I found an old .303 in one of the sheds and I done it up. We would do a bit of croc shooting at the week-ends. If you were lucky enough to get one it would help your ringer's wages a bit. One particular waterhole on Cabbage Tree Creek had a big salty in it. He used to come up his mud slide. I decided to sit up a tree and wait for him to surface. I waited for about four hours. Then there was a bit of a movement in the deep water, twenty or thirty feet out. His nose come up and part of his head. Then he went under again and I thought, 'Hell! He's gone!' But then he comes up again and now he's about three feet off the bank. Just gradually he starts coming up out of the water. He drags himself up until he could just put his head down on the dry bank. I waited a bit hoping he'd come up further, but he didn't. I thought, 'Well, if I hang around any longer he might go!' so I put a shot into him, just behind the eye. You only get one shot at a crocodile; you miss and they're gone! They've got a very small brain, even a sixteen footer. You've got to hit it, first go. If you didn't, that was it.

We used to skin them from the top of the back, right down and around the belly. I got about three weeks' wages out of that one. A salty was worth about $3.60 an inch so they were good money. We used to get fresh-water crocs as well, but they were only worth about $1.60 an inch. We didn't get that many because there were still shooters about then and the crocodile, he becomes very cunning. We would dry-salt the skins and wrap them in a moist potato bag. Clydey Lunn, the truckie from Chillagoe, used to cart them in to the buyer in Cairns for us, though he'd whinge a bit about the salt getting into his truck.

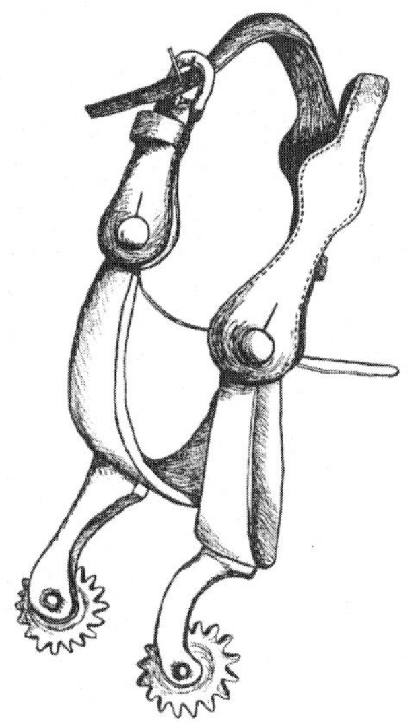

One time we were camped out at Pear Tree; a pretty big camp; drafting yards and all. We had old Wilson Horace, a real good old blackfellow and one day he got me on one side, and he whispered to me, 'Hey! Kerry! You know how to read?' I said, 'Yeah! I know how to read.' He said, 'I got a letter in here. Ole Kreidemann give 'im to me but I can't read 'im.' And he said, 'I doan wanna ask them other blackfellows how to read, y'know.' So I said, 'Yeah. Righto. Give's a look at it.' And I opened it up. And I'll never forget the handwriting in it. It was copybook perfect. Probably the best handwriting I've ever seen. But what was written was all Murrie. There were probably four or five pages to it and while I was reading it out to him, Old Wilson would laugh like hell! But then he'd think to himself that the other blackfellows might be watching and he'd stop.

I read it to him a couple of times and then a couple of weeks later he rode up beside me. I could see him coming and I knew he had something on his mind. He said to me, 'You know how to write, Kerry? You know how to write?' I said, 'Yeah. I know how to write. Not much good but I know how.' So I wrote a letter for him and read it back to him and then I give it to Kreidemann to put in the mail-bag. Wilson was a decent old man. For years afterwards, every time I was up that way I would call in and see him.

The mouth of the Topsy Creek, near Mitchell River Mission, the scene of the boat capsize.

One Easter week-end – we never worked over Easter – the whole station decided to go for a bit of a fishing outing to the mouth of Topsy Creek. We went down to Mitchell River Mission and teamed up with a couple of white families and some blackfellows from there. Arthur White was in charge of the cattle side of things at the mission and he had a little aluminium ten-footer. He freighted us all across to the Rutland side of Topsy Creek to where the best barra fishing was, a rocky sort of place, all petrified shell-grit turned into rock. Whitey ran us across in the dinghy, a couple at a time, and we settled in to fish for the day. We caught a lot of fish and the blackfellows speared a lot of fish and crabs.

Late afternoon when the tide was starting to run out, we decided to call it a day and head back. So old Whitey took the different boatloads of people back. On the last trip there was Rob Kreidemann and his two little kids, Margaret and David, and myself, and as well, there was Norm Smith, the cook, and one of the blackfellows. I had young David on my lap. He would have been two, maybe three year old. Robert was sitting beside me in this bloody jam-tin of a boat and he had his daughter, Margaret; she might have been three or four, on his lap. We got out, maybe halfway across the creek, probably twenty or thirty yards, and there was too many of us in this little boat and there was hardly any freeboard. When we got into the tidal current the force of it hit the side of the boat and tipped us right over.

I had jeans on and a long-sleeved shirt and my hat and sandshoe-boots. The last thing I heard as we went over was Robert singing out to me, 'Can you swim, Kerry?' I don't know whether I answered him or not but when I come up I still had a grip on little David by one arm. The boat didn't sink; it just tipped upside down. So I slung this little David up on to the bottom of the boat. And Robert did the same with little Margaret. Whitey and the blackfellow took off, straight into the shore. We were right in the mouth of the creek and the problem was the tide rushing out was washing the upturned boat and us out into the Gulf, out into the open sea. So we reckoned, well, we've got to let the boat go and try to make it into the bank. So that's what we did.

It was a pretty tough swim. I'd never been a strong swimmer, but when you've got a little kid to think about, well, you've got to! The trouble was I couldn't get these mongrel sandshoe-boots off. Every time I'd go to reach down to hook them off, I'd sort've half sink. And I couldn't scrape them off. But, anyhow, I just kept him up. I held on to his little arm with one hand and sort've swam with the other. Me and Robert kept together, side by side. He said, 'We've got to stay together!' and old Norm Smith – a terrific old fellow Norm was – he said, 'I'll stay with the two of youse. And whoever knocks up I'll bloody take over from!' And we somehow got in close to this rocky bank and Norm took over from me and we hoisted the kids up; slung them up high on to these rocks. And, I tell you! Wasn't it good to feel the bank!

We were pretty lucky, because as the tide was going out, it developed a big-sand bar in the sea out off the mouth of the river. And the upturned boat got washed up on to this sand-bar. It was a long way round but one of the blackfellows jogged around and got out on to this bar and somehow grabbed the boat. But the oars had gone and the outboard wouldn't start. We retrieved a big fishing-line and tied it on and hauled it upstream, and on the slack of the tide, paddled with our hands and got across. I'd lost my hat but I still had these mongrel sandshoe boots! We'd lost all our fish of course. But that didn't matter. There could have been lives lost.

10

Tommy Saville

ॐ ॐ ॐ

Introduction

There is something of a mystery about the opening of Tommy Saville's story. I met Tommy on the Meals on Wheels run from Camooweal hospital with Lorna Freckleton. Tommy Saville was a resident at the Old People's Home, a frail, gentle little man in a seemingly too-large bed. Courteously, he accepted that, 'Yes, please,' he would have the soup, and 'Yes, please,' the beef, and, 'Oh, Yes, please,' the pudding, at the same time ordering his two lanky dogs to get out of our way. I then asked Tommy if I might come back later to talk to him about his experiences in the droving days. Tommy agreed, seeming to know that, little and old as he might be, he had achieved a certain status in the township.

Later, cattleman Ray Fryer returned with me to tape an interview. I believed that Tommy would feel more comfortable talking about his droving days with another cattleman there. On the tapes Tommy begins his story; 'My old Mum was up at Lawn Hill, camped. I was just a little kid. And these drovers, they come riding into the camp. They picked me up, by my arm like that and slung me up on a horse. And they took me away with them. When I was working they would have to saddle my horse for me and lift me up. I was too little. I never seen my old Mum again.' When I exclaimed in horror, 'Never saw your mother again!' Tommy repeated, 'Never.' And yet, in the account, recorded by Bruce Simpson and Professor Bill Gammage of the National University's Australian Drovers' Project the year previously, Tommy related that he 'grew up around here' meaning Camooweal. For technical reasons it is that version which is presented here.

So which is the correct version? Tommy is dead now. Well into his early-nineties, affectionately regarded by those who knew him as something of an icon of the old droving days, Tommy died in 2005 in Mount Isa hospital. Perhaps in making the tapes with Ray Fryer and myself, he sensed sympathetic listeners and gave the true version of being 'removed' from his family, as he remembered it. Because Ray Fryer, 'six foot four and big with it', a respected founding member of the Camooweal Drovers' Camp Festival was present, Tommy would not have taken us for credulous listeners. But, perhaps, when interviewed by the team from the University, with their impressive recording equipment, he had felt that he should give a politically correct version. I use a hand-held micro-cassette recorder for the very reason that it is less intrusive. Ray and I were simply visitors at Tommy's bedside in the Home, his dogs beside him, the occasional friend or relative dropping in to say 'G'day, Old Man'. It was all very informal; a relaxed and comfortable situation where perhaps a painful memory was more easily shared.

But at the time, Ray Fryer remarked that Tommy's standard of spoken English 'must have been from growing up in a drovers' camp'. All that can now be said is that we are all glad to have known Tommy even briefly and to have enjoyed listening to him tell of life in the long-ago of the droving days; of notable boss drovers, camp cooks, night horses, rushes, of flooded rivers, of bullocks good and bad and of the slow twelve week trips on 'drovers' time' when the two hour night watches of the resting cattle were set from sundown. Tommy Saville remains a worthy representative of the hundreds of Aboriginal stockmen who played a significant part in the development of the cattle industry across Australia's north.

Six o'Clock Sundown

Tommy Saville

'On Rocklands we never killed a stranger'

I was born at Lawn Hill[1]. We been coming out of Lawn Hill country to come down here.

Well, in them days when I was a kid there was only buggy and horses. We had to change; come down looking for work.

My father, he did stock work most of his life. He worked his way down to Lawn Hill and that's where he picked up with my old Mum. My Mum's name was Lena. She could have an Aboriginal name but I never heard it. There was two of them; a sister was name Megan. She was married to an old Yellafella called Paddy Daley. They were young girls in them days. They come in off Highland Plain to Lawn Hill.

But my people, my Dad and Mum, they never talk about those old days before station

[1] Lawn Hill station in the Gulf

work. But Dad, he was a good stockman. He used to do a bit of horse breaking on different stations. A lot of horses on Rocklands, those old days. Good horse country. They don't use them now. I was sort of reared on Rocklands. I was a bit of a kid, y'know. I started work there. I can't tell what year; how old I was. But I remember the old boys used to saddle me horse up and lift me on. I couldn't get up. Yeah. Until I got strong enough, y' know.

Them times there was one old boy called Archie. And old boy called Tim. Old boy called Tippo. All there, those old boys, old local fellas. Head stockman used to be there, old Barney Lewis. Fellow called Jago was all-right manager. He was Returned Soldier. From the First World War. Yeah. And then he retired. Then old Robey[2] took over; Robey Miller. He used to drove off Rockland. Drove down to Tambo. I didn't go on the road with him. No, I've been with old Jack Carroll. From Rocklands to Tambo. Old Jack drove off Rocklands for a long time. Oh, long before. I was only a kid. Before I started work. Yeah. Even old Walter Cann. They was old timers there. There for a long time, them two. That's way back in them old days.

That other fellow used to be there, old Tommy Neade. Old boy called Paddy Lloyd. Yeah. He used to be the old cowboy; work around the station; milk the cows. There'd be a good few fellas in the camp, yeah; it'd be about nine or ten, eleven, maybe seventeen.

All bronco work then. You get on the old bronco horse and you got to rope them, (the calves); pull them up to the bronco ramp. There was about five or six men on the ground, catching. I did a bit of catching. You go until you do your round. You do your fifty. The other fella have a go. Good catchers. Hard those days. Yeah. But they used to be good, them days, y'know. Some day you might brand two hundred. Some day you might do three hundred, three fifty. Good way to brand cattle. But now it's all cradle[3], eh? Most places.

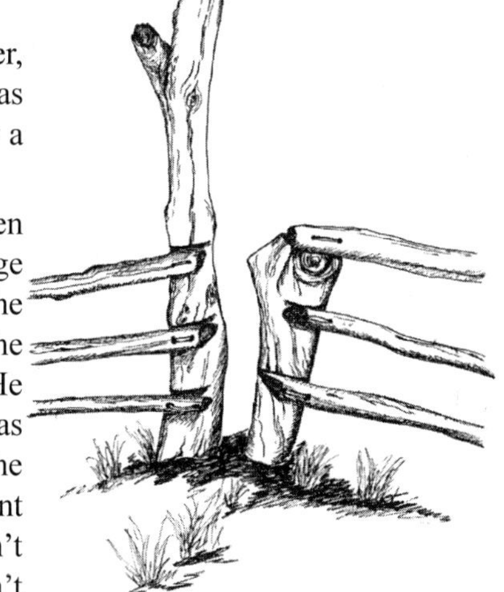

My family, I only got me niece and me brother, Ned Saville. He only a young fellow. When he was a kid he was droving. He went with old Fin Finley a couple of years.

The best man on a bad horse would have been old Barney Lewis. All them old people, old George Lewis and all them, all good. He was running the camp there for a long time. His brother, he was the youngest fellow, Elmore Lewis, and he got killed. He left Rocklands. He went out in the Territory. He was chasing a mob of wild cattle and in the thick grass, the cane grass, y'know, he didn't know what was in front of him. There's a big, deep gully, and he couldn't stop, and the horse tried to jump it but he couldn't

---

[2] Robey Miller, manager of Rocklands station, Camooweal, 1945 – 1972

[3] Cradle; hinged apparatus for throwing calves on to their side for branding, ear-marking and castration.

make it. Hit the bank on the other side and the horse broke his neck and fell on top of him. He was there a couple of days under the horse. Terribly dead before they found him. The maggots were going through him, the old horse, y' know, and him.

Didn't get much money working on Rocklands. None when we first started off. We were sort of Under the Act[4] you know? Might get ten pound, twenty pound or something; in the hand at Christmas time. Or when you come in for Camooweal races. We had plenty of tucker. Tucker was all right. And the races come, just a couple of days off for the races. Back again. They used to have a good race here in Camooweal one time. Only rode in the the last race; the dark fellas' race, y' know. Boys used to bring horses, station horses, y' know, for them. Headingly, Barkly, all them places, Austral.

Us fellows never drank alcohol those days. I used to drink a bit. But it made me crook, y' know. That turned me off altogether. A lot of them now, I don't think they've done a day's work, if you ask me. The young fellas now, a lot of them go out, might stay out on the station a couple of week or a week and turn around and say, 'This is too hard for me. I'll go back and live on the Social Service'. No Social Service in my day. No, nothing. We had to work for our living. Only all horse work. No motorbikes. A horse was better.

I been droving with old Pic Willet. A coupla trip with him I did, from Alroy. And took a mob from Brunette, one part of it. Droving is all right, but it's too cold. You get down inside there[5] you get some cold winds. Cold nights. But especially with west to south wind. Bitter winter rain, oh! I think back now. Yeah. Well, some time it take him eleven week, some time twelve weeks. All depend, you know, what the drought look like. Some time it might be dry, you know; you got to travel a bit to get to the next feed.

Old Pic, he keep a good tucker camp. Yeah. When I was with old Pic I used to have to do the dog watch. And I done a bit of everything; mustering, horse tailing. Yeah. And I'd cook supper before I'd go to watch. And when I come off watch then wash up and all that. Get up in the morning and cook breakfast and call him. Then I had to go on watch.

When you cook and do that dog watch it gives you bit of a break; six o'clock sundown[6]. Yeah. The dog watch, well, that's the one between six and seven, before the main watches start. Just short watches till things are getting organized. While the people are having their supper. Two hour watches except for the dog watch. Depend on how many men you had, how long the watch. Short-handed you did more time. Yeah. The horse-tailer usually did first watch. He get up at half past three or four o'clock in the morning and he go out and muster the other horses, might be forty, fifty, or more. And the boss usually did the last watch. Yeah, early morning.

Some time they play up, the old bullocks; they rush. One time we got to the Hamilton

[4] Under the Act; The Protection of Aborigines Act under which Aborigines and part-Aborigines were Wards of the State. Their wages were paid to a local official, usually a police officer, known as the Protector of Aborigines, who then paid them an allowance on application and issued clothing and blankets etc. Remaining monies were, hypothetically, banked on their behalf. Restrictions on the sale of alcohol also applied.

[5] on the inland stock routes.

[6] 'Six o'clock sundown'; 'drovers' time', the time from which the routine watches of the cattle throughout the night were timed for the duration of the trip.

and a bloody sheep got in them.Yeah! Well, they played up all night. That's when I was with old Jack Carroll. They might just race from here to there. They don't go far. But the bad ones, that Wave Hill mob; once they start, they go; go for miles. They'd gallop, yeah. Some of them old boys they used to sing around 'em; quiet 'em down. Sing corroboree, y' know. Well, I couldn't sing corroboree; I never learned. I'd hum a bit of a song around, y' know. Let them bullocks know you were riding around them.

You got to have about four or five night horses for night watch. Night horse, you might have two tied up at night. Well, he knows his work. If the cattle rush, he's good at night. You gallop and there might be a gully there, well, he jumps that gully and all that. Sometimes they make a mistake, they might hit a hole, eh, put his foot in a hole and go over and that's it.

There was a few old boys around Camooweal here who stuck with drovers a long time. Smiler, he come from Wave Hill. Old boy called Jack O'Keefe. He was with Keithy for a long time. Boy called Captain and his brother, Banjo Sam. And Banjo Finley. Banjo Finley was old Pop Finley's right hand man. He reared him on Thorntonia; that's where he was managing, the old fella.

Well, the last time I were broncoing they had them blue Percherons[7], you know, from Brunette. They were big horses; good horses. Well, he knows his work well too, old bronco horse. You just ride him into the cattle, rope the calf. Yeah! Rope him, Yeah! Pull 'em up to the ramp-post; then the boys put the leg rope on; the hind leg rope. Catch 'em with the hind leg and the other fellow gets the front leg. Grab his tail, pull him down; pull his legs out under him. That's the worst job, the leg roping. Then you earmark him with the big pliers, in the earhole. Yeah! And then brand him! And the head stockman does the cutting, the castrating.

Tommy was a skilled camp cook. The two camp-ovens half-buried in ashes were for baking bread or damper.

They used to dehorn 'em, too. I reckon that was bad, that. Oh, yeah! Flies, y' know! And in the wet weather, the blowflies blowing and all that. Poor buggers! Sometimes we used to put tar and fat, y' know, after you'd dehorn 'em.

We didn't draft the calves off. Put 'em all in. The lot. Cows and calves. Might be about a hundred, more. Sometime might be two hundred. But the most we done on Rockland, we done five hundred. One day we started; all day and all night; and all the next day. And that was five blokes on the ground and two on horses! Yeah! Catching!

[7] Percheron; a compact, heavy breed of work-horse, originally bred in le Perche region of north-west France.

When they cut 'em, take their balls out, sometimes we used to eat 'em. Not the big one, they're a bit strong. The little ones, y' know; they're good. Cook 'em on the branding fire. Good tucker. Them days there was no fridge or anything then, y' know, eh. We got mostly salt beef.

Rocklands, it'd be this side of the Northern Territory border there, and y'see, in the Wet time, the flood washed the fences down. Well, their cattle come through on to Rockland and Rockland cattle go through back in to their country; different place where the flood break the fences, y' know, so no fences. The cattle go in and out.

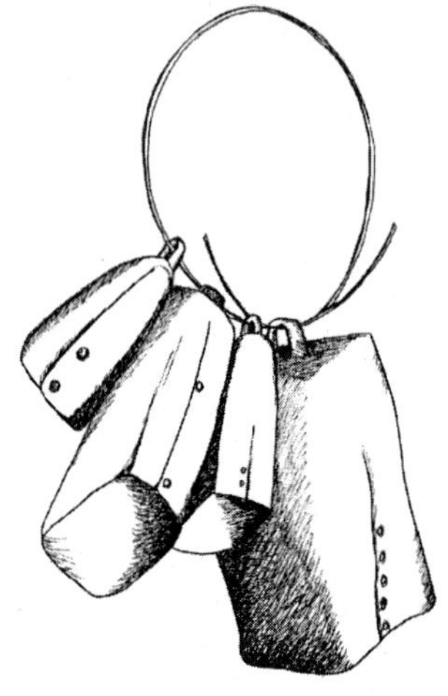

There'd be a muster, y' know, bring the cattle back. You just go out and join up with the other big stock camp, might be Avon (Downs). And Austral (Downs). Austral people come up the river. We all joined up in one big camp. And attending a muster there wasn't any arguments about the cattle. Sometimes them other place, well, they make a mistake, y'know. You can't help it. They might brand a Rockland calf, or Rockland might brand their calf. Well, they got to wait till they grow up. They take him back, when it leaves its mother. So, let 'em run with their mothers. Yeah. You bring the cattle back again and then there's a bloke do the fence, fix the fence up after.

Two old fella used to do the fencing. They used to have a wagon in them days. Old fella called Billy Booth and Sid Booth. And after, a bloke called Sid Johnson. He used to go out and do the fences.

On Rocklands we never killed a stranger. Maybe the old butcher might some time when he can't find a Rocky fat. Our butcher was an old cowboy fella called Didgery Jack. He used to work around the house, you know, clean up the big house and all around. Feed the pigs with the scraps. They used to have pigs there then. He'd kill a bullock; string the bullock up on a gallows when he killed; them old time gallows. Might be once a week. That's in the winter. And then in summer maybe two a week. Kill this week and again in another couple of days; kill a good fat one.

On stock camps you just have what they call a gambel. A stick, y' know. You shoot the bullock, put him on his back, take the hide out, put a bit of a cut above the hock to put the stick and you turn him over again and then cut him up; cut him up on the ground; spread the greenhide out so the meat won't get dirt, y' know. Save the hide. Make greenhide rope them days.

I done a bit of cooking with old Pic. And a bit out here at Rockland on the stock camp. When we haven't got a cook at the station, well, I had to do the cooking. I make everything. Cook a bit of pudding, dried fruit sometime and tinned fruit, custard. Maybe damper; yeast bread. The old time yeast, you had to boil it then put it in a bottle. You can put a bit of potatoes in with it but you gotta put the cork on pretty tight. When it dries up, well, it sort've blow the cork out. But then they brought in that Easy Bake, that dry balm stuff.

And making bread in the camp. When it come up, you work it once, roll it, put it back in the bucket till it come up again. You roll it again about three times. You rise it up again, then you roll it and put it in the oven, cut it up into pieces. Cut it up in little pieces and put 'em in the big oven, cast-iron oven. Well, I don't mind the old bush bread now and again or a damper. You might make three loaves in a big camp oven. If you got a small oven, well, you only just make one. And, them days you had the old coffee tin, y' know, and what I did, was in the middle I'd put a coffee tin to make it cook inside. I'd make bread might be two days, three days. If you made a good batch the blokes would hoe into it. It wouldn't last long. They got good feed of beef, too, sometimes jam.

Me, I didn't go much for bush tucker. A couple of times I had a feed of old goanna. But I haven't seen one for years, goanna. They're all died out. They've been dropping 1080[8] for the dingoes. Old goanna pick up something too at times, y' know; pick up that 1080. They chew the fat and that's it. There's not as many kite hawks around now. They come down and grab the bait, too.

There's not many fish in the Georgina these days. Maybe something wrong. A lot of them been dying, I think. I don't think they've been catching any lately. Must be some sickness. Maybe the Diamantina, too. The old Georgina only got water here and there's none between here and Lake Nash.

I been here a long time. The biggest flood on the Georgina was one time it nearly come halfway up to the old Freckleton store. That's halfway up the street. But I seen the flood when the dip-yard was the only high land. That was a fair flood. The river in that big flood, it'd be a fair way across it. It doesn't flood out on the other side, only on this side. Because of the high bank on that other side. But that flood it mainly came out to the town side. A lot of houses got water in them. See, there's Kaiser Creek and the Templeton and Gidgea Creek and the Ranken and times they're all in flood, well, back up to the Georgina, the water can't get away.

Tommy was an experienced stockman. He understood every aspect of the cattle industry.

When I was a kid here I can just remember a lot of old bagmen used to camp on the river, y' know. Old buggy men. Some with a spread cart, some pack, (with pack-horses) and some old foot-men. One old foot-man got caught in the flood. Poor old fella had to climb up the tree, halfway up. I think he was up there two days. They got him down after it. Poor

[8] 1080; A commercially produced poison bait scattered aerially to control dingoes.

old fella. And a Yellafella[9] called Georgie Wing and an old dark boy and that old boy called Thomas, well, they swam the river to get this old boy, swimming back across town side. Well, they swam in the middle and the old boy must have got a cramp. He drowned, poor bugger. Yeah, he drowned. Tommy was his name; Old Tommy Neade. He was married to the old fellow's daughter. And when they found him, he was way down near where Kaiser Creek junctions in. He got washed down to there.

Rockland's horses, they'd have a root. Some of them with a buck-jumper temper. I could hang up a bit m'self. Well, you had to ride or fall off if you don't stop on. You had to ride 'em those days. But some time you might get a new chum, a young fella, well, he got to learn, y'know. But I don't know about these young fellas these days, whether you can learn 'em or not. I don't know. I think they're more or less basically in motorbikes now.

We never had much time off in them days. You had to go out. Well, we were happy with it. Them days things was a bit hard and not like now, y' know. You couldn't get that and get this, what you wanted. They were sort've short of everything, y' know. But from that day on it was getting better and better; you can get whatever you want. Those days, we were happy. I think back now, it used to be good. Them old days, y'know, it's good to talk about.

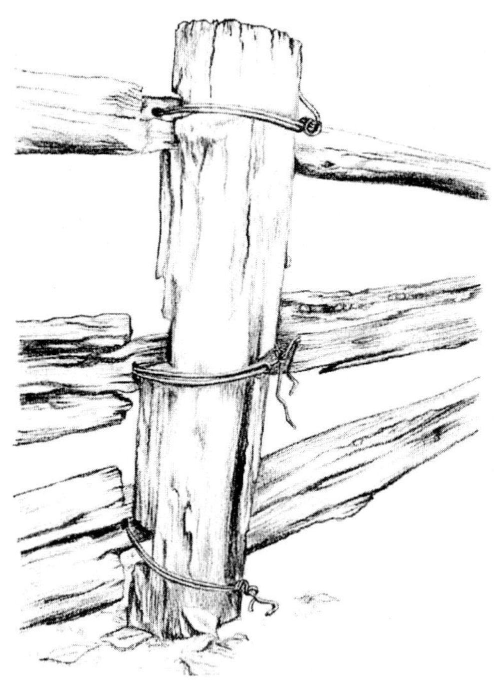

[9] Yellafella; colloquial usage for Mixed Race; not offensive in the north-west.

11

Wayne McCulloch

ॐ ॐ ॐ

Introduction

Wayne McCulloch has a gift for telling a story that is not only a gripping yarn but conveys a serious amount of information about the 'game' that he has loved since boyhood. His accounts of horse-tailing, cutting out from a mob and throwing a bullock from either a fast moving horse or on foot are of text-book quality for the step by step procedures outlined but told with such easy-going humour that the reader remains almost unaware that here is a man sharing the learning experiences of a lifetime so that the methodology of the old-style handling of cattle will not be lost for ever.

Wayne was born with an innate love of horses. His empathetic understanding of them shines through his account of his earlier years as a horse-tailer on Keeroongooloo in the Channel Country and is probably why he is remembered with huge respect across the inland as a horse-tailer rather than the head stockman and pastoral transport businessman that he later became. Wayne found himself involved in the transition period of the cattle industry from horses to mechanical handling and transportation. He realized that to survive he would have to let his horse plant go and switch to motorbikes. He learned the hard way that you could not leave the bike to pick its own way through the mulga; 'You hit one log and bung! You go again!' Then came the day that, on his expensive, gleaming, brand new bike, he found himself face to face with the piker bullock 'with a head as big as a forty-four gallon drum!' and discovered that 'Fear will put all sorts of wings on your feet.'

I met Wayne at Charlie and Pauline Rayment's property, Eildon Park, south of Winton. When I asked if I could tape some of his memories of life in the cattle industry we sat in the stripey shade under the back landing and Wayne, eyes half closed after a lifetime in the Outback's harsh distances and making roll-your-owns as he yarned, recounted some of his life experiences as the sun swung round. Suddenly, he exclaimed, 'But I've got to give Old Charlie a hand load his cattle, eh!' and was gone. I felt privileged to have spent time in the company of this legendary horseman. And, of course, we all followed up to the yards to watch the loading

The Horse-Tailer

Wayne McCulloch

'It was a specialist game – without the horses nothing happened'

One of my ancestors was with the first blokes across the Barkly Tableland into the Kimberley, not far behind Nat Buchanan. That's according to our family tree. But I was born in Brisbane and grew up a little city kid. But as far back as I can remember all I wanted was to be with stock. If there was a horse within a two mile radius I'd walk till I found it and get up on him with a bit of string around his neck. I used to go to sleep with a photo under me pillow of a horse, hoping that when I woke up in the morning there'd be a horse at the foot of the bed. I wanted to get out of Brisbane as soon as I could and go bush.

I was sweating on turning fifteen so I could leave school but my Old Fellow had a yarn to me. He said, 'Wayne, if you don't pass Junior you can forget about going anywhere. You've got to get a Junior Certificate first.' So I studied pretty hard and surprised myself. I got a hell of a good pass, and then I bolted.

I got a job on a well-known property, Coochin Coochin[1], in the Fassifern valley. Old Bill Bell was a gentleman; dressed well, always wore white moleskins, but there was toughness and hardness about him. His handshake really struck a chord in me and I've emulated it all my life. And any young fellows that have worked for me through the years I've taught them to shake hands like a man, not like some soppy sort. But Old Bill could see that Coochin Coochin was a bit small for me so he offered me a job on Gamboon at Eidsvold, in the stock camp. He said, 'They ride horses three weeks straight up there; all day, every day.' I just couldn't wait to get there. But then they put me on a bloody tractor for six weeks ploughing. I said to Mr. Bell one morning, 'How much longer are you going to keep me on the tractor, Mr. Bell?' He said, 'Well, Wayne, there's still another three thousand acres to plough and you're doing good job'. See, I was seventeen then. And I said, 'Well, Mr. Bell, I'm going to have to finish up. I came here to do stock work not be a tractor driver.' So I gave me notice, and got a job on a place called Keeroongooloo, just south of Windorah on

[1] Coochin Coochin is one of the oldest surviving homesteads in Queensland. It lies nestled in the junction of the Great Divide and MacPherson ranges. The Visitors' book records many famous names including Agatha Christie, Lawrence Olivier and the Queen Mother. Coochin Coochin was originally used by George Leslie to rest his stock as they moved inland from Brisbane to the Darling Downs. The painter Conrad Martens visited Coochin when it was occupied by George Fairholme, a pioneer settler and close friend of the Leslies.

the edge of the Cooper.

And, Mate, I never dreamed what the outback was like. I had a Holden ute and I got lost getting from the homestead to the stock camp. The first day there I was half frightened of all these big tough blokes. I thought they'd make mince-meat of a city kid like me. And, none of them had been to town for a while and they wanted me to take 'em in. I wouldn't do it. And I went to walk away and get into me swag and one bloke grabbed hold of me. He said, 'You're taking us to town.' I said, 'I'm not.' and went to walk away. He swung me round by the shirt and ripped it off me back. It was a brand new RM Williams Kimberley shirt that I wore and wore and I was that wild I knocked him down and jumped all over him a bit.

The next morning, the head stockman, a fellow by the name of Merv Wortley; he had been away, and he turned up in the camp. Oh, Jesus! He was a massive man; six foot three and eighteen stone and he got hold of me, because I come up to about his belt buckle, and he said, 'What are you going to do, Young Fellow, be like all the rest of 'em? Come out here and stay a few months and go back and lairize round in a pair of high heeled boots and a ringer's hat and say you've been out west?' I said, 'No, I'm not going to do that, Mate. I'm going to learn this game and stay at it'. And he said, 'I'll make you a deal, Boy. You take notice of me and listen and I'll teach you everything I can, if you want. And I 'll shake your hand on that.' I put me hand out and I shook his hand.

Well, Mate, the next six months were the hardest of my life. I could have cried every day. He poured it into me, Mate, but I stuck it. And I learnt. He taught me how to ride bad bush horses, and as rough and tough as that old coot was, if you got on something he knew was going to be too good for you, he wouldn't have been the length of your stirrup leather away from you on a good horse, eh! And, if things got out of control, he'd just pluck you out of the saddle like a bloody feather, eh!

So I was horse-tailing and that gave me all day, every day and as much of the night as I wanted with the plant. I listened to these pretty handy old ringers and was privileged to learn as much as I did. They kept young fellas in line and you learned not to be cheeky and to do as you were told. There was just so much to learn and every time someone spoke to you it was the voice of experience. You know, they call a ringer an unskilled labourer but you'll never get a degree in a school like you learn in the stock camp. It's a specialist game. And, with horse-tailing the whole camp depends on it because without the horses nothing happens. I tried me hardest at that horse-tailing game. I really liked it.

The horse-tailer is the man responsible for all the horses for maybe eight or nine men in the camp; night horses, bronco horses, pack horses, camp horses, face horses.[2] It was the horse-tailer's job to take the fresh plant out from the station. He'd usually have one or two blokes with him just to help him get to the first camp; might be five mile away, might be fifty. And, once you'd got the horses to where you had to go, you were the only bloke ever touched 'em, unless you asked for a hand.

[2] Face horse; a skilled, experienced horse used to take a selected beast, one that had been 'cut out' from the mob, to what was termed 'the cut', the cattle that had already been cut out and were being held separately a short distance away. Beasts that balked and tried to break back to the main mob were shouldered by the face horse and physically pushed into the cut.

Every morning, before daylight you'd walk out with the bridle over your shoulder to where the horses were hobbled through the night. All night you would have been listening to the bells. In sixty horses I never had any more than five bells because listening to the old timers, bells split your mob up. And they were dead right. It might just look like a bell to most people, but every bell had its own distinctive ring. And you knew from lying in your swag of at night, when that bell rang there, 'Oh, yeah, that's Fantail and her mob.' Another bell you'd hear; 'Donk! Donk!' 'Oh, that's the old bronco horse. Well, so-and-so will be with him.'

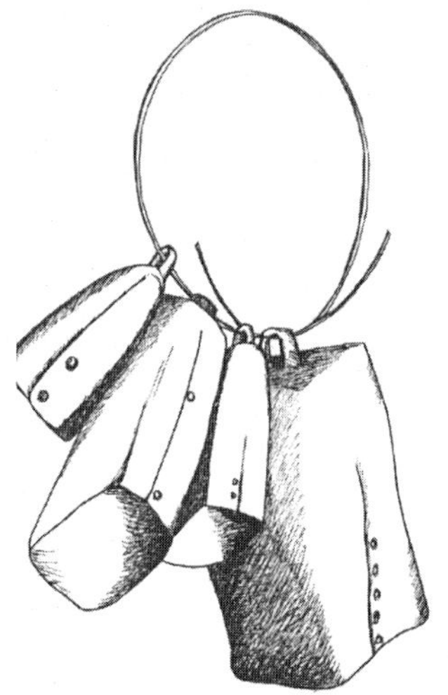

So, just from the sounds of the bells, when you got up in the morning you had a pretty fair idea which way you were heading. And you'd go out carrying your bridle and you'd find the horses - hopefully they wouldn't be spread out too much - and you'd poke around among 'em, leaving them hobbled until you found a horse you could ride bareback. And you'd un-hobble him and slip the hobbles through his neck strap and you'd lead him along and this is where the art come in because you had to know which horses to un-hobble first. If you un-hobbled the wrong horses and they started to walk, next thing all the plant is hopping in hobbles and you can't block the mongrels up and you've got a battle. You only learn that from knowing the horses.

We had different sorts of hobbles; green-hide hobbles with Turk's heads[3] on 'em, peg hobbles with a little peg of river wattle. You slid the peg through the slit in the leather and twisted it and slid it back and the hobble comes undone. I used to curse the bloke who invented greenhide hobbles. On a cold winter's mornin' when your hands are that cold they feel like lumps of wood and you're trying to get these big Turks' heads out from the slit in the green-hide and it's frozen hard, and maybe the horse is touchy around the feet too.

And then, if you were in early enough, when you'd bring the plant back to camp, you could grab a drink of tea before the ringers had finished cutting their lunch because you were the only man allowed in among the horses. The ringers would give you their bridles and you'd catch their horses for them. I made a point of it, of taking the bridle off the ringer, and bridling the horse for them and then handing it over to 'em.

Then, at the end of the day, I'd take the horses that were worked today, give 'em a good drink at the trough or the dam or waterhole and I'd take 'em and hobble them again for the night. Through the day I never used to hobble my horses. I just tailed them around and around. Some horse-tailers used to hobble 'em and then go back and lay down in the camp but the horses got leg weary too quick, from short stepping.

The camp horse was probably the most prized possession of the bloke who was allowed

[3] A decorative knot with a basket-weave pattern

to ride him. A camp horse would have come up through the ranks and showed a particular ability to anticipate a beast's movements and work it and cut it out of a mob. They'd had to have a good temperament and were treasured. The first camps I was ever in, when you started cutting out, it was the horse-tailer's job to take the camp horses over to the cattle. You led them over; never rode them over. You never put a leg over a camp horse. You just led 'em over to the mob with the halter on 'em or a bridle on 'em. And the head stockman would take charge then and he had his pet. And if there was one of the ringers who showed a particular aptitude toward cutting out, he was allowed a cutting-out horse. And once you were given a camp horse for the muster, that was your horse. Nine times out of ten it was your horse all the time you were on the station.

It might be about dinner time that they'd bring a mob in. Maybe you'd muster for two or three days in that light carrying country and you might have three hundred, maybe six hundred, head of cattle. You'd come into the water hole or bore about dinner time and give 'em a drink and a feed around the bore. If there was a mob of calves to be branded, the bullocks were always cut out of the breeders. They were never allowed in the bronco yard to be worked; they were always kept aside. They were moved to an open flat maybe only a few hundred yards away and the camp would just gather around 'em and pull 'em into a fairly tight mob, not jammed up tight, but pull 'em into an orderly mob.

The blokes doing that were riding what we call a face horse; probably the smartest horses next to the camp horse. Their job, when the camp horse cut a selected beast from the mob, was to take that beast away from the mob and put it with what they call the cut – the cattle that they were cutting out of the mob.

There might be one or two blokes holding the cut while the rest of the ringers held the cattle on camp. There might be one or two camp horses working and they'd bring the cattle out in a selected area called the face. The head stockman would delegate; 'You, you, and you, I want you on the face'. And that meant where a camp horse was going to cut out and bring the beasts out.

And, as they got the beast cut out of the mob, the face horse bloke had to be in a position to slip around behind the bullock and take him off the bloke and put him in with the cut. Usually that involved a bit of shouldering around until you got a little mob outside so that they'd stand.

A lot of camp horses probably started off as face-of-the-camp horses. Or even when they were broke in, one might show a little bit more aptitude for proppin' about. And you'd work him probably for twelve months and as he got worked, you saw whether he had what it took to watch a beast and start to act on his own judgement. And, if you had a colt that showed potential, the head stockman would say, 'Well, look, you can use that horse on the face for a bit if you want to try him'. So you were allowed to give him a go on the face and he might do one or two years on the face before you were allowed to put him in the cattle.

And the old way was at first you just rode him into the cattle and let him become used to the tightness of the mob around him because he'd never been jammed in among cattle before; it's new to him. So you let him get the feeling of the dust and the cattle bawling and bellowing close to him. You might do that half a dozen times; just ride him around. And the head stockman would say, 'Cut one out but take him at a walk'. And if you could get that beast out without reefing your horse around, the head stockman – he'd be a pretty cluey old coot - he's watching that horse's ears more than what you were doing.

And if he could see that horse was watching a beast and looked like it had a bit of potential coming up, he might let you walk one or two out after probably for a week or ten days. And then you'd ride him into the cattle when you were allowed to and you might cut one or two out. And you might do that for three months until the horse got to know what he was doing. So his life as a mustering horse was gone and he had graduated as a camp horse and starting to become a treasure to you.

Some of those old camp horses were pretty lively when they were on a beast, especially some of the touchier Channel bullocks. I speak from Channel Country experience. You'd get the odd one that was pretty mate-happy and didn't want to leave the mob. And I've seen a couple of blokes fall off a really smart camp horse that was working well. You get a movement out of a camp-horse when they're on a difficult beast that'll surprise the most experienced rider and they'll just slip you clean as a whistle, eh!

It happened to me once. Bloody oath! A mate of mine, a fellow by the name of Dick Smith, he had a big brown horse that I didn't like the look of. This big brown was half thoroughbred, half clumper and he looked to be a big dopey slow-moving coot of a thing. And Dick had had a mob of Sherwin bullocks on agistment on his property just north of Stonehenge and we'd mustered 'em to send 'em away. And, as we were yarding up, a big bullock sailed out, a Brahman-cross bullock, and he floated. Anyway, Dick and me, we went with him and, out of the corner of my eye as I went, I saw Dick jump off this little blue mare, his favourite, that he always skited about, and jump on this big old half-clumper brown horse that his missus had been riding.

And I thought, 'Gee, I'll have a shot at him about this! He got off the gun[4] to get on that ugly-lookin' thing!' Anyway, Dick locked onto this bullock's shoulder. I jumped off behind him and grabbed his tail and Dick pulled out of the road and I laid him on his ribs and tied him up. And, later, I said to Dick, 'Why did you jump off the pearl of them all and get on that brown thing to shoulder it?' And he said, 'Well, Wayne, When we get back to the yard there's a few strangers to cut out. So you slip up on him and try him.'

So when we got back to the yard I jumped up on this ugly old horse to cut out. And I thought, 'Yeah, you've got a bit of movement in this horse'. And Dick said, 'That horse is bludging on you, he's not trying'. He said, 'Here, take this jockey whip and give him a couple of cuts down the blade when you get your eye on the beast and you're just about to get to the face'. Dick's wife was a very capable dressage woman and she rode in one of those sliding-seat dressage saddles; no knee or thigh pads. So, I'm sitting up there in this little sliding-seat saddle and I cut a big lump of a heifer out and as I got her to the face, I give him a couple of live'ns with this jockey whip. And with my movement, the heifer jumped forward out of the mob. And this horse jumped with it. The heifer propped and doubled back and I went straight up over the brown's neck, full length of the reins, and landed on my feet out in front of him, holding him. And when I say I landed on my feet, I

[4] the best; 'gun shearer', 'gun ringer' etc.

had no say in where I went. It was just a fluke. And, Dick, well, the tears was running down his face. So, yeah, I've been slipped a couple of time, Mate. But that was the neatest.

A lot of times there'd be clean-skin cattle or just straight out rogue cattle that wouldn't stay in a mob and when you were mustering they'd just cut and head for the ridges. And the only way you can get 'em back, if your horse isn't capable of shouldering them back, was to pull 'em down and tie 'em up. There's a few ways of doing it. One, you could fly up beside 'em and, as you're shouldering 'em, grab 'em by the tail and then canter past 'em or gallop past while you've got hold of their tail and pull their butt end around up towards their head, and as you get 'em off balance, they'll roll. But, unless you're very slippery at getting out the saddle off a fast moving horse you're gonna miss him when he's on the ground. So one of your mates coming behind would have his horse set up and he'd just fly off as the bullock was hitting the ground, and he'll grab him by the back leg, lift it up high till you pulled up and then you'd strap the beast. If it was a real big beast, you'd strap him front and back legs.

That's throwing off a horse. The throwing off the ground was probably practised a bit more, particularly in timbered country where you couldn't get a properly good go at 'em. And there's a bit of a knack in it. There were a lot of times those beasts would be big buggers and they'd make a man look insignificant; full grown bulls and cows and big bullocks. They'd take off out of the mob at a flat gallop. Well, you'd get in behind 'em and send 'em a bit harder and a bit faster. You'd jam 'em and make 'em gallop. Well, in about two or three hundred yards, that'd blow the first wind out of 'em. And, as he hit what we used to call a high canter, just after the initial burst was gone out of him before he'd drop into a trot, you'd slip off your horse, run along behind him on foot and grab him by the tail – probably about the most frightening part of that is the last four foot, because, if they happen to prop, you're going to wear their head.

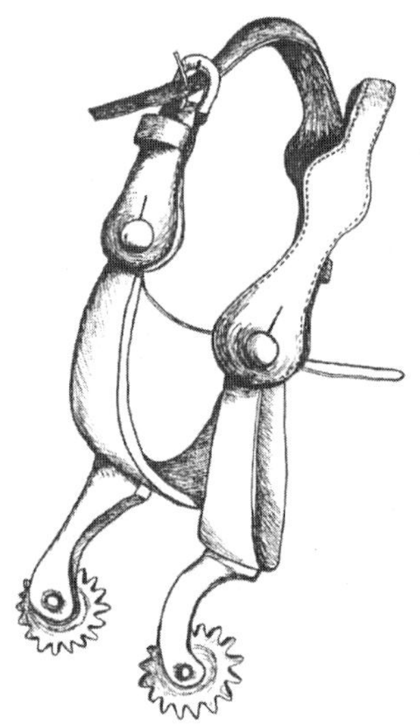

And then, hopefully, you've got him by the tail and you'd just take a double wrap of the hair of his tail, right on the end, around your hand so it wouldn't slip. And, when you had a good handful, you'd step out to the side and let him see you were there. And as he went to come around, there was a point when he lifted the near-side leg off the ground to hook at you. That's when you just stepped out a bit further and pulled, when he's got nothing to prop him up. If you got him the first time, it was easy. If you missed him the first time you were in for a bit of a battle because a bull weighing seven or eight hundred pound is ...Well, you're outweighed several times.

So you had to be skilful about it. When you were learning how to do it, there was always a real handy man on his horse beside you just in case you got into trouble. God, I can remember the first time big Merv Wortley put me off to a bullock at Boundary Bore, down at the bottom end of Keeroongooloo, just near the Malagarga boundary. There's a dog-netting fence – ran right down along the front edge of the Cooper there, eh. And we'd come out with a mob of bullocks from the channels – we were on bullock muster – and late in the afternoon about thirty big old bullocks come out of the ranges because on the eastern side of the netting fence, it ran back into scrub country.

These big old bullocks weren't supposed to be there. The manager, a fellow by the name of Fred Nissen, oh, a fantastic man, eh! he'd come down to the camp. He saw there was going to be a bit of fun involved here so he said could he have a lend of a horse.

Anyway, the whole camp plus the manager set out. These bullocks hadn't seen us. They were coming out on to a big open mulga flat. And we went around them and hit 'em before they got a drink of water, so they were going the right way; they weren't going back into the range. And there's two bullocks sailed out and away they went. And the manager said, 'I'll get this one'. And Merv Wortley said to me, and we're lapping along while he's talking, 'Here's your chance to make a bit of a name for yourself, Young Fellow. We're going after that one and you're going to pull it down'.

And I'm thinking to myself, 'Holy Smoke, look at the size of it! How's a skinny little blighter like me going to get that thing down?' And Old Wortley would try you to your limit to find out how good you were going to be, y' know.

And, he said, 'Righto, now, hit him. He's pumped down now. Jump off that horse and grab him by the tail and get him down'. Well, it was like a feather being flung around. And Old Wortley is yelling at me, 'You nearly got him, Mate! You nearly got him!' I'm thinking, 'I don't know what I've nearly got but I know I'm knocking up'. And I'm going around and around this little turkey bush, eh! And I couldn't get that blighter down. I had no idea, eh!

And, when Wortley saw I was just, you know, tongue out, trotting along behind, hanging on to the tail, he's saying, 'Don't let him go! Don't let him go! I was pretty fit but I was pumping down. Anyway, Wortley, he jumps off his horse and he says, 'Now, this is going to be pretty hard because you've let him get pumped down and he's just trotting along now and how am I going to get him down'. And he's feeding the fat into me and I'm feeling like I've let the man down, y' know.

And he said, 'Put a strap on his back leg.' Well, Wattle had hold of him because by this time the bullock is just standing there spread-legged. So I put a strap on one back leg. He said, 'Now you just sit back and hold that leg back with all your weight.' And Wattle kicked a bootful of dust out in front of him and as the bullock came around and took the weight off his back leg, I just fell straight over backwards because I was straining, eh!

And he said, 'Now this is where you get initiated because what we're going to do is we're going to lead him out.' We were still three or four hundred yards away from the netting fence and the gate. And he got his pocket-knife out and slit the bullock's nose; just a little gash, but wide enough to fit a bridle through and put the loose end of the bridge through the end of the Kimberley knot and pulled it tight. So then I had a six foot lead on this bullock, didn't I, and Wattle is giving me instructions. He was a hell of a good teacher. He said, 'Now, what you're going to do, Young Fella, is you're going to run along in front of this bullock and you're going to steer him. And I'm going to hang on to his tail and I'm going to anchor him so he can't get you and we're going to lead him over to that gate'. And

I'm thinking, 'You've got to be mad'. Because, when I stood up beside this bullock, he was taller than me and he had a head on him bigger than a forty-four gallon drum; a big poley bullock. Anyway, away I go like a bloody rabbit, eh! And old Wattle was pretty good over a hundred yards himself.

And we were going real good, eh! We were watching out of the comer of our eye and in the distance here comes the manager and his men with their lot. Wattle is saying 'Come on, Mate, we gotta beat 'em! We gotta beat 'em!' And we're going flat out! And we did! Yeah! There was pride in what you did and trying to let the other bloke see, 'Look, I'm as capable as you are!' There was a lot of competition and a lot of good humoured banter going on.

So that was my initiation into throwing bulls by the tail. Later, working with a bloke from down Augathella way by the name of Gordon Gadd - a very pretty man on the ground with a bad beast and nothing seemed to frighten him. He'd walk up to a beast that was bailed up, straight at its head, and, as it come for him, he'd just drop his hat on the ground and step aside as it come at him and get the tail and drop the beast in its tracks.

And, the more you learn, the more you realize that there is to learn. You can be with cattle for years and you still learn. But the one thing drummed into me by old Merv Wortley was, 'The best teacher you've got is your eyes and your ears'. He said, 'You'll never learn anything while you're talking.' I was running camps from when I was twenty-four and I suppose for the first five years I was just feeling my way, because being a capable ringer doesn't make you a good general in the field, good enough to make the decisions and organize the men. If you're in a responsible position, you've got to take the responsibility for the actions of the whole camp. It's your name on the line if something goes wrong with the stock or the camp comes adrift because you didn't have your foot on it. It was your name as the head stockman that was slurred and not the bloke that caused the trouble.

One time I was working on Connemara working with a bloke named Arthur Price on the BTECH[5] programme. Connemara was renowned for scrubbers as far back as you want to talk cattle country. And we're going to clean it up, eh! Arthur Price says, 'Oh, twelve, maybe eighteen months, we'll get 'em all'. About six years later and we're getting down to the bottom end of them! There's one paddock called the Big Bullock paddock; about three hundred square mile; a lot of scrub in it, a lot of open downs and a lot of pikers. We got the bulls, we got the clean-skin cows but that occasional old piker that pokes away on his own,

---

[5] BTEC; Brucellosis and Tuberculosis Eradication Campaign; introduced across Northern Australia in the 1960s to ensure Australian beef met international export standards

he's a different kettle of fish, eh! He's forgotten more about hiding than we know about finding him.

Tancreds owned Connemara then. It must have been about '85, '86. And they wanted to send a big mob of stores down, because we had heaps of feed; a beautiful season. It was drying out up in the Gulf and they wanted to send down about three thousand stores. They were a bit over weaner age; probably yearlings. The DPI had inspected this paddock and we'd run the grader around every bore and every water hole and left a broad open track so we could see if there was any cattle watering in it. We'd go around every day to check 'em to see if there were cattle tracks. And, if there was even one track that had crossed one of those graded lines, me and another bloke, John Egan, it was our job to go in and find the beast. John was a man of sixty-five, sixty-seven or so. And reliable! You could leave him with a mob of coachers and you could guarantee those coachers would be within a hundred yards of where you left him when you come back an hour, three hours later. A fantastic old chap.

Anyway, this time a cattle track turned up crossing one of these freshly graded tracks. It was of a big old hard-footed bullock. And, yeah, we got to find him, eh! The manager was away. He'd said just to keep an eye on the bullock paddock for any sign of tracks. So, Johnny and I, we were driving round in a vehicle, and we see this bullock track. We say, 'Not long gone, eh?' 'No, Mate, probably just a little while ago' and we pull the 303s out of the car and away we go on foot following his track, eh! Not real easy country, a lot of cap rock; a lot of stunted turpentine, running into belts of mulga. Hard tracking country. A lot of brumbies in that country too.

The manure was pretty fresh so we reckoned, 'We'll get this bloke real quick'. This was about eight o' clock in the morning. We walked and we walked and we walked and we got just the one fleeting glimpse of this old scrubber. We're sort of starting to look because the sun is right up above us. I said, 'Well, now, gees, I'm getting a bit hungry, Old Fella'. He said, 'Yeah, we've been walking for about four hours and it's going to be a four hour walk back'.

We were in a real tight little scrub running through red country. You knew he'd pulled up somewhere just ahead in that mulga. You knew you were pretty close to him. And your hair was sort've standing up on the back of your neck because you knew he was right there somewhere looking at you. And just ahead was something that just didn't look right and we're both looking at it and it turned out it was him, just standing watching us. And here's this sickle horn, one that comes around in front; this one horn up in the air and this sickle horn around in the front of his face. We are only fifteen feet from him. And by the time we woke up to it, you couldn't even bring your rifle up to fire. He was gone. And we sort of split too, because when that timber started crashing we didn't really know which way he was going. He floated.

So we went back to the truck and Johnny said, 'You know, it might be a good idea, Old Mate, if we run a couple of horses in and follow him along on horseback tomorrow'. So we did. And for six days we followed that bullock. In that time he earned our respect. It got to where we didn't even want to find him.

But that beast walked us around in a circle, about a three-mile radius. He led us a merry chase. He got that way that he'd walk along a pad on the cap rock, then he'd move off that pad and get on another one and go back the other way. I'm fair dinkum about this. He had us astounded. We saw him once or twice. And each time we found where he dropped manure it was getting harder and drier. We found places where he'd camped in the night and then just floated. Probably a 'roo or a wallaby or something had startled him and he'd just jumped.

On the sixth day, he left that three mile radius and headed straight. We knew we had him then. We'd rattled him that much he was cutting out for fresh country. He knew that country better than we did. The next morning we went to the water hole, just a little rock hole it was - and there was his fresh track. He'd just come in and he'd just gone. And we caught up with him within half a mile and, fair dinkum, it was sad, Mate. He was a massive bullock when we'd started. Now he was dried up, tucked up in the gut, eyes sunk, nose all dried out and half flakey from perish[6]. He'd had a bit of a drink of water but he just couldn't relax enough to have a big bellyful.

He'd bailed up in a little scrub. And, of course, we're riding along looking at the ground and we had it worked out that I did the looking out further and Johnny followed the track, in case we might just glimpse him going. But we didn't see him until we were right on top of him. He was laying down in this little thicket. As soon as he seen us, he hit his pins and up us!

Cattle at Eldon Park station, south of Winton

And, as he charged, I just leant out to one side with the .303 and squeezed the trigger. And down he went in the dust, mid-stride. And, you know, when we rode away, me and old John never talked for about two hours. Because all we wanted to do was to see that old fellow beat us and get away. He earned our respect.

And so, eventually, I had my own plant, thirty or so good working horses and a few breakers coming on and I decided to go contract mustering for myself. But it was a time of transition. In the end I couldn't get a job with me plant, eh! Horses had become obsolete. I realized I had to change to modern methods to stay in the game. So I bought a motorbike. I got more busters off that bloody motorbike in the first six weeks than I ever had from mustering. Because, working off horseback you could let the horse watch where he was going and watch the stock yourself.

[6] Dying of thirst

But when I tried the same thing on a motorbike, I'd be slipping in and out of the timber thinking I'm Evil Knevil and I found out I wasn't. I'd be watching the cattle and leaving the bike to pick its own track. The next thing you'd hit a log and, bung you go again! Fair dinkum, it is harder on a motorbike to keep a touchy mob together because you've got to watch where the bike is going, as well as what the stock are doing. A motorbike is a one-eyed sheep dog because, jeez, they're unforgiving bloody things. They won't duck a branch, won't jump a wash-out; won't jump a log. You've got to make 'em do everything.

One time when you were mustering your bullocks to turn off to the fat drover[7], they never got out of a walk. You knew they had another three or four weeks, maybe eight or twelve or fourteen weeks' walk before they got on the railway line. They didn't just go to the yard and jump on a truck and twenty-four hours later they're in Brisbane. So you had to nurse 'em. Now, these days you can trot your bullocks, get 'em there quicker, jam 'em in the yard and put 'em on a road-train and they've got their heads cut off in two days.

Vergemont was another bad-name place for cattle. For a few seasons I ran the camp there on contract. They used to get me in every time they mustered. There was a lot of scrubbers there. There was residue there from the days of the Camerons and we were cleaning them up; picking them up here and there. Once we were mustering a paddock called Wheelbarrow because Wheelbarrow Creek runs through it. I guess that's fairly original, eh!

It was a bad creek, a very difficult creek to get across because it was hard clay-pan country and the banks had these wash-aways about five or six feet deep and up to a half a mile long. And I've got this shiny, brand-new motorbike; the first brand-new motorbike I ever owned in me bloody life, eh! And it hurt me to buy it too, but never mind.

So I'm first day out on this out brand-new shiny machine, and we're mustering Wheelbarrow paddock and there were some big bullocks in there and they were rogues, big old piker bullocks. And, anyway, the boys had most of the mob in hand and I had a couple of us spread out behind, watching the helicopter in case he had trouble keeping the tail. We'd get in behind and send 'em along. And the helicopter, he's sitting back over one spot so I went back to see. We were all radio controlled too, y' know. They could tell you where to go and where the cattle were and give directions. When you couldn't even see the cattle, you could tell the blokes what to do.

So it's scrub country, pretty tight mulga all around and I rode back on to this bit of a wash-away and here's this big bullock, another one of them one-horn-down-and-one-horn-up mongrels. Every one of them I've run into seem to think they had a problem in their head; their brain was twisted as well as their horns. He was a massive bullock. So I'm chasing this big old fellow along. But after a bit he got sick of me and he bailed up. He good as said, 'This is as far as I'm going'. And from where I pulled up on my bike, about twenty feet or thirty feet away – it might have been a bit further – there was a big old coolabah, Mate. She was about two and a half foot through, and this bullock is standing a bit beyond

[7] Not an overweight drover but one who is taking charge of a mob of 'fat' cattle in prime condition ready for market. It was the drover's responsibility to ensure they reached the railhead in top condition and was a matter of pride among them to achieve best possible delivery weights and numbers. For this reason they would move the mob along skilfully and patiently, letting them feed and spell to maintain condition.

it. From where I was looking it was just on the other side of this wash-out; one of those deep narrow ones.

And I thought, 'You blighter, I'll give you curry if you jump across that and get me'. And, anyway, I walked up. The tree was on the right side of my vision and all I could see was the bullock and the cut-away. It wasn't until I was about eight feet from him that I realized he was standing right on this side of the wash-away and there was nothing to stop him galloping straight at me. And, of course, I'm coming at him with this stick in me hand, about four foot long, to throw at him, like I'm ten foot tall and bullet-proof.

I'm about four or five foot from the coolabah when I realize. And he's sending out the signals. His ears come up and he gets a bit of a quiver and he sort of comes up on his toes. I just said, 'Oh, shit!' And with that, it's on. And he comes straight at me. I ran around the tree but it was too big to duck around. He's got too much pace up. And I couldn't run that fast anyway! So I grabbed a branch and swung up over his head, which wasn't really difficult. Fear will put all sorts of wings in your feet.

And, when he missed me, he just looked across the flat another thirty or forty feet, and here's this shiny new motorbike there idling. And I'm thinking, 'Oh, no!' Well, he goes straight at it! He gets to the bike and he gets that hooky horn of his under the back mudguard and the other one hits the fuel tank and next thing there's my brand new motorbike going four feet into the air and down again, and the bullock, he's going the other way.

I tell you what, Mate! Give me horses anyday, eh!

12

Estelle Moody

ॐ ॐ ॐ

Introduction

Dark haired and vivacious, with sparkling eyes and an infectious laugh, Estelle Moody is the friend everyone would like to have. In any situation of need, Estelle is always willing to give of her concern, her time and her help. I had particular reason to be grateful to Estelle, when in 2006, for the launch in Charters Towers of Volume One of the 'From the Gulf to God Knows Where' series, Ray Fryer, of Tabletop Station, who normally undertakes the organization of such occasions, fell gravely ill. It seemed there would be no Launch. Such occasions do not organize themselves and meals for a hundred people do not happen without someone very capable being prepared and willing – not only willing, but happy – to rally some helpers and take over the catering side of things.

The result was that, come the night, Estelle and her merry band in the kitchen facilities of the Charters Towers Race Course seemed, with their laughter and camaraderie, to be having a much livelier time than the Launch audience. The aroma of the delicious dinner in preparation – roast local beef or corned brisket, followed by apple crumble or bread-and-butter pudding – were an added distraction. The closer the end of formalities drew, the more enthusiastic the applause at the end of each speech. Estelle had even the forethought to bring along her talented nephew Graham to provide lively Country and Western dinner music. That is Estelle; always to be found in the thick of things, surrounded by friends, good humour and laughter.

Estelle's memories of her time as the wife of the manager of Anthony's Lagoon provide a cameo of life in the Big House on large outback properties in the 1950s. However, since that time, education for Aboriginal children in the Northern Territory has improved. The 1960s saw the introduction of air-conditioned, self-contained mobile schools for Aboriginal children on pastoral properties with secondary education provided at boarding schools in Darwin and Alice Springs. Many Aboriginal students now go on to Technical and Further Education and to university.

ॐ ॐ ॐ

The Manager's Wife

Estelle Moody

'a wonderful life together'

My husband, Kev, and I were on Douglas Downs, near Dajarra, for four very happy years. Then Jim Newman, who owned the property, decided to sell because of his health. Kev applied for the position of manager of Anthony's Lagoon, in the Northern Territory, owned by the Australian Pastoral Company in Brisbane. One morning, the phone rang and I answered it. They told me that Kev had been appointed. When Kev came in from out on the property, he was wild with excitement to think he was going to such a large, well-known station in the Northern Territory, where he had always wanted to go. He went into Mount Isa, and they interviewed him and told him that he was to start in October.

I was equally excited. I always trusted Kev's judgement and it was time to move on. Kev went on ahead. His Mum said she would love to go for a holiday so she came with me to help look after the children. When we arrived in Mount Isa, Kev came across from Anthony's by vehicle and met us at the railway station.

It was four hour's travelling time out across the Barkly, up through Camooweal and across the Queensland border into the Northern Territory to the Anthony's turn-off.

The road from the turn-off was quite a good well-formed dirt road. On the way we passed through Alexandria Downs where they gave us a lovely lunch and made us feel very welcome. That was the first time I had ever seen dark girls pulling punkhas to cool you while you ate.

When we arrived at Anthony's it was already quite late in the afternoon but two Bush Nurses had gone over from Brunette Downs and had prepared such a feast for us! And Burkie Cant, the former manager was still there, covering, until Kev had settled into his new position. We felt so special, arriving after our long drive from Mount Isa to such a lovely welcome.

The house had a large kitchen at the back with a big combustion stove, a large dining room with a long table that seated about twenty, a sleep-out on one side and on the western side, a long front verandah with polished boards and cane furniture, suitable for the climate. On the southern side were the bedrooms and bathrooms and toilets; a country home, well constructed and well painted and maintained.

It was a big house to keep clean and there were four Aboriginal girls to help; Mavis and Daisy who waited on the table and then Ivy and Mabel who were the kitchen girls. The meals were cooked over at the kitchen, which was a separate building[1] and the girls had to carry the food across. Then they put it in the oven in the pantry to keep warm. The girls wore starched, ironed uniforms, a white dress with a green apron and green cap, which gave them a certain status among their own people. The laundress was a half-caste girl, Edna, who was excellent. She was married to one of the stockmen.

When they came up to the house in the morning the girls would be freshly showered and you could always smell the California Poppy hair-oil. In winter they would have not just a coat on but always a blanket draped around their shoulders as well. When they went back to the camp of a night time they would take back any food that was left over from the evening meal and share it with their families. It was a well-kept camp and the natives were supplied with tea and sugar, flour, jam and meat and there was a station store that carried tinned food and tobacco and dresses and shirts and stockman's hats and boots and sandshoes of every size.

The garden was filled with large shade trees, Athol pines and oleanders and poincianas under which we had our garden table and chairs. Beyond the fence was open downs country as far as the eye could see.

You couldn't see the lagoon from the house. I never went there. It didn't have very nice banks. I preferred to sit out in the garden, especially having a small baby and little children. It was too hot and windy. But the natives used to go down there and they'd catch mussels and cook them up for a feast. Lloyd would go down with them and would come back with mussels to cook. The lagoon was about a half a mile from the homestead. The natives told Kev it was very deep in the middle, fifteen or twenty feet. There was always bird-life on it. The lagoon was never ever dry in the years we were there. That area is famous for its ribbon-stone and there was ribbon-stone all round the lagoon. Ribbon-stone is a very hard stone with fine bands of different colours; pinks, blacks, browns and purples and it polishes up beautifully.

Paul and Jacob were the gardening boys and looked after the grounds and also the tennis court. In the cooler months they grew good vegetables, beans and cabbage and tomatoes and so on, but nothing would grow in the hotter months. There were no house cows or goats. We never had fresh milk; always powdered Sunshine.

On one occasion Paul and Jacob went out with a cross-cut saw to do a job and mid-morning, Paul came in with a dreadful gash about seven inches long up the inside of his forearm. Kev got the Flying Doctor medical kit out and got the gauze jelly that is in every medical kit and strapped the wound with plaster and bandaged it and told Paul to leave it wrapped and not to get it wet. About five days later Kev undid it and the wound was healing beautifully, with no sign of infection.

Mail Day was Friday. It was an important day. The perishables, the fresh fruit and

[1] Detached kitchens were a feature of outback homesteads. Should the kitchen catch fire, in an age of wood-burning stoves, the homestead itself could be saved. Such kitchens were connected to the main house by a covered walkway called 'the landing'. Bob Forster, in *From the Gulf to God Knows Where, Volume 1*, tells an amusing tale of the landing at Wongali station.

vegetables – Yum! – and the mail-bag came on the same flight, from Mount Isa. I'd be longing for letters from home. The book-keeper would sort out the mail. Then for reading there'd be the *Women's Weekly* for me and for Kev the *North Queensland Register* and the *Country Life*. We'd sit together in the lounge room at night after dinner and read. That was the only time he had spare. We didn't have radio reception to listen to the wireless but Kev loved music and he would play his LPs of *Oklahoma* and *My Fair Lady* and *The Sound of Music*. He had all the records of Peter Dawson and Richard Tauber.

And there'd be the glossy catalogues from the big stores down south, David Jones and Myers. The catalogues would have little 'feelers' of cloth inside so that you could get some idea of what the fabric was like. I'd send away for clothing from the catalogues and then couldn't wait for the parcels to arrive; little elastic-side boots for Lloyd and Jumping Jack boots with ankle support for Mark.

Ivy, Daisy, and Gladys, House-girls on Antony's Lagoon.

The book-keeper also looked after the Outpost radio and took the incoming and outgoing traffic each day. The store and the radio room were in a separate building away from the house. There was a 'galah' session when all the voices would come in for a chat session. I never listened because with small children and a big house to run I was always on the go.

Every morning the smoko bell went at nine o'clock because the men were on the job by six o'clock and were ready for a cuppa by then. Kev believed in making an early start and finishing at five or six in the afternoon depending on the job. The men would come trooping in for smoko on the side verandah where the table would be set up ready with fresh bread every day and every second day the cook, who was the head-stockman's wife, would make sweet buns or bun-loaf. There were always biscuits in the biscuit tin and if we had unexpected visitors she would make pikelets or scones within minutes and she always had a fruit cake on hand.

Dinner at night was at seven when the cook would ring the gong for the men to come in and I had a little bell at the table for the girls to change the plates. The two jackaroos lived at the homestead and had their own rooms on one side. The book-keeper also had his meals with us; dinner at night and lunch. The men wore jackets and ties in winter but not in the hotter months.

We often got parties of overseas visitors who the company would have organized to come out and have a look at an Australian cattle station. For these we would have a barbecue out on the lawn and afterwards a sing-along with perhaps some Slim Dusty records. They seldom stayed overnight but would fly out on the rest of their journey before sundown. We would get lovely Thank You letters afterwards and sometimes very nice gifts.

The Flying Doctor used to come once a month and stay overnight. It was a special occasion. All the natives would have a scrub-up and put on clean clothes and the children would have clean clothes and they'd all wait for the plane to fly over and land. They would all be given whatever injections were necessary, polio or triple antigen and the mothers would be checked and the children's ears and chests. The natives were all very healthy except for the snotty noses! If they were bitten by anything or hurt themselves they would come up to the homestead and say, 'Missus. Me like Band Aid,' and I would hand out a packet. Not long after we arrived at Anthony's I found I was pregnant with my third child but apart from the Flying Doctor who came in once a month, I never saw a doctor until I was six weeks off having our beautiful little daughter Devita.

Once we had to take Mark into Tennant Creek when he was a baby when he had severe conjunctivitis. His eyes were stuck together and we had to bathe them with warm salty water first thing in the morning so he could open them. And the eye itself was terribly bloodshot. After four or five days we knew we would have to take him into Tennant Creek for medical treatment. It was a four hour drive into Tennant. Kev always made sure we had plenty of water and there'd always be a couple of packets of Arnott's Arrowroot biscuits and ginger-nuts in the glove-box for the children in case we broke down. The country was not as open as the Barkly. It was more timbered, with several dry crossings on the way. But it was a good built-up gravel road.

And, poor darling, when we were in the doctor's it took three of us, Kev and the nurse and myself, to hold him down, it was so painful. They had to force his eyes open. He screamed the whole time! He was only a baby really; not even two years old. I thought the doctor was going to pop the eye out of his head! I was sick in the stomach when I saw what he had to do. He was rolling it round and swabbing it to get all the infection out. Then he gave us Golden Eye ointment and we were told to keep bathing it with warm salty water. He told us that if the infection wasn't watched it could develop into trachoma. I attributed it to the flies and the dry, harsh summer heat. When we'd seen the doctor we did our shopping and then started on our way home.

We had lunch at Rockhampton Downs and then Kev saw clouds coming up and he said, 'It looks as though we're in for a storm. We will have to move on.' And he was right. There was a storm and there was water, water everywhere and though we were in a four wheel drive vehicle we got hopelessly bogged. I was about seven months pregnant with Devita at this stage. Kev estimated we were about ten mile from home. He said, 'When we don't turn up they will send out a vehicle to look for us.' When it stopped raining he found us a stony ridge because the children were too cramped up in the vehicle. We put a rug down on the wet soil to sit on while we waited. At about ten o'clock at night we could see the lights in the distance. Lloyd jumped up and down yelling, 'They're coming, Dad! They're coming!' When we got back to the homestead and had put the boys to bed I made a cup of tea, and oh, wasn't it the best cup of tea we ever had! Paul and Jacob took the station truck back out next day to pull the Toyota out of the bog.

Another time Lloyd had an accident at Avon Downs. Our friends there had small cattle-dog puppies and Lloyd was playing happily with them. When he ran they all chased after him nipping at his heels so he ran to the fence and climbed up to get away from them. It was steel Weldmesh fencing and near the top there was a metal spike with one piece sticking up. And when he turned to look down at the puppies, the spike of Weldmesh caught him right in the middle of his forehead. It left a gash an inch and a half long between his eyes. It was a deep wound but we were so far from medical help that we had to deal with it ourselves. Lloyd was a brave little fellow but when they put the iodine on, oh! the screams!

Later as it started to heal, proud flesh began growing on the wound. The policeman, Peter Ralph, from Anthony's Lagoon police station, which was about half a mile away from the homestead, came over and he brought bluestone with him. Bluestone is a powder that eats away any proud flesh which forms when a wound is not healing naturally. We had to treat the wound with it though I was terrified that it would affect his eyesight. Lloyd was so brave because it would have burnt terribly. Peter Ralph came over every day to keep a watchful eye on the wound and it healed up beautifully in due course. Kev was out on the cattle camp at the time.

But the worst thing that happened while we at Anthony's was the death of one of the little native children. There were sixteen to twenty native children on Anthony's when we were there but unfortunately there was no school for them. The little girl that died was a five or six year-old named Kathie, Daisy's daughter. When we had been there about twelve months Kathie got into the kitchen scrap-bin and picked out some of the food and ate it and got food-poisoning. We battled to save her for three days. Her stomach swelled up terribly. She should have had a stomach pump put on her. We couldn't get the Flying Doctor to come in quickly enough during the night. We were in constant contact with the Flying Doctor and the policeman, Peter Ralph, came and sat with us, but in the end we lost her. All the natives were wailing and beating with sticks all night long. It was just terrible. The Flying Doctor came out and took the body in to do an autopsy. When they sent her back they had wrapped her up in a white sheet. The natives made their own preparations for the burial to be held on a secret native site. The white staff were not invited. There was no religious ceremony. I wouldn't say the natives were exactly primitive but they had their own beliefs as the tribes do and they carried their own traditions out. They took her out to one of the far ridges and buried her there.

Lloyd Moody and friend playing 'horses', wearing fly-veils as a protection against 'sandy-blight'.

Lloyd loved all the native children and Kathie had been his play-mate so he was sad and upset. He used to go and sit next to Daisy when she came up to the house and he would pat her on the hand and sing to her.

There was less cattle work during the wet season. Including the native stockmen there were about seventy men on Anthony's but come the Wet most of the white stockmen, would be gone down south, the natives would be gone to Borroloola on walkabout and Kev had more time to spend at home. He would catch up on book-work and any jobs that needed doing around the station; supervising the men that chose to stay on, maintaining the yards, doing any painting that needed to be done, any dripping taps, leaking tanks, anything that needed touching up with paint; any odd jobs at all. We would be looking for plenty of reading material.

One time Kev was pulling the bore at the homestead and caught his left hand in the rope and took the top of the third finger off. I had Mark as a toddler so Kev got in the Toyota and drove himself all the way into Mount Isa with the joint of his finger wrapped up in cotton wool. They couldn't stitch it back on and he had a terrible time with it. He had to go down to Townsville to have skin grafts on his hand.

Before they went on walkabout at Christmas, the natives would put on a big corroboree night and invite all the whites down to the corroboree ground they had in a special clearing with a big fire in the middle. We would take folding chairs down. They'd be all painted up and it would go on for a couple of hours and they would play the didgeridoo. The house-girls would take part, laughing and giggling. They had special corroboree skirts that a former manager's wife had made them, three tiered ankle-length ones gathered on to a waistband with matching bra-tops. The men had their faces painted and head-dresses of feathers and their legs painted white and the girls had feathers on a band in their hair but they didn't paint their faces.

Once the corroboree night was over they would all be taken over to Borroloola, about a three hour's drive away, on the big station truck and they would stay there until the cattle-work started again in February, when Kev would take the truck over to bring them back. But some of them might make their own way back before then.

I always believed that through life you have got to support your husband in whatever he undertakes and if he is happy, you are happy. No matter what job Kev took on he gave it one hundred percent and he expected his men to give a hundred percent also. He always had a clear mind and he was never afraid of responsibility. He wasn't hard on the men and always worked with them and they respected him for that. He was a wonderful horseman and had good management skills. It wasn't in his nature to be grumpy. If ever we had an argument, which wasn't often, before he came in of an evening he would pick a flower out of the garden and give it to me and it would melt my heart and all would be forgiven. We had a wonderful life together.

13

Mac Core

ॐॐॐ

Introduction

As I never met noted North Queensland cattleman, Mac Core, in person, it would be better to let Mac's daughter, Jenny Roberts, introduce her father.

'Dad was a people's person. Anyone who visited Mount Full Stop station will remember his warm welcome, courteous attention, cheerful disposition and his sincerity. He made people feel special because he was truly interested in everyone he met.' Jenny then quotes another great North Queenslander, Harry Clarke, of Fanning River, 'It didn't matter where you met Mac; at Government House or out in the mustering camp, he was always the same. He treated everyone with respect and as an equal.'

Mac Core loved racing and was a member of the North Queensland Amateur Race Club from 1937 onwards, becoming president in 1979 and racing his horses at venues ranging from isolated picnic meetings in the Gulf, to urban Townsville and Cairns. Mac also served on camp-drafting and rodeo committees, acting as pick-up man when required. Closest to his heart was his involvement with Ewan Race Club and as its President he initiated moving the track to Spyglass Station on the Lynd Highway so that trucks and horse-floats would not have to negotiate the narrow Paluma Range road.

I had always hoped to be able to include this remarkable man's story in this volume and was saddened to learn of his death. I was grateful on phoning the Australian National Library in Canberra to be told that Mac Core had in fact been interviewed the previous year by Bruce Simpson and Professor Bill Gammage of the Australian National University. The following account of Mac's life is based on their material, supplemented with additional information supplied by his family. For further reading, the story of Mac Core's mother, Mary Ada Core, 'A Fast and Spendid Ride', in Volume One of this series, will be of interest, as her father, William McDowall was an early pioneer of the north, including Christmas Creek station, mentioned in Mac's story.

Beyond Blue Range

Mac Core - Pastoralist

'We had a good brand, ZZ1; the old Christmas Creek brand'

I've been involved in the cattle industry all my life. I was born in Charters Towers on the third of April, 1920. I got the name 'Mac' from my Mother's initials. I grew up on Blue Range station on the Upper Burdekin, north-west of Charters Towers. Originally, Blue Range was part of Christmas Creek. After the First World War the Lands Department decided on a Soldier Settlement Scheme and my father drew Blue Range, the homestead block, in the ballot.

About the time that I was born, Mother and Father bought a large house in Charters Towers, two storeys, with verandahs all round. They dismantled it and moved it to Blue Range on a horse wagon. They got carpenters in to re-erect it and that became Blue Range homestead.

Then Father and Mother[1] bought in cattle from different properties to build up the herd, all Devon Shorthorn. Early in the piece, mother's father, William McDowall, had bought a Brahman bull from Melbourne Zoo whose mother had been brought from India in calf to a Brahman bull. As a weaner that calf was shipped to Townsville and for a while they had him as an exhibit and people would pay a couple of bob to go in and have a look at this 'pre-historic animal'.

To get him up to Christmas Creek, he was walked up with the packhorses. He was a white bull and so quiet that he used to come into the Christmas Creek homestead and lie down on the ant-bed floor. Christmas Creek homestead was seven miles from ours at Blue Range. That was the first Brahman bull to ever sire calves in Australia; the start of the Brahman herd. They used to call them 'zebus'.

Later another Brahman bull came to the Melbourne Zoo and old Grandfather McDowall acquired him also but my mother told me that he was a very vicious bull. It was a bit of a mystery what happened to him in the end but she thinks that Grandfather might have shot him.

This was in 1930, when I was ten years old and starting to take a bit of notice. About that

[1] See Chapter 13, *A Fast and Splendid Ride* , in Volume One of *From the Gulf to God Knows Where*, which relates the life-story of Mary Ada Core's girlhood experiences growing up on cattle properties owned by her father William McDowall in North Queensland.

time Mother and Father bought Christmas Creek. The purchase price was £5,000 with two thousand head of cattle on it. This was at the height of the Great Depression. After that the two properties were managed from Blue Range and the Christmas Creek homestead was used as mustering quarters when we mustered in that area.

It was obvious that there was the exotic strain in the herd though we didn't get any more bulls until later on. Then Frank Frazer, a merchant from Ingham – he had Burnside Stud – and Ken Atkinson of Wairuna at Mount Garnet and a chap named De Landelles of Cherokee station outside Emu Park, got a shipment of a half a dozen Brahman bulls and a couple of Brahman cows from India. We bought the progeny from that shipment and introduced them into our herd. Father had also kept every bull calf of the original bull he had got from Melbourne. The quality of those cattle wasn't equal to the quality of Brahman cattle today but they were drought resistant and tick resistant to a degree. Tick resistance was a great thing for the northern cattle industry and it was due to the venture these early cattlemen took with the introduction of Brahman blood.

And, yes, it was a bit of a gamble! When old Grandfather McDowall brought that original bull to Christmas Creek it was rumoured that he wouldn't be able to cross it with a British breed; with his Devon Shorthorns; that it would be like a donkey and a mule and wouldn't be able to reproduce. They had a lot of theories, those old chaps in those days. But Grandfather gave the lie to that.

Mount Full Stop homestead.

We didn't have a big Aboriginal mustering camp on Blue Range like they did on places further up in the Gulf but we had a few families that lived and worked there. They had properly built cottages. I grew up with the kids. My special mates were the Kennedy kids, Alwyn, Paddy, Kenny and Woggie. We learned to ride early in life, as bush kids do, and gave a hand in all the station activities but we still had time for some fun. Once Woggie and I shot a crow with a shanghai down the river. We found an old tin for a billy and made a little fire and cooked it and ate it. But I can't say I'd recommend it! But sad to say, those children didn't get any schooling, and a lot of them couldn't read or write. But growing up with them I learned how to track; how to track a horse that got away with a saddle or a couple of bullocks that might have strayed. They wouldn't be looking at the footprint. They'd be looking fifty yards ahead, at a disturbed leaf or a stick or a bit of grass. Their eyesight was wonderful. All the knowledge of their race was geared to survival. If they were tracking a kangaroo for food it was pretty important for them to have these tracking skills and I picked up a lot from them. And they had knowledge of the country – not only the full bloods but the part-coloureds as well – and this knowledge meant that they were very efficient in mustering.

As stockmen, they were excellent because they could recognize patterns. Once they saw a calf with his mother they would always remember which cow it belonged to at mothering-up. Mother and Dad were very particular about mothering-up calves after branding. You had to take them out and hold them around a water-hole or the river and see that the calves got their mothers and that there were no calves coming back to the yards, or just letting the bush cattle trot away from the yards.

My sister Olga and I did all our primary schooling by Correspondence and when we had done the Scholarship exam we were sent away to Warwick; myself to Scots College and Olga to the Presbyterian Girls' School. I loved sport and got into the athletics and swimming teams but I never learned much about the spelling side of things! We stayed there three years and only got home at Christmas because of the distance.

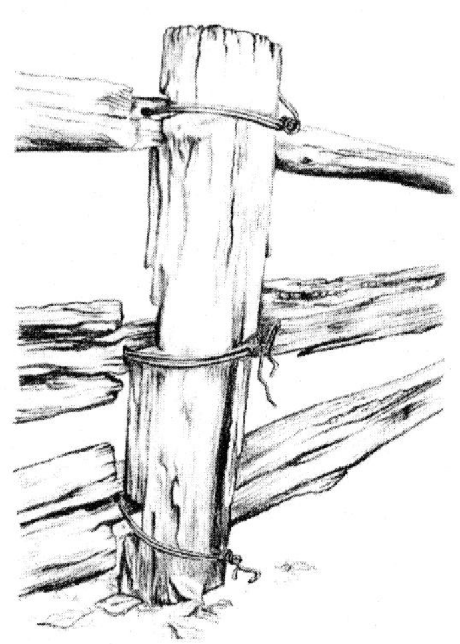

Then, when I was fifteen, well, I was the only son, so I was supposed to be running the mustering camp. There was a very capable half-caste man – he also had some Chinese in him – Alwyn Kennedy. A very capable horseman. He ran the mustering camp for about twelve months after I left school. Then they told me that I had to start running it. I wasn't very qualified but this Alwyn Kennedy and I got along fine and he was a very great help to me. Blue Range was then eight hundred and seventy-one square miles and we turned off about four thousand calves a year. I could never have managed without Alwyn's guidance and he has remained a lifelong friend.

Alwyn Kennedy would have been the best horseman I ever saw. None of his horses ever had sore backs and all his horses were quiet to catch and quiet to shoe. A good horseman is not just the person on the horse's back. The horse has got to respect him for saddling up and shoeing and general quietness and fellowship. Alwyn Kennedy may have been part Aboriginal, part Chinese, but he was a white man as far as manners and decency were concerned. He was the best man I ever worked with[2].

We had a big camp, probably about fifty percent part-Aboriginal people. They were great bush men, great horsemen and a friendly race of people. Unfortunately, something seems to have gone wrong with them now and they stick to the town and don't care about

[2] Mac Core is paid a reciprocal compliment by Alwyn Kennedy's wife, Maisie Kennedy, in her book *Born a Half-caste* (Australian Institute of Aboriginal and Torres Strait Islander Studies; Canberra, 1985). '*By now Mac had taken over as head stockman and we still worked long hours. No-one minded as the Cores were family to us as Mac was to prove over the years. He was also a good friend, a good mate, and if he couldn't do you a good turn he wouldn't do you a dirty one. We were all happy and the Cores worked along with us no matter how late. Mac Core is one of the whitest of white men you could ever meet and know and we all loved him.*'

the bush at all. But the Aborigines were a very great help to the pastoral industry in the early days with their knowledge of the bush and the hardships of the country.

There'd be about twelve to fifteen men in the mustering camp at Blue Range. It was comfortable working. You would each be allocated your team of horses for the muster. You shod them up yourself; all cold shoeing; no furnace. We didn't trouble with a toe-clip on the shoe, and having to make the groove in the front of the hoof for it to fit. We used to knock that clip back into the groove because that's where the shoe would wear out firstly, on the tip. A lot of rivalry went on, in fun. 'Oh, a shoe came off your horse! You can't shoe! If you'd have shod it properly it wouldn't have come off!' We'd get a lot of laughs out of it. But in that rough basalt country it didn't matter how well you shod your horse, at certain times and in certain country, a horse will lose shoes.

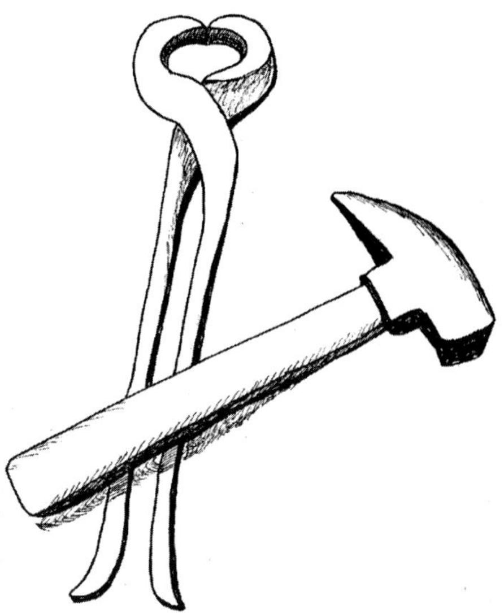

And if you had shod your horse up and he developed a sore back, well, you had to pull the shoes off him and let him go. And I noticed over the years that irrespective of the build of the saddle or the counter-lining there were some men who couldn't help but give a horse a sore back, including a lot of light men.

Each horse had a pair of hobbles and a neck strap. You put that strap on the day you shod him and you never took it off and they had their hobbles on that strap for the rest of the muster. But after I felt my way a bit at running the place I didn't go in for this hobbling horses very much. Horses always turned towards home; particularly fresh horses. You'd take them to a fresh mustering camp and they'd be thinking about home. They'd always be wanting to go back. You could have a couple of men out of your mustering team away looking for horses. So I tried to modernize the place a bit and I built horse-paddocks at all the different yards, which made it a bit easier, and I put in dams.

We had yards at the camps; but not very well-built ones. We did some broncoing out in the bush, particularly when the dry season was on and you only mustered the cattle into the wire yards. We had what we called a stockyard grip, with a rope around a pulley wheel. The wheel had locking tags on the inside so that it could only go one way. The calves would be dragged up by the bronco horse, with the rope coming through the rail, to this stockyard grip.

Later, the branding cradle came in – a very acceptable piece of machinery. You can do one a minute with them. It had always been drilled into me; 'Don't go slapping the brand on. The brand was made to go on neatly and not to be blotched when it heals up.' I like things to be neat and well done. We had a good brand; ZZ1, the old Christmas Creek brand, and we carried that on, of course, at Blue Range, after the purchase; a beautiful brand,

ZZ1; all straight. Horizontals are the ones to get for a good straight line brand; horizontal V or B. With the horizontal B, the old saying was, 'The tits are up' or 'The tits are down'. Altogether we had Blue Range, Christmas Creek and another place called Gadara. We used to do it all with the one mustering camp.

We bred our own horses by Thoroughbred stallions from England[3], imported as the station sire. You get many types of Thoroughbreds but they were great horses to ride all day. They were our foundation stock. And when the brumbies first got started in the north they were only station horses that got away, basically Thoroughbreds, and even today, though they may have lost some of their size and conformation, they're still useable horses in a mustering camp. Now they have the Australian stock horse, and the quarter horse. I've seen the quarter horse cutting out and he is superb but I'm not in a position to say whether he can do a full day's muster. I still prefer the Thoroughbred. I won only one Australian Championship and that was the Camp Draft at Mareeba in 1955 on a Thoroughbred mare I bred myself called Mermaid, so I'm sticking with that.

Originally, Christmas Creek was the old McDowall property where my mother lived. Then after she married my father, George Core, he took up Blue Range. When my father died in 1965, Blue Range was divided. Now my sister has Blue Range and my wife and the three children and I moved, first to an old mustering camp called Tin Hut, where we lived until I established the new place at Mount Full Stop just down the river. Tin Hut was just a tiny mustering hut where we kept our food when we were mustering that area. The kids used to love to come out to visit the camp when we were mustering. One time during the Wet we got caught on the wrong side of the river. The river rose during the day and we could see we were in for a decent sort of a swim. I asked them if they were up for it. Jennie would have been about twelve and David maybe nine. They looked at this dark flowing muddy water and looked a bit dubious. I decided it was a bit too good for them, so I swam the river, got some bread and beef and tied it in my shirt on my head and swam back. The mossies were bad but they got a fire going and put some green branches on it to make a smoke and settled down for a hard night. They were good kids. They knew how to do it tough without whingeing.

The Upper Burdekin, in the Dry.

The Mount Full Stop homestead has a beautiful view out over the junction of the Clarke

[3] A british breed, the ancestry of which can be traced to English mares and Arab stallions.

and the Burdekin. It's named Mount Full Stop because it is very obvious that at some time in the distant past that line of mountains stopped the river; then the river must have broken through. Half the mountain is standing on one side of the river and the other half has been washed away. At Hell's Gates, four or five miles down the river, they were going to build a dam at one time, to channel the Clarke into the Cooper basin. It was a scheme thought up by Dr. Bradfield[4], but by now the costs have escalated so much that it may not be feasible.

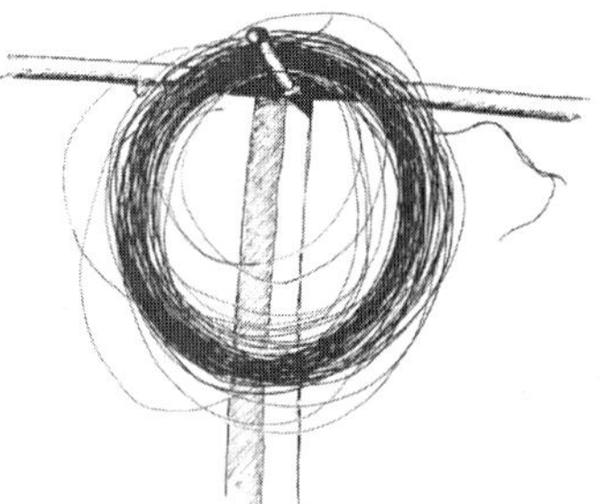

At Blue Range and with most of those properties on the Upper Burdekin, bushfires were not much of a hazard. There are big tributaries in that Burdekin country so that if you got a fire from a lightning strike you could burn back off the creek into the face of it. And the ash was good for the re-growth. Towards the end of the Dry, when you were hopeful of getting some rainfall, you might go out and burn areas off, but you wouldn't let your country get completely burnt out. Some people still believe that the old grass is meant to fall and rot into the ground and that is the fertilizer for the new grass but I was brought up by both my mother and father to believe that you have got to burn your country to sweeten it up to get new grass. The tribes up there in the Gulf and the Peninsula used to burn off sections of their country to get green re-growth to attract kangaroos. Then they'd stalk up on them from tree to tree and could spear them from a hundred yards. We might get a few storms as early as October, November and when you saw that, then you were hopeful of getting a good Wet, through from December to March. I have only seen one year when we didn't get any rain at all.

The herd we have at Mount Full Stop is three-quarter Brahman and almost one hundred percent white. I got a Shorthorn throw-back in the mustering camp and I decided that I would breed the horns off them. I bought Polled Brahman bulls to breed with the Mount Full Stop cows and culled progeny that had horns. But it is very hard to get a one hundred percent poll herd. I was doing quite well and had them down to about eighty-five to ninety percent poll. When my son David took over he introduced Brahman bulls from the sale. Some breeders have a very unique way of taking the horns off the bulls so they look as if they're polled. The percentage of polled cattle in the Mount Full Stop herd is now around seventy percent. This remains quite an achievement for a breed that is predominantly horned.

There was one time when I had a horse I was riding that was horned by a cow. We were on dinner camp and the cattle began to move away. My daughter Jennie worked in the mustering camp with us for many years and my own horse must have been a bit touchy or something so I got on to Jennie's horse to turn the cattle back. One cow broke from the lead

[4] Queensland born John Bradfield (1867 – 1943) was a brilliant engineer who was involved in major projects such as the construction of the Burranjuck Dam, the Sydney underground railway, the Sydney Harbour Bridge, Brisbane's Storey bridge and the University of Queensland. In his later years he advocated a scheme which became known as the Bradfield Scheme, of damming Queensland's coastal rivers in order to turn their waters into those of the dry inland. Among other honoured positions John Bradfield was a member of the Senate of Sydney University (1913 – 43) and a member of the Australian National Research Council.

and I let her go while I turned the others. Then I went after this cow and I jumped off to throw her. But I missed her tail as she came at me and she charged straight up to the horse and ripped its stomach out. I had to destroy that horse. That was one of the saddest things that I've had to do; to shoot a good horse of Jennie's.

There used to be a bit of poddy-dodging going on in the Upper Burdekin country and I could never understand it. It was more or less 'You pinch my calf and brand it, and I'll pinch your calf and brand it. You kill my bullock for beef, I'll kill your bullock for beef.' At the end of the year you would be square, so what the hell! But poddy-dodging has just about gone out with the blades now. If you make a genuine mistake and brand your neighbour's calf, well, you get him another calf. We're all mates. We meet at the bush race meetings; Mt Garnet and Einasleigh, Oak Park and Ewan and the Townsville Amateurs and at the rodeo's and camp-drafts. We have a scotch or three, swap a few yarns, sing all the old favourite songs, '*Sweet Peggy O'Neill*' and '*Watermelon Wine*' and dance with all the pretty girls. The Upper Burdekin's a pretty happy area. We love the place. I'm never happy for long away from it.

14

Reg Hart

ॐ ॐ ॐ

Introduction

Reg Hart was one of the old drovers I would have loved to have met while I was off-siding for the real workers at the Drover's Camp Festival in Camooweal, 2002. Sadly, Reg died before I was able to make contact with him. But, fortunately for our Outback heritage, Professor Bill Gammage and ex-drover and bush-poet, Bruce Simpson had interviewed Reg for the Australian Drovers' Project of the National Library. They have generously allowed me to edit the transcripts of their material for inclusion here.

Reg Hart's story is of significance not only for his lucid account of droving in the 1930s when 'times were rough', and some of the characters in the game even rougher, but, also, from a literary point of view, because it exemplifies the difference between the spoken and the written word in the recording of social history. Reg, having received an above average education by the standards of his time, wrote a short account of his days as a drover, as an addendum to the tape-recorded material he provided for the National Library. Although the written account is more succinct it lacks the immediacy of the oral version, and we lose the charm of 'hearing' actual words spoken long ago by people long forgotten. In Reg's oral account we can hear them speak to us in their own words across the decades; his mother's dismayed, 'You're thin, Boy!'; the old quart-pot drover's foolish sooling of his dogs on to the sheep; the 'No fightim' you!' of the infuriated Aboriginal stockmen, short-changed of decent rations; and the twenty-year-old Reg's dry warning to the stingie boss drover, 'You'd better move on! You've got a short life span here!' For a brief moment we are not merely reading a print version of someone's life, but are actually back there, witnessing events as they happen, sharing the hard times of the Depression years with them. This is the unique appeal of oral history. The spoken word takes you there.

Another important aspect of Reg Hart's story is that, although in the opening paragraph he establishes that he is 'of Aboriginal extraction', he then gets on and tells his story without making an issue of it, except when, near the end of his life he is introduced by a friend in the racing fraternity as 'the whitest man I ever knew'. With the confidence born of knowing his own worth, Reg joins in the appreciative laughter and accepts the comment as the compliment it is intended to be. Reg Hart was a man that all men were glad to shake hands with and call friend.

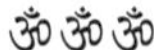

The Diamantina Drover

Reg Hart

'Keep your eyes open, Son. And your mouth shut.'

My father, William 'Billy' Hart, was born in Charleville in 1885 and my mother in 1895. My mother was formerly Topsy Wells. Both my parents were of Aboriginal extraction. My father had no education whatsoever. My mother had very limited education from a travelling school-teacher around the early 1900s along with other children who lived on sheep and cattle stations. They got married and I was born in 1915.

My father was a stockman and horse-breaker for the stations around Charleville, at Dillahlah and Gowrie, so my early years were spent living in a tent as we moved between stations by a horse-drawn buggy. In between times, my father also did some kangaroo shooting and so there was plenty of kangaroo meat for tucker. But that was my early days. When I was about five and a half we moved into town and by the time I was six I was at Charleville State School and that was where I stayed till 1930. My last years at school were spent learning typewriting, Pitman shorthand and book-keeping and so on. My parents made sure I had a reasonable education.

This was about 1928, just at the beginning of the Great Depression and things were always a bit tight with us because my father worked off his own resources. Times were hard on all families. I can recall I used to get the horses and the sulky at the weekend, take a fishing line, a butcher's knife and a rifle and come home with some fish and maybe a rabbit. Rabbits were a great standby in those days. You could have roast rabbit or stewed rabbit. They went over well. All over Australia unemployment was at its peak. Swagmen were on all the roads carrying their swags.

In August 1930 my father said to me, 'I'll have to take you away from school, Boy, because you're not going to go any further when there's no jobs.' So my school-days were at an end. He took me away and he placed me with a local drover called Jack Drennan from Charleville and that was my first learning experience in the cattle game. We went up to the head of the Warrego and picked up with twelve hundred head of mixed cattle including calves from a property called Canoe on the south-west side of the Carnarvon Range. And

I ended up going with Jack down the Warrego and down through Thargomindah and in through Adelaide Gates. We got near White Cliffs in New South Wales and the cattle were bought by a station called Cobham Lakes.

To go from my school days to this kind of life was very hard for me to adjust to. All day and night we had that mob of cattle for three months. I was there for learning experience only. I was fed my meals and given clothing but no pay. But then a bit later, as a sixteen year old, I got ten shillings a week and my keep.

After that I continued working with other drovers. Times were bad. And in between I was working for what I call quart-pot drovers. One of them was Tom Felsman. He was about six foot five and he smoked cigars and he wore a vest and a tie. He was the boss and things were very tight. He must have been travelling on a mean budget because there was not much to eat. When I come home after one trip my mother looked at me and she said, 'You're thin! Boy!' I said, 'Look at the dog! He's leaning up against me. There was no meat for him either!'

And this Tom Felsman when he'd finished at night he would go to his wagonette. He had a little box there and he'd pull out either a bottle of brandy or a bottle of whisky and he'd have a nip. One day he said to me, 'Reg, I'll have to give up drinking.' I said, 'Why?' He said, 'I'm drinking far too much. The bottle's nearly empty.' I didn't tell him the cook was opening it too.

Freckletons' store, Camooweal, is now a Heritage Centre with exhibits of the droving era. In its heyday Camooweal was an important centre for drovers, many of whom had their homes and families there.

He was one of those characters you couldn't talk to. He said to me one day, 'Reg, you go on ahead and have a look at that water-hole and tell me how we should water these sheep.' I went and had a look and I come back and I said to him, 'It's pretty boggy. We'll have to be careful. You don't hurry the sheep. Just let them walk their way in and I'll be down there and I'll be watching them and steering them to places that are best to drink.' And I said to him, 'Don't you sool those dogs on to them, Tom!' He said, 'Leave it to me! I won't.' But next thing he's, 'Bring 'em up there! Bring em up there!' to the dogs and the dogs are barking and the sheep are pushing and there's sheep bogged everywhere.

In 1932 my father joined up with Albert Clark and we took the droving plant – my dad and I and a cook – with a wagon and spare horses out to Dalgonally on the Flinders. When we got there my dad and I worked in the stock camp helping with the mustering until the rest of the team came. By the time the others got there, we had all our cattle ready.

Those Dalgonally bullocks weren't all that hard to handle. They didn't jump that much. But we had an unusual experience on that trip. We'd only gone to Gilliat and there was a young chap, about my own age – I didn't know him at all – he just joined us that day. Someone brought him out from Julia Creek to make an extra hand. I don't know what happened because they warned me not to come around to see what was going on. But we were putting the cattle on camp. It was just on dark and they scattered and I tried to block some of them but this young chap had unsaddled his horse and he was sitting on it and the horse might have been touchy around the head and reared over on him, or something, when he put his hand around its ears. I don't know how it happened. But the poor devil was killed.

So someone had to go up to Gilliat and Tommy Scanlon, the hotel-keeper there, come down. He had a car and he went and got the police out of Julia Creek. And I never even knew the poor fellow's name; never even got to know him, because he was working on one side of the cattle and I was on the other. I was always kept with the boss around the back because my father said I lacked experience to get up near the lead because when you work a lead mob you've got to learn to spread them out to feed. So this poor devil, he was only there with us for might have been half a day and he got killed. He was some mother's son. The police took his body away. I never even got to say good-bye to him. The bush has a lot of tragedies, eh! But that was one of the saddest things I've ever known.

So, anyway, we took those cattle down to Boatman station out of Charleville. That's another Dalgonally company station. We dropped them off there in the mulga country and we had a few days off; maybe about a week. Then we went back and picked up more cattle from Boatman and moved on. The stores only went there to rest. We moved them on down past Gunnedah to Werris Creek so they would fatten up for the markets down in New South Wales. That was in 1932, that trip.

In 1935, Dougal Cameron got a contract to move cattle from Wave Hill in the Territory. It was a large property and carried about sixty-five thousand head of cattle. Dougal Cameron had a wagonette made from a cut-down Cobb & Co. coach and it still had the thorough braces on it. They were springs made of leather, not steel. Dougal and my father went on ahead. And then I flew up in a Qantas plane. In those days, Qantas had a mail run, a hop, step and jump sort of thing from Tambo, Blackall, Longreach and Cloncurry all the way to Darwin. It was an eight-seater passenger plane. So I flew from Charleville to Camooweal.

Including my father there were seven of us; two white men and the rest of us were of Aboriginal descent, either half-caste Aborigines or Aborigines. One white man and one white cook and the rest of us coloured. We drove those bullocks across the Territory via the Murranji Track. Then from Newcastle Waters and via Brunette Downs and Anthony's Lagoon and down the Ranken. We headed east towards the Queensland border north of Urandangie. We followed the stock routes that offered grass and water for our mob of bullocks. And round Boulia the grass cut out, so to follow the grass we headed across to Winton and down through Longreach and down the Thompson south to Windorah; then via Quilpie and Cunnamulla. We ended up delivering those bullocks near Walgett in New South Wales. That droving trip took nine months to complete. I was completely worn out. I'd do my watch of the cattle and then I'd go to sleep in my boots and in my sleep I'd be taking my boots off and putting them back on. I didn't know what I was doing in the finish.

But we had a lot of luck along the way. We took delivery of fifteen hundred and twenty five and we delivered fifteen hundred and twenty five. Because when we come through the Murranji, we found some Wave Hill bullocks that got away from somebody else. These extra bullocks kept our numbers up when we had losses. My father never missed a trick like that. You got paid on the number you delivered, not the number you took delivery of. A contract drover got so much a head per hundred mile. At first we were getting one and threepence per head per hundred mile but eventually we got one and four pence per head per hundred. Kidman men were on about a penny less. So you had to make sure you got the numbers there.

My dad was one of the best stockmen I ever knew. He knew practically everything and he taught me. By the time I was eighteen or nineteen I was castrating sheep, cattle and horses. I could read the weight of a live bullock. If a buyer wanted to know the weight and he said, 'Well, what do you reckon?' I could read it by the cod and the body. I could shoe horses and I could break in horses. I used to do all the inoculating for pleuro – pleuropneumonia, a serious cattle disease, before we left Alroy. Generally, I learned very quickly. My father was a smart teacher; he had a stock-whip seven foot long. Just a flick; only a flick. But that was enough to say, 'You're not going too good.'

One of the first things my father told me when I went out bush was 'Keep your eyes open, Son. Keep your ears open and your mouth shut. And you listen and learn only off the people that got on.' I never forgot those words. It stood me in good stead all my life.

Then Dougal Cameron took sick and died and he willed all his droving plant to my father at a nominal cost of two pounds a head for the horses and nothing for the rest of the gear. So we ended up with one hundred and twenty-five head of horses and a wagonette and a team of eleven pack-horses and pack-saddles and all the rest of the gear.

So in 1936 we went to Alroy Downs and started working for Dolf Schmidt. The Schmidt Company also owned Galway station in the Cooper Channel Country and other sheep and cattle properties on the Warrego River between Charleville and Cunnamulla. We took cattle from Alroy down to Yambuccoona on agistment. Those Alroy cattle were a bit touchy early on because they were used to that open country and watering on bores and as soon as you got them into timbered country, they were very timid.

I've heard people say; and Dolf Schmidt told me, 'Your father's the best drover I ever had. When he takes cattle down and they go into the paddock there, they take two months less to recover from the trip. They respond quickly and fatten quickly. He'll do me any time.'

I believe my father's secret was that when he watered the cattle he always picked a camp where there was abundance of grass. The cattle fed off the camp and they got dew with the grass. He never walked them and put them on dry grass because they didn't eat well when they were thirsty.

And the next year I went back out to Alroy and worked there until the season started. Jack Crouch was there then and Owen Lewis was the head stockman so I joined the stock camp and we done the mustering. One time I saved Owen from – well, – getting into bother with the Aborigines. He wasn't speaking to them too kindly. And he wasn't treating them with respect. And, well, poor food. He'd say, 'That's good enough for the darkies', or, 'That's good enough for the boongs'. I said to him, 'That's going to get you into trouble one day, Owen.' He said, 'They haven't got the guts.'

One day he said to me, 'You head on ahead down to so-and-so. You come round that way and I'll send the others and we'll meet at the bore. I'll tell Tommy and Jackie to go with you.' So I went on my way and I only went about half a mile, I suppose, and I thought, 'There's nobody following me. I'd better go back.'

And there are twelve black boys around Owen and he was in the middle. And they've got a piece of gidyea wood. Two of them are in the middle with a piece of wood about two foot long and they are trying to measure Owen up. He was doing a bit of fancy footwork. He didn't know which way to duck. So I galloped in among them with the stock whip, cracking it round their ears. They all scattered, yabbering at me in their own language. 'No worry! No fight'm yu! No nothin' yu!'

I said, 'No. But you hurt that man there, that Big Fellow Crouch come out and he'll bring his rifle and he'll just go bang, bang, bang, bang. No more gin. No more piccaninny.' And I told them, 'You wait till you get back to the station. You tell that Big Fellow Crouch.' You had to talk to them like that because that's the way they spoke.

So they all settled down, and I said to Owen, 'I think you've got a short lifespan here. You'd better move on.' He was a coward really. But I think I just come back at the right moment because the same thing happened to Tommy Neverns on Alexandria but they didn't miss him. He was the camp cook there and he was found dead with head injuries.

In 1937 Dolf Schmidt gave me my first mob as Boss Drover. He gave Dad one mob and I had one mob, a week behind my father, to take a mob of twelve hundred and fifty bullocks off Alroy to South Galway in the Cooper area. At the time I was twenty-one years of age and I considered it some achievement to be entrusted with the responsibility of such a mob when most boss drovers in the 1930s were all aged about sixty years old.

Anyway, when we got to Boulia, Mr Donahue, the storekeeper, met me. He said, 'I've got bad news for you.' He said 'Your father's gone to Cloncurry hospital. One of his stockmen pulled out, got up the pub and got drunk. And he had a grudge against your father apparently. And when your father tied his horse up to the store he come down, and when your father was talking to me inside, he pulled the saddle off and got his pocket knife out and cut the counter-lining on the saddle. And when your father went out he stabbed him four times. And your father pulled a paling off the fence and whacked into him. If I hadn't come out I'm sure he would have killed him. Because the fellow had a bit of drink in him by then, see.'

The upshot was that Dad was three or four days in Cloncurry hospital getting patched up. They got him back to his camp and then six months later he had to go back to Cloncurry for the court case. The fellow got six months in Stuart Creek gaol in Townsville and ever since has the nick-name 'Stabber'.

They were rough times. We had problems with the men, particularly from the Northern Territory and the border. If they were good drinkers they'd only go as far as Boulia or Camooweal and then they had enough money to buy grog and they'd go back home again. Getting them past the pubs was always a problem. For that reason we used to try and pick our labour from Charleville or South West Queensland; then we had strong prospects that they would stay on the job; Georgie Begg and George Day, and a little fellow with squinty eyes, a little skinny, jockey bloke, Mick Sweeney; they were reliable. And now and again we got a couple of black boys. One of them was named Pilot and he was an excellent horse-tailer.

So that was my first mob as Boss Drover. I stayed at Alroy and continued working for the Schmidt Company until the war broke out. A lot of stockmen joined up but work on western grazing properties was declared an essential industry while the war was on and Manpower exempted me. I was committed to work for the Schmidt family until the end of the war.

In 1941 I got married. I had to leave my wife at my mother's in Charleville. My father had a heart attack and went to Brisbane for medical attention. Then eventually the horses were sold and the house in Charleville. I was still committed by Manpower to stay with the Schmidt family, so then, later on my wife joined me on South Galway on the Cooper and then down the Warrego at Bandu station until the war was over. By that time we had two little girls and another baby in arms. My wife said to me, 'There's not much future for us in Charleville with three girls so we'll go to Brisbane.' So we went to Brisbane and settled in around Hendra. Then I found I was the proverbial square peg in a round hole. All I wanted was to get back to the bush.

It took me a while but after twelve months a friend of mine from Charleville rang me up. He said, 'I've got a horse here, out of a good mare. Would you like to take it?' I said, 'Yes,' straight away. I took out an owner-trainer's licence and rode it at track-work myself at Doomden. So there was my wife and myself and three kids and we're trying to pay the rent on an old rattle-trap, broken-down house; patches in my pants; holes in their shoes; and I'm trying to ride at track-work and train a horse. But, eventually, that horse won me five races. Plus a couple of places at Eagle Farm. And from then on I never looked back. Once you've been a stockman and a horse-breaker you notice things. I became pretty proficient at reading a racehorse. My father was a great horseman and very knowledgeable and I learned a lot from him. But the main thing I learned in the bush was to stand on my own two feet.

I've seen a lot since I gave up droving down the Georgina and the Diamantina. Our droving wagonettte that my father and I used on our droving trips has been restored to its former state of being a Cobb & Co coach that was used around the Charleville district during the 1900s. It is now on display at the Cobb & Co Museum in Toowoomba. I appreciate the fact that in some small way my father and I have contributed to the history of our past.

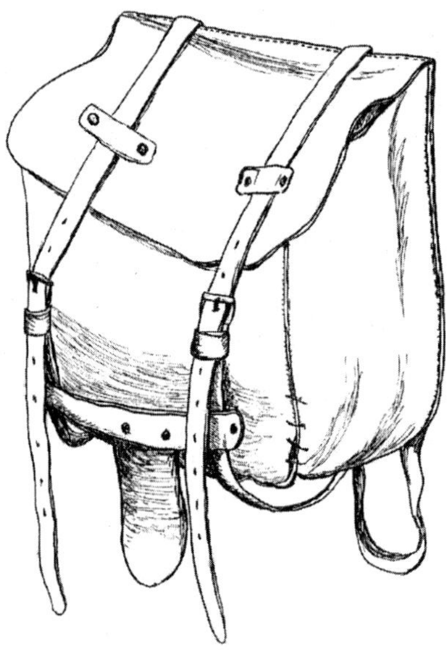

15

Edna Zigenbine

ॐ ॐ ॐ

Introduction

I first met Edna Zigenbine at the Drovers' Camp Festival in Camooweal in 2004 and knew her to be another of the legendary figures of the droving era. Slight of build and weathered of complexion, Edna is respected by every cattleman of the north for her lifetime of experience in the droving industry, including her many crossings of the notorious Murranji Track. She speaks of those years in typically understated manner; almost dismissive of the experience, describing the infamous bullwaddi trees of the Murranji as '...branchy old things...could be a bit dangerous to gallop through if you had to.'

At no time in the telling of her life-story does Edna dramatize her extraordinary feats of courage and endurance or make them appear more than every-day routine, seeming unaware that she is a one in a million among generations of women before and after her, literally a legend in her own life-time. In fact Edna lives a secluded life in her adopted home-town, Mt Isa, and can hardly be prevailed upon to tell her story at all, let alone to record it for posterity.

The account of Edna's life presented here is a blend of material which I recorded at Camooweal with a pocket-cassette, an interview with her by Judith Hosier on behalf of the Australian Stockman's Hall of Fame at Longreach, an extract from an article titled 'Ruby Zigenbine – Wife, Drovers' Cook and Mother' in 'Cattle Pads', the magazine of the Drovers' Camp Festival, October 2005, and the personal recollections of seventy-five-year-old Rodney Watson, a Camooweal-based drover of the period, who remembers Edna as a girl. For the use of these additional sources of information I express my deep appreciation, confident that we are each of us pleased to play a part in helping to establish Edna Zigenbine as the noteworthy Australian she deserves to be.

ॐ ॐ ॐ

Reared On The Road

Edna Zigenbine

'I just kept on droving'

I was born in Thargamindah in 1926. My father, Harry Zigenbine, was droving for Sydney Kidman. My mother, Ruby, was a Sydney girl and she met my father when she was working at the hospital in Cloncurry. Dad was kangaroo shooting round there but they went droving straight after they were married.

Mum had eight of us kids so it must have been a bit tough for her. I'm about the middle. There are four older than me. There were four boys and four girls; an even number. All born on the road. And reared on the road. Mum only had one baby in hospital. All the rest of us were born without any medical help. She had two stillborn babies and they had to lie beside her on the ground until she was well enough to get up and bury them.

I was riding from five years old. We went along day by day and we reckoned it was a great life. We didn't worry about any schooling, only what Mum might tell us if she had time. If we wanted to learn to read we practised on the jam-tin labels and sometimes a paper. Mum was a good camp cook. She always made sure us kids got plenty of good food; stews and curries. Plenty of meat. She made her own bread and brownies in the camp ovens. Most of the bores would be about ten mile apart and Mum'd do the washing when we got there and hang it on the barbed-wire fence to dry. Sometimes it was so cold in the morning the dog dishes and wash bowls would be frozen. Sometimes if there was a dust storm it'd be that dark it wouldn't break daylight till nine o'clock or ten. It'd get that way you couldn't hardly see to move. The horses and cattle'd just turn their tail to the wind until it was over.

We all stayed with the droving plant, grew up with it. It was a family affair. Wherever Dad went we followed along. Mum drove the wagon. It had rubber-wheels and was comfortable. We all had four or five horses each and we'd ride them alternate days. Never rode the same horse two days running. We broke our own ponies in and started shoeing our own horses. But my eldest sister, she got married young, and she broke away, and my eldest brother, he did a few trips with us and then he broke away. Most of stayed together. Then there was only me and Dad and Andy and Joe and Mavis and Jack. Just the four or five of us left. Usually Dad would get a couple of extra blokes there with us.

Then Mum came to Butru near Duchess, just a bit of a township with a railway siding and lived there for eight or nine years, or Mum and the youngest did.

And then Dad started droving for Vestys in the Territory, moving their cattle mostly from Wave Hill to Morstone[1]. Each trip would take about fifteen or sixteen weeks.

We might take a mob of fats from Morstone to the railhead at Dajarra, or from Morstone to Kajabbi. Them days we'd only do about two trips a year. Might be fifteen hundred head in a mob. Dad drove for Vestys for years and then we went away up to Bedford in Western Australia and took the mob from there and brought them down to Dajarra and then me and Dad went and brought another mob from Banka Banka.

We come through the Murranji Track from 1942 right up to 1950. It's got a bit of a reputation because it's so scrubby; scrubby country; bullwaddi and lancewood. You always had a man in the lead, stringing them out through there[2]. Bullwaddi is a damned branchy old thing; branches out right from the bottom up. That's why it gets so dangerous if you've got to gallop through it. But the Murranji's alright. It's not that difficult to keep the mob together. It you had a bad mob of cattle it would be bad of a night but most of them old Wave Hill cattle were pretty good. They never used to rush on us. Only maybe, sometimes of a morning, they might jump up if a kangaroo went through them, or something. That's about the only thing that would start them.

I had to take over Dad's plant in 1950 because Dad got sick. That was his last trip. He had to go to hospital in Tennant (Creek). We was bringing a mob down from Bedford through the Murranji. When I seen how things were I took over. I brought the mob in and delivered at Dajarra. I was a bit young running the plant m'self but it was OK. It was a bit worrying at times. I had the brother that comes next to me with me and we didn't get on too good about a few things. He was camp cook and he was working against me half the time. But we managed. I did a lot of the cooking m'self. I was used to it. I used to cook for Dad a lot. Most of the time there would have been five of us. Sometimes down to four. I had three blackfellas working for me at one part of it. One of them left me at Elliot but the other two old 'fellas, they stuck with me. They were good old 'fellas. Fifteen hundred head of cattle. Watching them at night was the worst part. Long hours. You had to be there all the time.

Bullwaddi normally grows densely and its interlacing branches form an impenetrable barrier to the horseman. This isolated specimen is unusual.

I drove for Banka Banka, Helen Springs, Morstone. They're all the one company. Or was. Every year

[1] A Vesty's fattening property north of Camooweal.

[2] In *From the Gulf to God Knows Where, Volume One,* Bluey Ellis describes the Murranji Track; 'The government had bull-dozed this track through but only wide enough for a vehicle; no ten chain road. The cattle had to string out.' Of bullwaddi scrub he says, 'Bullwaddi is terrible stuff; at about nine or ten feet it bows over and forms a barrier of interlacing tunnels that cattle can push through but not a man on horse-back.'

there used to be drovers come in from Wave Hill, one behind the other. You had to keep your cattle separate. You might talk to one another but you had to keep apart; keep a day behind one another. You might sometimes be a few hours behind one another but most times it was a day behind. When there's a bore I'd water today at that bore and I'd go out that afternoon and the next drover would come in and he'd water and go out. You worked it like that all the time. One day behind the other.

You couldn't go just anywhere. You had to follow the stock route. If you got off it some of them (the property owners) didn't like it. There wasn't much difference in the Territory because it was all just plains, anyway. You had to let the property owners or managers know you were coming through when you could but apart from that they never worried about you much as long as you kept the rules. But say there'd been a shower and there might be a bit of feed off the stock-route a bit, well, you might sneak off there for the sake of your cattle and horses. We often done that.

You couldn't just camp if there was a bit of feed because you had to keep your mileage up, unless your cattle were sick and you had to pull up. But it was better for yourself to keep to your mileage because you had to truck at a certain time. If you had to be at say, Dajarra at a certain date to load, and the trucks are booked, well, you had to be there. The trucking date mightn't have been arranged before you left but it would've been, after, and along the road they'd let you know, and then you had a deadline for your delivery. So you had to keep to the regulation; the nine or ten mile a day. And it was better for yourself, because if you pulled up for a week and rested, well, that's money out of your own pocket. You got so much a mile. Say you were averaging your nine mile a day, or ten mile a day – all depends on the stock-route – you got so much a head, a mile. You always counted the cattle when you took delivery; and counted every week. You'd keep checking your count.

So if you'd pulled up for a day's spell, that was your bad luck. You had to pay the wages of the men. Unless you were quarantined, say, with redwater or pleuro, well, then the owners of the cattle had to pay you.[3]

You got paid when you reached the railhead. You counted when you delivered and you got paid on the count. Mostly the owners depended on you to do the trucking, though the agent might be there. You'd have to be there and do it yourself. You were still the boss and you'd see the cattle were loaded properly on the rail; and you were satisfied. If the cattle were already sold, well, the agent would be there and he'd pay you.

The cattle we brought in from Wave Hill, well, they were stores. We'd deliver to Morstone and they'd be left there and they would fatten them there. Then they'd go from Morstone as fats to the railhead at Dajarra and down to the meat-works that way. Once we took a mob down to Kajabbi to the railhead. They were going straight to the meatworks. But by the time they got from Wave Hill to Morstone, they're not fat, poor devils. They're pretty bloody poor.

We never had too many rushes. The Banka Bankas rushed a fair bit on us. Them Bankas

[3] Redwater, a tick-borne disease, and pleuro-pneumonia; if cattle were sick with these it was the owners' financial responsibility, not the drovers'.

always rushed the first week but then they settled down. A rush is a bit frightening, alright. If you've got fifteen hundred bullocks on camp and they rush! Out on the downs it's not so bad, but if you're in timber country it's frightening. We had a bad night once. One of the worst nights I can remember. It was at Newcastle (Newcastle Waters). It was rainy. It rained bad and they rushed and headed straight for the bullwaddi scrub. Anything can start'em rushing and it all depends on the cattle, too. A stormy night. Or lightning. A flash of lightning and they'll go. Or something startles them. Might be a kangaroo or something jumps into the buggers, or something like that. Some stations have cattle that'll always rush. That station that Dad used to drove off, bloody Alroy; them cattle, it didn't take much to start them. They were very, very jumpy. They call them sort a 'jumpy mob'. They would jump at anything. Anything at all. They might go three or four times a night.

And you get what you call 'hollow' ground, or drummy ground. It makes a bit of noise. A horse walking on it, or something like that, will make cattle jump up and start galloping. And limestone country. Limestone country's not much good. It's a horrible place. You slip on it, y'know. Very dangerous for your night horse. My Dad, when he was droving when I was only a little thing, before I got with him, he nearly got killed in limestone country. They had a few mobs of rushing buggers and a mare got killed on top of him one night, down the Ranken there somewhere. They were Alroy cows and they were buggers to rush and the mare fell with him in the limestone rocks.

One time my sister was on watch and the mob rushed. There was just the two of us. I don't know how we never lost the lot but we never. It was that dark we couldn't even see 'em. A shocking night. One of the worst nights I've known. We cut about twenty-eight, twenty-nine off the lead. They must have been way out in front and we were after the big mob and blocked the big mob, singing out and yelling and cracking the whips, and swung the mob around, swung 'em back towards the camp; rung'em back round on to the camp. We must have just chopped them twenty-eight fellas off. They got away on us, anyhow. But we got 'em next day. We tracked 'em down and got 'em.

But, droving, day from day, it's much the same. You get up in the morning. You generally wake the cook and the horse-tailer about half-past four. The horse-tailer goes and gets the horses and the cook gets up and gets the breakfast. And the men get up at five and they have their brekky and cut their dinner, whatever they want. The horse-tailer's there by then with the horses and you get your day horse and away you go. And as soon as you ever got ready, say, half past five, six o'clock, you take the cattle off camp. And you feed 'em along all day; a man on each wing, if you've got the men. If you've only got a couple, well, there'll be one on the tail and he'll do the wing; just ride up and sing out and crack the whip if he wants them to go over; once you just turn 'em they'll go over. The cattle get broken in after a while. You let them feed out; give them a bit of a spread and let them feed along.

There's always a man in the lead when you're stringing them on to water. You might get a mile-long string. It all depends on the water. If you've got a long stage, a dry stage, well, when you get close to the water, you've got to cut 'em up; might be into fifties or a hundred at a time, they get a good drink. And when they've had a drink, well, you push them on out a bit. Then you cut another fifty or a hundred out and let them go in. You can't let them all go in at once or they hurt one another. It might take you an hour and a half, two hours to water them all.

Abandoned mill on the Barkly stock route.

We never had to bail water out of any of those old wells for the cattle. Only one year there, coming down from Morstone, we had to bail water for the horses. They always had to have a drink but the cattle never got a drink there. Never had to do that. Cattle can do a dry stage.

Depends how far the waters are apart. You feed 'em along for a couple of hours, and the horse-tailer would bring the horses along and the cook would bring the camp along. If you had a truck he'd bring that along. If you had pack-horses, well, they'd have to be packed up. The cook and the horse-tailer would do that. I was horse-tailing and m'brother was cook.[4] You just work together as a team. You got a good mate, well, you've got a good mate. You get off camp early and get on to camp early and let your day horses go. They're hobbled out and the night horses are caught by that time. You might get on camp round four o'clock and then you let your cattle feed close to, all round the camp. Round about six o'clock they might start poking in on the camp. They get used to it after a while, cattle do. They know where they've got to lay and they just come in on it. When you've got 'em quietened down they're only a bit away from your camp.

It's the boss's place to watch the horses till the horse-tailer's ready. The horse-tailer does the first watch. And you have your camp behind your cattle. You have your cattle out in a ring, a big ring, out in front. One fellow's got to ride around 'em all night. You have your different hours to go on, out on watch. And he's out for two hours and he comes in and he calls another bloke. Or maybe two and a half hours; depends how many's in the camp. Sometimes the cook does a watch. Sometimes he doesn't; depends how many you got in camp. You might have three or four night-horses tied up. All depends on whether your cattle are quiet or not. If your cattle are bad you'd have three or four. If the cattle are quiet you might only have the two at a time. The old night-horse, he's got to be special. He's got

[4] Skilled understanding was required in 'packing' pack-horses. The weight in each pack had to be evenly distributed so as not to cause injury to the horses' backs.

to be sure-footed and he's got to know what he's doing. They get very attached to the game, the old night-horse.

Then I went back out to Bedford and got cattle from Bedford and I just kept on droving. I met my husband, John Jessop, in Winton and got married and then we kept on droving a few years. I did most of the cooking. We drove from Helen Springs a lot. After m'husband and I give up droving we come in here and then we spilt up. See, I never had no schooling and I said to myself, 'My son's going to have schooling if it's the last thing I do! So I'm going to town and I'm going to settle in town.' So I come in here to Mount Isa and bought a house and put my son to school and I've been here ever since. I got a good job. I worked for the Council as pound-keeper and did that for over twenty-five years. So I was still working with horses.

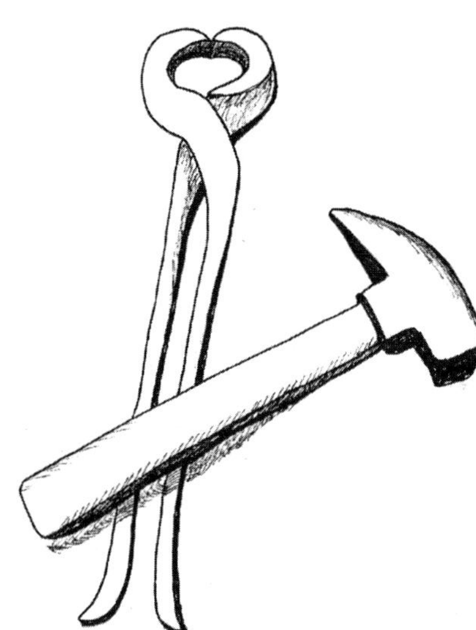

16

Ross Leake - Grazier

ॐॐॐ

Introduction

Is there any sound more heartening than the laughter of cattlemen swapping yarns of the mates they have known, of the times that were bad or the seasons were good. Visitors to the lovely new homestead of Ross and Jill Leake, on the outskirts of Charters Towers, approach eagerly, knowing that not only the warmth of genuine western hospitality awaits them but laughter and companionable talk as well.

Ross Leake, a tall, fine-looking man in his early sixties, is a descendant of two noted pioneering families, the Allinghams and the Blacks. In a place of honour on the sideboard was displayed a tiny leather-covered prayer book that had been Violet Black's at boarding school. There was also, ready to hand, a first edition of 'North Queensland Pioneers - by J. Black of Pajingo' dedicated to 'The pioneers of North Queensland of Yesterday, Today and Tomorrow' with a contents listing of notable families such as the Atkinsons, the Clarke's, the Daintrees and the Garbutts.

Ross's attractive wife, Jill, is also the grand-daughter of pioneers, having grown up on Cressy, south of Richmond, owned by her family, the Logans, who overlanded stock and wagons in the early 1900s.

We had a wonderful day's tape-recording on the front verandah, well provided for from the kitchen with a continuous supply of refreshments, our work punctuated at intervals by shouts of, 'Alf! Get back here!' Alf, a hyper-energized Jack Russell, was bent upon intercepting flights of galahs, low-flying Cessnas, crows, or any approaching vehicle. Alf has a long pedigree but selective hearing. Ross says the thing Jill and he have discovered about owning a Jack Russell is that you only call them when they are coming directly towards you.

ॐॐॐ

A Man Among Men

Ross Leake

'You've got to be ready to learn.'

There were no artificial waters in the early days of the North and the pioneers had to follow water. My mother's family, the Allinghams, came up overland in the late 1850s from the New England Tableland and took up country on the Burdekin. My great grandmother, Jane Black, wrote a book about it.[1]

I grew up on Kentle Downs, south of Hughenden on the old Muttaburra road. Dad bought Kentle in 1936. His father had married a school-teacher from Maxwelton and they bought four aggregations south of Richmond. But it didn't rain for a number of years and he got behind the eight ball where the banks were concerned. So he borrowed a heap of money and bought a lot of sheep. The very next year the sheep all got washed away. He sold that place and went to Torrens Creek and bought a property called Cranford. Later he sold that and bought Kentle. At first they lived in the shearing shed but it got burnt down. Kentle homestead was built in 1944 and added to in 1952.

Then Dad bought the operation next door, Jireena, off two old blokes called Dibbs and Lamont. Lamont did not drink at all and Dibbs was drunk everyday. And in one of the old station diaries we found there, written day after day, in Lamont's beautiful copper-plate hand-writing, was; 'pulled the bore'; 'mustered sheep'; 'cleaned out the bore-drain'; and every day's entry ended, 'And George Dibbs drunk again.' Lamont gave diary-keeping away and George Dibbs took it over. And in his scrawly old hand-writing at the end of each day's work, he would write, 'And Lamont sober again'.

Old George Dibbs was a legend. We were very good friends with the Browns of Bogunda and spent a lot of time there. We used to go over for Christmas and we'd have to cross Towerhill Creek at Jireena. One time we got to the crossing and here's George, sitting in the middle of the creek up to his chest in water. He had a bottle of rum in one hand and a pannikin in the other. He'd pour a bit of rum into the pannikin and then dip it in the creek to add the water. And the problem for us was how were we going to cross the creek in time for Christmas dinner when George Dibbs is sitting in the middle of the crossing and won't budge! Luckily, Ben Brown arrived from the Bogunda side to see where we'd got to, and

[1] Black, Jane. *The Pioneers of North Queensland*

he sees how things are. So he calls out, 'What time is it?' And old George just reaches underwater and pulls out this big old pocket-watch and says, 'It must be dinner time!' and he off. That's how we got across the creek for Christmas dinner on Bogunda.

We had a neighbour who had a remarkable knack of 'acquiring' stuff. During the war he 'acquired' a Tiger Moth from the American air-force. He and Dad taught themselves to fly. No landing strip; just the paddock! But those old Moths, you could put them down practically anywhere. They only do about forty miles an hour.

This chap also 'acquired' a Canadian Blitz in boxes. Even the chassis wasn't bolted. The starter-motor was still in grease-proof paper. And he constructed this Blitz from scratch; riveted the chassis, put the diff together, got all the wheel-springs in; like a big meccano set. It took him four years to do it. And then he said to my father, 'Come over, Mick! You've got to meet my Mabel.' That's what he called this Blitz. And he started her up and said to Dad, 'Well! What do you think!' And Dad said, 'Mate, you've done a brilliant job. But how're you going to get the flaming thing out of the shed?' He'd built it long-ways across! He had to pull the shed down to get it out!

During the Shearers' Strike Jack Schultz had a Proctor and he and my father and Monty Geary and the Dalgetty's agent from Hughenden went out and I suppose they'd sunk a bottle of Scotch or two, but it was the middle of a stinking hot day and they took off. Well, this Proctor wouldn't fly. It got up to about a hundred foot and that was about it. There's no lift in the air when it gets to a certain temperature. So they're coming in to crash and old Monty Geary's sitting in the back seat, and he says, 'Dear Mister Jesus. If you ever took it in your heart to do old Mont a good turn, now's your chance!' They crashed alright. But not one of them got a scratch! The lot of them walked away!

My father was involved in the Australian Graziers' Association, and he was away a lot. My earliest recollections of Kentle are of Mum running the place with two men to help.

I went to school at All Souls when I was five years old. My panama hat came down over my ears and my strides were down to my knees! Mum believed in buying things a bit on the big side for me to get a bit of wear out of. I didn't feel too good about boarding school for the first few months. When you started in those days, it wasn't in Grade One. First there was Prep One and Prep Two, then Prep Three and Prep Four the next year. After I'd been there for six months I started to get the hang of it. After two or three years I was well and truly broken in. By the time I got into Grade Four I was practically an Old Boy!

There were plenty of other little kids my age; Arthur Wearing, Robert Conn, Gordon Hassett – his father managed Chudleigh Park – Lux Lethbridge; all kids we knew from round our district. There was a junior dormitory for all the little kids. I ended up loving the place; played a lot of sport; made it into the tennis team and the cricket team. I had my brother David there, four years behind me. There was none of this 'Leake Senior' and 'Leake Junior' business. We were Springer and Sprunger![2]

We had the greatest man that ever walked on two legs as our head master; Canon Cedric Hurt. He was a gentleman; English. He had a tremendous understanding of the character

[2] If the humour of this at first escapes you, try putting the surname after it.

of each of those three or four hundred boys at the school. He could do more damage with words than he would have with a cane. By the time you left his office he would have convinced you that whatever you'd been up to was wrong. And he knew every one of us by name.

But after him we had a fellow named Mattingly. He had come out of the navy and he brought a very stern regime to the school. He wanted to run it like a navy vessel. He tried to change things too quickly. By the end of the year he didn't have a prefect left. And when you are a kid at school the big fellows, the footballers and cricketers and swimmers, they're your heroes. When they decided to jack up, us young fellows thought, 'This is great! We'll be in this too!'

I don't know where Mattingly went wrong but I know where I did. I was running a book! My mates and I; Herb Evatts, the Anderson boys from Tobermorey, over on the border, and a couple of others. It was good money! Every pocket-money day we would lay the odds and the kids would give us tuppence or threepence and we'd lay it on the horses. We made quite a lot of money out of it! Bookmaking isn't a criminal offence. Except maybe if you happen to be at a Church of England boys' boarding school!

I went as far as Grade Eleven. At the end of that year I didn't exactly get kicked out but I was told very politely that it might be better if I didn't come back. I was more concerned about what Mum and Dad would think than I was about Brother Mattingly. When the letter arrived home that was it! I was put to work and not allowed off the place for six months. Which didn't do me any harm. Now I am Vice Chairman of the School Board of Governors!

My father had a heart attack and died in 1967. Jack Wearing – a great man – became our mentor. My brother and I took over the place, working in partnership. Jack tried to help us not to pull the wrong rein. We were still in sheep at this stage but in the end we went broke. We'd had three deaths in seven years. The succession duties they had in those days! After each death we would have to pay the probate again. We bought the property three times over, in seven years. We owed the Federal government more than the place was worth.

Then came the cattle crash of 1974, and that's what put us back on our feet – the cattle crash. I ran into a chap named Sylvester out at Cloncurry – I was only a young man then and he was a lot older, so I was inclined to listen to what he had to say. He said to me, 'Boy, whatever you've got to spare, start trading in cattle. Don't breed any more cows. Don't breed calves. Go buying and trading.' So my brother and I had a bit of a talk about it and we sold whatever we could. Fortunately the seasons went with us. All through the '70s we had a run of good seasons.

In '78 it neglected to rain and we took sixteen hundred head of bullocks to Boulia. Ever since then I have had fond memories of Boulia. Great fattening country! We sold a thousand at three hundred dollars a head which enabled us to pay off all our debts. It took six or seven years to do it but it was the cattle slump that put us on our feet.

We built up a pretty good herd of cows, but not without a few hiccoughs. At one stage we thought we had imported every infertility disease that was ever known to the cattle industry; fibriosis, tricominosis; abortion diseases. The bull is the carrier and he shifts it from cow to cow. You can test for it and eradicate it. So that took a few years. Then we went in for controlled breeding.

I realize now that breeding was a mistake. Kentle was pretty good country; handy country. We should have been paying somebody else to breed the cattle and we should have been fattening. The country was too good for breeders. It was fattening country. We used controlled mating. We preg-tested all the cows. If we had three hundred cows in a paddock we got three hundred calves. We would pull the weaners off depending on the season. If the cows were prime fat and milking like hell, we would leave the weaners on them. We have taken weaners off at up to three hundred kilograms. But we've also taken them off in a bad year at a hundred and fifty.

We made our own hay; round bales; Flinders grass, preferably. We had big coolers[3] seven hundred yards square; five plain wires, two electrified – where we used to feed the weaners. But that turned out to be a mistake. It was just so simple to take the tractor down with the forks on it and dump ten or twenty bales around. But it meant you weren't seeing enough of your weaners. We found that with the square bales when you've got to walk around and get the strings off and they're trying to get the hay from under you, they get used to you and quieten down a lot more. We thought we were saving time and money just chucking these big round bales into the coolers but it turned out it wasn't the best way to go about it. You learn these things as you go along.

The electric fences were to educate them not to go anywhere near a fence. It works, because, over the years we have taken a lot of cattle away on agistment and we get all our cattle back. They don't go near fences. They have learned to respect them. We have had cattle on agistment as far south as Meandara and Blackall, out at Boulia, up in the desert country; a lot of different areas. Nutritionwise, Boulia would be some of the best country you'd see in Queensland. And the further down that Channel system you go the better the country gets.

There's a story down there in the Channel Country that if a beast gets on the end of a tarvine – that's a plant that grows along the ground with sticky flowers that get in your socks – by the time he gets to the root end, he's fat! The lower the rainfall the better the country. It doesn't get leached. They might only get four inches of rain but that flood-out country

[3] yards built for a specific purpose such as feeding livestock

has the silvery Mitchell grass, and barley Mitchell. Wherever you see barley Mitchell you know you are in good country. And I've seen spinifex well over six foot tall. If you drive cattle though spinifex when it's seeded, you'll see them turn their heads sideways and strip the seed off. In the old days those old teamsters used to strip the seed off it and use it for feed for their working horses. They called it desert oats.

Generally speaking, the higher the rainfall the worse the country. Close to the coast the grass gets long but it has no protein value in it. But by the same token, in the Channel Country they need big areas. That Boulia country might only get ten inches a year but it is built for light rainfall. And it's my observation that black soil country needs two or three inches of rain to get it started but that's all it takes for Mitchell grass. Apart from the Channel Country the best area of black soil country in the north would be around Corfield. They turn off magnificent bullocks from that area.

We were using Droughtmaster bulls. We bought a herd of Brahmans from a chap named Cyril Chaplin at Cloncurry. He had a Brahman stud down at Giru. When he sold out we bought all his cows. Excellent cows! And with the Droughtmaster bulls over them we produced pretty good progeny. Colour never worried us, though with the Droughtmaster bulls the herd mainly tended to red.

'Get a run of good seasons in that downs country you haven't got enough money to stock it!'

We ran big numbers of cattle. When you get a run of good seasons in that downs country you haven't got enough money to stock it! Plenty of years we'd run a beast to ten acres. And we improved the place to the extent that Jill and I could just about run it on our own. We had put in good watering points and improved the pasture. We had lanes everywhere. I could muster a paddock by myself; could start them along in the lane and they would just trot off to the next water; or wherever I wanted them. So what if the mob was a mile long! They'd just trot along these lanes. Or along to these beautiful big yards that I built. I'd just tail them along.

But what I didn't realize was that when the time came, after about four or five years, when they had to go on agistment, well they had never been herded up. When we tried to muster them the conventional way, we ran into trouble. They wouldn't block up. They'd never been taught. We realized using the lanes had let them learn bad habits. So from then on, when we put them in a lane, we put someone in front of them. When we took them out of the paddock we put someone in front of them. That way they learned.

I bought my brother out in 1987. Jill was very much involved in the cattle work. She'd been brought up to it, growing up on Cressy. We used to employ some people, but, really, we had a wonderful neighbourhood. If Arthur Wearing wanted a hand, or Kelly Davidson wanted a hand, or Toby Rogers, or ourselves, say, when we branding; four or five of these fellas would give a hand. And then we'd go over when they were shearing and give them a hand. The give and take system worked pretty well. It saved labour costs.

On Kentle we had an irrigation dam we built ourselves. We dammed a creek underneath the wall; just a natural, desert wall. You drop down over it on the road from Prairie to Hughenden. It went through the eastern side of Kentle. That dam was big enough to water-ski on. Two times round was two and a half miles. We all water-skiid. The Browns had an even better one over on Lammermoor.

Jill was a brilliant gardener. We had about two acres of lawns, and mainly trees; Cook trees, cedars, gums. Out there you grow what grows. Garden flowers don't do all that well in that black soil. With that amount of lawn Jill needed a ride-on mower but taking care of the garden, constantly changing the sprinklers, was a pleasure to her. My mother had started the garden back in the early days but water was always the key issue. Jill had a six thousand gallon tank off the bore. She could empty that every day. And when she'd run that tank dry that was it. She couldn't extend the garden any further.

We pulled a lot of the country and seeded it to buffel. We were the first people out there to use dry lick. Dick Kelso was the one who put us on to it. We were dung-sampling. Nowadays everybody is talking about dung-sampling but we were involved in it ages ago. Up here, if you get a standard supplement from a stock and station agent you might be paying for minerals you don't need. With dung-sampling you collect eight or ten sample pats from around each of your watering points and send them away. Ours used to go to Toowoomba. They tell you what your cattle are deficient in and what supplements they need. Then you get a supplement mix made up to your own requirements. The downs country was never short of phosphates. It is phosphorus-rich. It was mainly nitrogen that we were chasing; and a bit of copper and sulphur. And then if we were down on protein we might feed some copra meal.

We had a telephone line that was built by a bloke known as Wire Wheels Robinson. He used to hit the bottle a bit. When he was sixty miles out of town the line was as straight as a dye but as it got closer to town it got a bit of a wobble up. Every time it broke down we used to have to go along the line and find the break. But all the breaks were very close to town. It was very hard to convince the women that fixing the phone line was thirsty work.

Jill and I have two children, Michael and Tracey. When they were little slips of things they used to go to a school over on Cameron Downs; a pastoral school, run by the state, with about eight or nine kids from about Grade One to Grade Seven; just bush kids with no idea about flash clothes or Nike gear. Jill and a couple of other mothers from around the area took it in turns to run the kids the twelve miles across. They'd meet up at the junction and do the school run turn and turn about. Then when ours got up a bit they went away to St Gabriels All Souls in Charters Towers. They had a pretty fair introduction to the place because some of the teachers were still there from my day! But Tracey ended up School Captain. St Gabes had an Exchange programme and Tracey spent six months in England, at a school called Charters Ancaster College, in Sussex. It was a tremendous experience for her.

But talk about aristocrats! Tracey was interviewed by the parents of the girls who were to come back out here. They refused to believe that we had forty-seven thousand acres at Kentle. These were colonels and ships' captains but they had no idea of the distances and conditions in Australia. Tracey told them, 'But in Australia our place is only a small operation!'

So we got three English girls in place of Tracey. And those girls couldn't believe the size of everything. When they arrived we were driving them home from Townsville to Hughenden and we passed three cars one after the other. I could see these girls were a bit toffee-nosed, so, just teasing, I said, 'The traffic wouldn't be as thick as this in London, would it?' One immediately burst into tears. They wondered where on earth we were taking them!

And when we got them home it wasn't too good either. We tried to feed them roast beef and they were vegetarians; so that didn't turn out. We were at a loss how to entertain them. But we had a tennis-court so I said, 'Would anybody like a game of tennis?' One girl said, 'Yes. I would.' So we turned the lights on. We had a girl, Debbie Brown, working for us. I said to Mother, 'You and Debbie better play together. I'll help this child. We'll let her serve first.' The ball went past at three hundred mile an hour. Four aces later that was the end of that game. Six love, the set. The ability of that child! As we were walking back inside the house, I said, 'You're not too bad!' She said, 'I have my private coach.' She was the Minor Junior Champion of England!

Our kids both rode from when they were tiny. There wouldn't have been a day when they weren't out riding bareback. I was leading Michael in a Show event when he was about three and he was grizzling at being led so I unclipped the lead and told him, 'You're on your own!' During the drought I used to tell them to keep to a trot. And they would go over the bank of the dam behind the house, trot, trot, trot and then when they were out of sight, they'd go flat! Then they'd come back again later, over the wall of the dam, trot, trot, trot. It used to make Jill and me laugh. They never thought we were a wake-up to them. But we made sure they had decent ponies and we followed the shows and gymkanas all over the countryside.

We've had a few accidents, a few bad moments, on the place. Jill and I had only been married twenty-four hours and I fell under a trailer. That was a bit of a scary one. My brother David and I were carting rock with this little dog-trailer. We got a flat and when I tried to jack the wheel up it slipped and rolled backwards and tipped the lot on top of me. David raced back home and told Jilly I was dead. So she was practically a widow on Day One of things.

And another time I had the two kids with me and we were up in the scrub country and I had a buster. I'd promised the kids that they only had to help me shift some cattle into the next paddock and we could go pig-catching. My horse tripped over an ant-bed and fell on me. I'd done my shoulder and was a bit dozy. So the kids propped me up against a tree. Then they caught my horse and got the saddle off him and laid me up against the saddle. Then they trotted off home, seven or eight miles or so, to get help. Tracey told us that

Michael cried all the way home. He reckoned, 'I suppose this means we won't be able to go pig-catching this afternoon!'

And when we did go pig-catching I let the two kids loose after all these little suckers and all they could run down were these two little runts. So we took them home and the kids are going to raise these pigs. They lugged all these bricks up and built a pig-sty on the front lawn next to the tennis court! So after a while the novelty wore off and we had a bit of an altercation. I said, 'Those pigs have got to go! They said, 'No! No!' I said, 'Well, shift them down and we'll put them in the stallion stall.' After a few more days they lost interest again so I thought, 'Right! That's it!' and went down and opened the gate. One pig bolted for the scrub. But the other fellow, he smells feed where the horses had spilt it under their feed tins. So he pulls up and has a bit of a feed. And he seems to think, 'This doesn't seem like a bad place!' So he stays. And after a bit he starts to think he's a horse! We'd go mustering and next thing, 'Hoink! Hoink! Hoink!' and it's this bloody pig! He's coming too!

At this time the kids were training their ponies every day, trotting round the cooler three or four times. And to stop them fighting we'd send Michael round one way and Tracey round the other. And this little pig, away he'd go after one of them. And where the two of them would cross, Pig'd go 'Hoink! Hoink! Hoink!' at the other pony. This blasted pig!

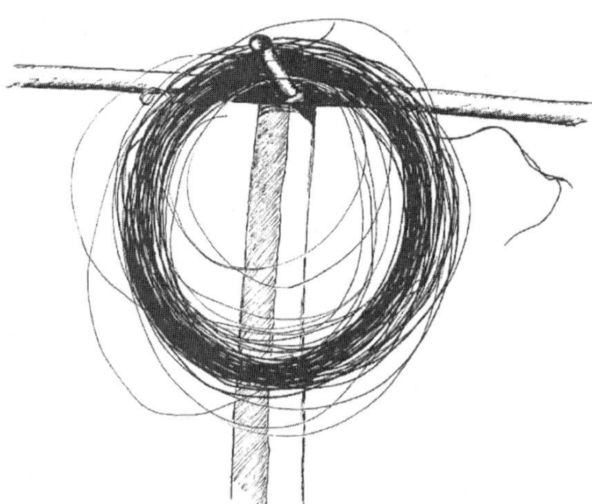

But in the end we had to give him away. We didn't have a house-yard and he'd get into the vegetable garden and root it up; into the lawn and rip it up; into the chook yard. You couldn't keep him out! He was destroying the place. So the day came when the neighbours came to collect him to be made into pork. They couldn't catch him so we made the kids lead their ponies with the pig following along behind up into the old pig-sty so they could corner him there. The kids were bawling their eyes out! And when the neighbours drove away with him, there we were all standing around with faces a yard long having Three Minutes Silence for this bloody pig!

Over the years we made a lot of money out of sheep. We dealt in sheep in bad times. When it got dry we would take our cattle away on agistment and when they had left there was always sheep feed left in the paddocks. When it got very dry, sheep places would be practically giving sheep away and then later when it rained the price would go up. So sheep have been very good to us. Nobody will criticize sheep to me. But all the same I don't think northern Australia is sheep country. We don't get the wool cuts or the lambing percentages. One year we took cattle on agistment to a place named Murramurra on the Nemoi River. All mulga country. The biggest sheep I've ever seen in my life! They were giants! And the year we were there they marked 110% lambs. Twins everywhere! You don't get that up here. You'll be lucky to get 80%.

And the dingoes are always a problem. Old Jack Wearing was going to show me how to catch dogs, but all I learned was how to walk! We'd walk for eight miles. Jack'd be telling me that a dog had scratched itself here, or gone up this gorge or that. His method was to work out the pattern the dog had; that and his secret decoy. There was no way he was going to tell you the recipe of that bloody decoy! But did it stink! So we'd walk eight miles. We'd just about get to the point where Jack was going to set his traps and he'd say to me, 'Right! You go on back and get the motor!' Even then I wasn't allowed anywhere near the trap-setting side of things because of leaving my scent and so on. So all I learned to do with old Jack was walk! But he was a good old dogger, old Jack!

When you're on the land you've got to be ready to learn. Especially when you're in an area like we were, where you only get two and a half good years out of five. I believe the time has come when people on the land have to think of some form of diversification for when the seasons are bad. Certainly any young fellow going on the land today should have some form of alternative trade. I've seen a lot of changes. One of the best would have been when Rural Power was put through; pulling all the windmills down and putting electric pumps down the bores! That and road-trains. In 1978 when we wanted to shift cattle to Boulia we couldn't get a road train for love nor money. We had to get them from South Australia. Now you can ring up and in a week or ten days you can be shifting your stock.

I wouldn't change much in my life. But I'll tell you what! I wish to God I had known when I was a young fellow what I know now! I always said that I would be a cunning old bugger by the time I got to seventy but I think I'd better stretch that out to eighty now!

17

'Scrubba' Watkins

ॐ ॐ ॐ

Introduction

'I'm Scrubba Watkins and I was never a Boss Drover!' began 'Scrubba' Watkins, addressing the crowd at the closing ceremony of the Camooweal Drover's Camp Festival in August, 2005. The audience roared appreciatively, as 'Scrubba' knew they would, a 'scrubber' being a wily old bull that has eluded many a muster and intends to elude many more. Then, despite his assertion that he had never been a Boss Drover he gave a succinct and entertaining account of his years in the droving industry and was roundly applauded.

Later when I asked if I could record his story I said, 'What's all this 'Scrubba' business? You were never christened 'Scrubba', now, were you? What does your wife call you?' With a grin Scrubba admitted, 'Nah! She calls me 'Jack'. I said, 'Okay. Then I'll call you 'Jack' too, shall I?' But, strangely, although 'Jack' seemed the polite and reasonable way to address this striking-looking cattleman at our first meeting, 'Scrubba' soon seemed more natural. 'Scrubba' it became.

Scrubba had driven from his home, 'Ringer's Retreat' in Renmark, South Australia, to attend the Drovers' Camp Festival, accompanied by his eldest daughter, Lynne. The interview took place in the cool of early morning on the scrap of lawn at the back of the pub, for even in August the daytime temperature in Camooweal, seven miles from the Northern Territory border, starts shifting towards the thirties. Background effects included the snarls of passing double-decker road-trains, the early morning screechings of parakeets – the mighty Georgina being a short walk away – and the melodramatics of a gang of street dogs in pursuit of the hotel cat. But Scrubba's sense of humour, his vitality and his enthusiasm for the history of the droving industry as he had known it, enabled the interview to go ahead as though we were in the most state-of-the-art recording studio.

A touching moment was Scrubba's description of coming home one day to find his young wife in tears over their toddler babies. She told him that she had been remembering the time when she had been 'removed' from her parents as a little girl and had realized the broken-

heartedness they must have felt, thinking, 'Supposing it was my babies!' In recounting this incident, Scrubba struggled to maintain his own composure. I thought all the more highly of him for his compassionate heart.

By the mid-thirties of his life, with a young and growing family to educate, Scrubba had realized that it was time to give the droving life away. He moved to Alice Springs, bought himself a typewriter and taught himself to read and write. The years of disciplined hard living and self-reliance in the drovers' camp stood him in good stead. By 1967 he was managing his own transport company, specializing in truck, taxi, coach and specialist car-hire services for the tourist industry. His business card reads simply, 'Legion Group of Companies. Jack A. Watkins; Chairman of Directors.'

Never A Boss Drover

Jack 'Scrubba' Watson - Drover

'A good cattle-man is a quiet bloke'

Now, don't get me wrong! I was never a Boss Drover. Never wanted to be one. We couldn't all be bosses. There wouldn't be any Boss Drovers if it wasn't for blokes like us!

I did my first trip droving when I was eleven. I was born at Beltana, a railway siding about five hundred miles north of Adelaide, in South Australia, on the original narrow-gauge line from Port Augusta to Alice Springs. The house was on the bank of the creek and it had a wild peach tree, a 'quandong', and a well. And up on the hill was the little old one-room school and the police station. Beltana was mainly a siding for loading bales of wool from Beltana station, one of the biggest sheep properties in South Australia. My dad was an engine-driver for the Commonwealth Railways but my life as a kid was always with some kind of stock; donkey teams and camels and horses. So it was inevitable that one day I would jump that train up to Marree to go droving. You could walk as fast as the train went so I don't know why I bothered to catch it. And from there I went out on the mail truck to my first job on Mungerannie station.

My first trip was with Boss Drover Gordy Oldfield with Clifton Hills bullocks from just below the Queensland border. So there was Gordy, Tom Singer, Henry Singer, Siddie Branson, Tommy Campster and m'self. This is 1939 and I wasn't twelve until we reached Marree at the end of the Birdsville Track. That was September 1939, the year that war broke out. These boys were all older than me. They all went away to war, of course. Some of them came back and some of them didn't.

Because I was so young they wouldn't let me watch the cattle of a night time. There was plenty of young fellows like me in the game who hadn't had enough experience to be real good at the job. So to keep us on and make us feel important we were wood-and-water boys, or wood-and-water 'joeys'. We had to keep the billy-cans for the cook filled and drag the wood up and make the fire for him. And watch the cattle on dinner-camp after they've been watered, while the droving blokes had their lunch and a bit of a camp. But I always wanted to be one of the big blokes and do a stint on night watch.

I would have got maybe be five shillings a week. But those years, through the Depression, I never worried about nothing. I had m'swag and there was always plenty to eat; meat and damper and a cuppa tea. So what the hell would I want money for! I often ask myself, did I ever get paid? And if I did, what did I do with it? I don't remember money until I was maybe twenty years old. I didn't smoke and I didn't drink so I had no use for it. I was happy.

But then later when I grewed up and I got to doing night-watching cattle, well, it's pretty damned boring! I've often been asked 'What you think about when you are riding cattle of a night time?' Well, you can work it out for yourself; what a silly bastard you are for being there! And then when the cattle rush of a night and you're trying to turn them! Those cattle rushes get pretty hairy in scrubby country when you've got bad bullocks. You get ready to give it away, but, no, it's the only job you know so you stick to it and just hope the next lot of bullocks is better than the last lot.

The tiny township of Camooweal on the Georgina River, seven miles from the Northern Territory border, was once an important destination for drovers. The curve in the recently built high-level bridge was put in to avoid a rock site of cultural significance to local Aboriginals.

Then I done two trips with Dick Palmer, an Alice Springs drover, and a trip with a drover called Dick Smith. They were good blokes; half caste; coloured people, as I call them. To me they were nature's gentlemen. Very good blokes. They never let you down, y'know. They looked after little blokes and taught us all they knew. This is about the mid -forties and I'm still just a lad. I was always ready to learn off them.

You get different experiences on different tracks; quiet cattle, good cattle, bad cattle. Certain stations seem to turn off bad cattle. Newrie station, now, they always seemed to be bad cattle. We called them 'galloping Newries'. And Elsey cattle were never known to be quiet. But you could have a quiet mob that you would think nothing would stir up but then if something frightens them in the night time they can be just as bad as the bad cattle. But when we are talking bad cattle, they are jumping all the time. They even rush in the daytime. Anything to gallop at, they gallop.

When a mob rushes you have to gallop a bit y'self. You keep out from them until you hit the lead and you're yelling and swinging your whip and gradually you swing the leaders right around and bend them around towards the rear. Then they will start going round and ringing in a circle until it's that damned dusty they choke themselves down. Then you've got to watch that they don't break out somewhere else. But mainly, nine times out of ten, once they start circling they will stop there. They think they're following the leader, see!

One mob of Elsey bullocks, we came down the Stuart stock route – or you can call it the North South stock route; it follows the old telegraph line down right through and if you wanted to follow it all the way it would go through to Quorn. We watered the mob at Aileron, took 'em down through Native Gap about sixty miles north of Alice Springs and out on to the big spinifex flat there and they galloped all night. The next day we took 'em in to Connor's Well to water early as we had a long drive to do. And it could be about fifteen, twenty mile further on to a big Mitchell grass plain where there was a lot of stone to see if being on stone would quieten 'em down. It quietened 'em down, alright. They were that sore-footed in the morning they could hardly walk into McGrath's Flat for a drink of water! Yeah! From then on down there was a lot of stone and a bit of sand and by the time they got to the trucking yards at Alice they could hardly walk.

But, then, thousands of mobs of cattle have been on the stock routes over the years and you only ever hear about the bad ones. You might have one bad mob for the whole year.

We always had to carry a little anvil and horse shoes if we were going into stony country to keep our horses shod or they'd go lame. We'd carry that in our pack-bags. In my time we only ever had pack-horses but later on we were lucky enough to have a wagon and some camels pulling it. Or we'd use our bronco horses to pull the wagon. You'd pick good reliable ones to carry the water canteens; five gallons each side. They would have probably the lightest job but you couldn't afford to have them go bush with your water; no more than you could with your tucker-bags. Your bags of self-raising flour, they were fifty pound. And if you had tins of jam and so on, well, there was a bit of weight.

Scrubba's plant, watering at White Stone rock hole on Anningie station.

Cattle from the west and north-west of Newcastle Waters would generally go east across the Barkly into Camooweal or Dajarra or Urandangie. That's why the pub at Newcastle is called the Junction. It's the junction where the Murranji Track comes in from the west and meets the North South stock route, also known as the Stuart stock route, which heads south to Alice Springs rail-head trucking yards. The original Murranji used to follow the Buchanan from VRD and Wave Hill in to Dunmara. That's a fair way round. By going on the Murranji they cut off a lot of miles. So rather than go all the way round they used to take a chance with this new track. But there's not much clearance along it where you can camp of a night time. It's all that thick, branchy bullwaddi and lancewood scrub.

You like to have your cattle somewhere out in the open of a night, a soft camp with a few trees around, where you can put your packs behind you and make your fire where the cattle can see. So if they do rush they won't come over the top of you. Or that's the theory. It doesn't always work that way. But nine times out of ten they won't come near. And you put your horses behind you. That's part of the night bloke's job, when he's riding camp at night; to make sure your hobbled horses don't come round in front of the camp. Because when cattle rush, they're not going to stop and go around some hobbled horses. And the next thing you know you got a mob of dead horses. So that's part of the night-watch bloke's job; riding around watching the cattle and singing and making sure them hobbled horses are kept back behind the camp. If they start coming around between the camp and the cattle he has to keep pushing them back.

I lost one of my best cutting horses like that. He was a horse I never hobbled and he strayed around in front of the camp. The cattle jumped and I found him in the morning, dead. They'd gone over him. I called him Roachie. And, cutting out, he would go up and put his nose on the bullock's tail as much as asking me if that was the one I wanted. And I would just nudge him with my knee and he'd push him out of the mob. His name was Roachie because a roach-back horse has a short back; his front legs and his back legs are closer together.[1] It's just like they have had a piece cut out of their back and they've been joined together again. They're only a little short horse. They can spin on threepence and give you tuppence change. In my time I'd only ever seen this one. He was the best horse I ever had for cutting out. And I can tell you this; when you are cutting out, you are only as good as your horse. The whole thing revolves around a good horse.

When you're cutting-out, you give a big bullock a reasonable time to get out; you don't push him out. You give him a chance to see the other mob, and ninety-nine times out of a hundred he will run across. Big bullocks have got their mates and there would be some of his mates that when they saw him go, the next thing you see is all these big bullocks going over, following him. If you're a good cattleman you watch for signs like that. If you've got these big fat bullocks you don't want to be galloping them all round the country losing weight. You let them take their time and you don't rush them. And nine times out of ten none of the others will go from the mob, just that bullock and his mates. And if others follow, well, that's when the face-men move in and turn them back. And, say that big bullock didn't want to go across. He might get out halfway across and then decide to swing round back into the mob again. That's when you use your good cutting horse. He can swing on his hind legs, left and

[1] '*Short backs and perfect shoulders that are priceless on a camp*'; 'From the Gulf' by Will Oglivie

right, and block him getting back. Then the face-blokes move in and push him across. You don't go galloping them. A good cattleman is a quiet bloke.

And when you are droving bullocks, well you put them on camp of a night, just as the sun is going down and get them settled down. Then you might ride into the camp for a cup of tea but you never get off your horse between the fire and the cattle. If they see that shadow it might make them jump. And you don't tie your horse up and walk across in front of the fire. You keep your horse with you. Cattle don't like blokes on foot. It's alright if you're walking with your horse. They accept that. But not you on your own. They will jump any time for that. And when you get on him again, you go to one side of the fire or the other. You never come out in front of the fire and get on him there. If they see the horse and all of a sudden they see a bloke jump up on him, well, they'll go! Different things like that will frighten them.

The N.T., Queensland Border fence, and the '*sunlit plains extended*' of the Barkly Tableland.

When cattle have done a dry stage it is a good thing in a kind of way because they are walking and smelling for water and that keeps them occupied. It's when the mongrels are laying down and there's not a sound, and butter wouldn't melt in their mouth, that's when you've got to be on your toes. The slightest thing, a stick snapping, or a rat in the grass and they'll be on their feet and off.

But if you were lucky enough and the waters were about ten mile apart, that was ideal. You'd camp halfway in between. You'd feed 'em for five mile; and then your dinner-camp would be on the water, maybe two or three hours. And then they'd be feeding the next five mile to the night camp. So you were doing your gazetted ten mile a day.

But in some places your waters might be thirty mile apart. You would dinner-camp on the water the first day and then move them out about a third of the distance. Then the next day is a dry stage for them. They might be a bit restless that night. You keep an eye on them otherwise they might disappear. You might have to push them along a bit the next day. You would try to keep the minimum number of blokes on horses with them so the horses can go back for a drink or go on ahead to water with the horse-tailer. The horses you've got with you, you give them a bit of a drink in your hat out of the canteens. Just so long as he can wet his lip a horse will make do. Then the next day you are heading into water. That last stage you might have to do up to fifteen mile.

As for getting to a watering point and it's dry, well, if ever it come to that you would give your job away. That's the responsibility of the Boss Drover; to send a man, generally the horse-tailer, on ahead and let the station know you're coming through and to make sure the water is there. It's the responsibility of the station owner to make sure of the water. Then he'd usually come out to see you through, because he wouldn't trust you. He thinks you might take half his cattle, or knock off a couple of good killers. Some of them would send a bloke out and he would camp with you and see you through. They might be thinking to themselves, 'You don't want to trust old Jack, Mate!'

The government put those bores down in the early days when the stock routes were first gazetted. The pity of it now is that a lot of those government wells and bores are completely neglected. Not even the stations are using them.

I've had a few falls off horses but the worst one was when I was on the face-of-the-camp on Anningie, about two hundred mile north-west of Alice Springs. A face-of-the-camp horse has to be pretty good; gallop pretty fast. But this time, mine tried to spin and he got his legs tangled up under him and down he went and I'm under him. He got up straight away but I knew I'd done my leg. But lucky I didn't get my foot caught up in the stirrup. The blokes just splinted my leg up with a couple of mulga sticks and took me into Tea Tree and the ambulance from Alice Springs come up. Anningie turn-off is about ten mile north of Tea Tree and then another fifty mile into the station so I would have done sixty mile in the back of the ute, then another hundred and twenty into Alice Springs in the ambulance. I was in hospital quite a few weeks. They didn't do too good a job of fixing my leg because later on I had to have a hip replacement where it didn't fit into the hip socket properly. I never went back to finish that trip but afterwards I went back out to Anningie and did station work there for Jim Davey. 'Ironbark' they called him; 'Ironbark' Jim Davey. He was a good boss; the best boss I ever had.

Scrubba on Roachie, his favorite cutting-out horse, killed in a night rush.

I done a lot of station work and I liked it but I always preferred the droving. If I was working on a station and a drover came by and he was a bloke short, well, I would go with him; just to go somewhere different. That's how I covered so much country. The longest trip I ever done was four months; from Singleton, just south of Tennant Creek, down through Alice Springs, down to Granite Downs. It was a long trip because it was '54, a bad year. The drought was on. The drought had started in the 'fifties and was getting bad, '52 and '53. There was very little feed on the road but it got a bit better south of Alice Springs.

Normally with bullocks on the road you are supposed to do ten mile a day. That's the gazetted distance. You can't dawdle on station owners' properties. And you can't go off the gazetted stock route. Or you're not supposed to. I've been known to, once or twice. So you used to do eight or ten mile a day. That's if the waters were available. If not, of course, you would have to do more. But we had cows and calves and weak steers, so we were lucky on this trip to Granite Downs if we done five mile a day. You don't shift pregnant cows because if they have a calf on the road you have to knock it on the head before she turns around and licks it or smells it and whistle the cow on and burn the calf, otherwise you might as well shoot 'em both. You would get her going but the first chance she got she would try to get back. And you can't just leave her there. She would perish. Having weakened beasts was why we took so long. But once we got south of the Alice if we come across a bit of decent grass and a decent well we might put in a couple of days there. On that particular trip we were in no big hurry. We were shifting cattle from one of the owner's properties to another one; from Singleton and Anningie down to Granite Downs. So we were station drovers, not on contract, and we could take our time.

I never wanted to be a Boss Drover. I was quite happy to be what I was. I've been head stockman; Stirling, Granite Downs, 'Ningie, Willowrah. I loved cattle work. I loved the life. And I tell you what, I'd go back droving again tomorrow! But if I did, I reckon I'd settle for being the wood-and-water boy again!

18

Brenda Wilson

ॐ ॐ ॐ

Introduction

Central Mount Stuart, a blue hump on the western horizon from the Stuart Highway, is not the geographic centre of Australia. Technically, the geographic centre is about sixty kilometres to the south-west. But when you stand on the summit of the mountain that John McDouall Stuart named Mount Sturt in honour of his old leader, Charles Sturt, but which was subsequently re-named Mount Stuart, you cannot help but feel awed. For three hundred and sixty degrees, shimmers a horizon of immense and inscrutable distance, and you are at the heart of it.

Brenda and Nic Wilson and I climbed Central Mount Stuart together in 1991 and reached the site of the cairn where McDouall Stuart and his second-in-command, William Kekwick, had planted the Union Jack in 1862. We then set out to follow the remains of the historic 'O.T.' – the Overland Telegraph Line – through semi-desert country, skirting Lake Eyre, as far as Beltana in the north of South Australia, where, in a stony hillside cemetery, we located Kekwick's grave.

Despite these shared adventures and years of friendship, I realized when I came to write this account of Brenda's time as a nursing sister at the Australian Inland Mission hospital at Fitzroy Crossing in the Kimberleys, that I knew very little about her life. Brenda is a person of wisdom and compassion and never talks of herself. So it was only in putting together this cameo of her time at Fitzroy Crossing that I learned that she had spent a lifetime serving isolated and vulnerable people across Australia's north.

In 1963 she helped to set up the Australian Inland Mission hospital at Kununurra, in the Kimberleys, which used materials dismantled from the AIM hospital at Beltana. Beltana had been the first posting of John Flynn, the founding superintendent of both the Australian Inland Mission and the Royal Flying Doctor Service. Later Brenda worked, again for AIM, at the Rio Tinto mining township of Mary Kathleen in North West Queensland. This was followed by years of service with another AIM initiative, the Far North Children's Health

Scheme. Finally, with the Department of Health in the Northern Territory, she worked with Dr. John Hargrave, noted for his work among leprosy patients, in particular with the Aborigines of Australia's Top End.

Brenda sees nothing unusual about her years of service in the Outback, saying only, in her practical, down-to-earth manner, 'There's nothing out of the ordinary about anything I ever did. Plenty of other girls did the same.'

ॐ ॐ ॐ

A Purpose and a Calling

Brenda Wilson – Bush Nurse

'I always seemed to fall for the teeth'

People ask, 'How did you become interested in working in the bush?' Well, as a child I always loved being in the bush near our home in Sydney. We lived in a suburb in between two rivers, the Lane Cove and the Parramatta. There was lots of bush in our area and my playmate and I loved to go down near the Lane Cove River and light a little fire and boil the billy. On one occasion we almost ran into a circle of men tossing coins in the air. It was a two-up game. Two-up was illegal and we were terribly frightened. The men didn't even see us. They were too intent on watching the coins going up and down and laying their bets. But we were convinced they would chase after us and we fled through the bush for dear life.

I went to 'SCEGGS.' – the Sydney Church of England Girls' Grammar School – at Darlinghurst for eight years. Each day I had to travel by bus, ferry and train, which probably made me independent about travelling on my own. Then, about 1945, I decided that I wanted to be a nurse. I applied to the 'PA', the Royal Prince Alfred Hospital. In those days there was a long waiting list, so I took a position as a governess on a sheep and wheat station called Maneroo outside Moree for six months. There were four children ranging in age from nine down to the baby, eighteen months. That was a great experience of both children and the bush. Sometimes I would lie on the creek bank and look up at the filigree pattern made by the sunlight and shadows through the leaves of the trees and think how much I loved life away from the city.

The baby Charlotte had a mind of her own and a very strong cry. One day she was supposed to be sleeping in her pram outside on the verandah. Suddenly I realized that her cries had turned from crossness at being in her pram to shrieks of pain. Somehow she had pulled the net into the pram and stuffed it into her mouth and a burr had stuck in her throat. I realized at once that she was choking, so, without benefit of any nursing training, I instinctively grabbed her, turned her upside down and slapped her firmly on the back. Out of her throat streamed her last milk feed plus the burr.

Next, still waiting to get into 'PA', I spent three months as a nursing aide at a small hospital in Berry. One day, holding a basin while a patient vomited into it after her appendix operation, I realized my own stomach was turning. So, that afternoon I went across to where I could see the hills and I thought deeply, 'Now, I either go to Prince Alfred or I don't.' And made my decision. I would go to Prince Alfred and train as a qualified nurse. So I went. And I did my General Certificate and Midwifery and then, up to Brisbane, where I did my Maternal and Child Welfare.

In Brisbane I became very good friends with a girl called Jean Neill. Jean had been inspired by a book called '*Flynn of the Inland*', about John Flynn[1], the Presbyterian Minister who had founded the Australian Inland Mission. We talked and talked about it together and after much thought we both felt we had a calling to offer ourselves to this service. We applied and were accepted. As part of the preparation we had to do a week's dental training, mainly extractions. We knew that in the Outback, dental problems were a cause of terrible suffering and that many people might need our help. Among other things we were warned about the dangers of doing a 'block', a 'block' being a mandibular nerve block, which seemed an enormous responsibility. You had to visualize the patient's head and face structure at the same time as trying to insert the needle. If you inserted it too low or too deep or too superficially the anaesthetic would be deposited too far from the nerve to be of any use, and there was a high rate of failure, even among professionals! The idea was not to hit the parotid gland, the salivary gland. None the less we knew we had no alternative. We had to do our best, in this and in everything.

Australian Inland Mission Hospital at Fitzroy Crossing. The heavy shutters were for protection agaist cyclones and dust storms.

Once our period of training for the Australian Inland Mission was completed we were told we had been appointed to Fitzroy Crossing in the Kimberleys and the long journey began. We travelled up to Townsville, changed trains and continued out to Mount Isa, a four day journey. We were met in Mount Isa by a Bush Brother[2] of the Anglican Church. He just couldn't understand why we were going to work for the Presbyterians! Then we went on to Darwin by a small

[1] The Reverend John Flynn (25 November 1880 – 5 May 1951); Australian Presbyterian minister, founder of the Royal Flying Doctor Service, the inaugural flight of which took place from Cloncurry in 1928. He was the first superintendent of the Australian Inland Mission. As well as tending to the spiritual needs of people living in the Outback, Flynn was aware of the need for medical care and established a number of bush hospitals. After his death his ashes were placed under a large memorial boulder outside Alice Springs

[2] Bush Brothers; Anglican Brotherhood of St. Barnabas, dedicated to working with people in the Outback.

plane and flew on to Derby in Western Australia. That night we stayed at a bush pub. We were sitting on our beds on opposite sides of our room when suddenly a fellow without a shirt on walked through, taking a short-cut out to his bed on the verandah. That was our introduction to casual outback ways.

The second night, another fellow brandishing a bottle of cherry brandy invited us to go out on to one of the boats with him. We may have looked naive but we weren't as green as that. We weren't wandering travellers. We had a purpose, a destination and, we felt, a calling.

Next day we flew on to Fitzroy Crossing[3]. The hospital was about three miles from the aerodrome, built at the top of the road that went down into the low-level bridge at the crossing. We were told that in the Wet the river was known to rise thirty feet over the bridge and spread over the countryside for miles. The town consisted of just two police houses, a post office, a pub and the hospital. That was it. At first we wondered how we would cope but we knew that other girls before us had done it and that so could we.

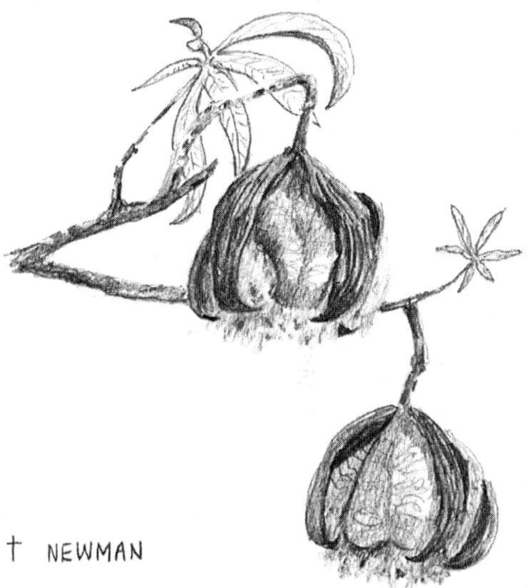

The hospital was made of galvanized-iron and timber with heavy push-out wooden shutters; the sort with a stick to keep open. We would soon learn that when dust storms arrived – you would see the wall of red dust approaching up-wind – the first thing to do was to rush upstairs and slam all the shutters down and lock them.

Downstairs there was a big cement-floored kitchen before us and off to one side a large dark store-room in which was kept six months' supply of everything we would need; flour, sugar, tea, hops for making bread, powdered milk and so on. Downstairs was the only area that had fly-screens. We didn't really need the powdered milk because there were goats in the area which the police staff used to milk, so we were given milk each day. There was also a Coolgardie safe and a kerosene refrigerator. The Coolgardie safe was kept cool by filling the tank at the top with water which as it trickled down over hessian bags kept things beautifully cool by evaporation. Outside there was a bough-shed where we could sit to have a cup of tea.

[3] Fitzroy Crossing, 2, 685 kilometres north of Perth, and originally settled as a suitable place to cross the huge Fitzroy River, which during the wet season was capable of stranding travellers for weeks on end, is a predominantly Aboriginal community. The Fitzroy River was named after Captain Robert Fitzroy, a previous commander of the H.M.S. Beagle, by Captain Stokes in 1838. The upper reaches were explored by Alexander Forrest in 1879, whose report on the potential pastoral value of the region led to the establishment of historic Gogo station, Fossil Downs and others, 20 kilometres downstream from the present township. The local Aborigines resisted the early pastoralists and the area saw some bloody skirmishes.

Beyond that was a toilet – a septic toilet, that is – and a shower-room; a cold shower, of course.

Across from the engine-shed which housed the two engines for power and water were the native-quarters and another large bough-shed. Most of the patients and their relatives and friends spent their days over there. There was also a large corrugated-iron shed, which was a shelter from the rain for them but they didn't use that very much. Even when Aborigines are sick they prefer to spend their time in the open air except for the very sick patients who were in the hospital, or in our bough-shed, where we could keep an eye on them. It was all basic but we knew that AIM hospitals were really only outposts and that any critically ill patients would be evacuated by air to Derby. That was John Flynn's original vision; to cast '*a mantle of safety*' over the Outback.

When we arrived we were met by the two sisters we were replacing. There was an Aboriginal couple, Stella and Joe, to help around the place. In the big storeroom I found a primus stove. I thought 'Aha!' because I like my early morning cup of tea and I knew the big old stove in the kitchen would be pretty slow to heat a kettle. On the first morning I pumped up the primus and got the kettle on the go. I was filling the tea-pot when Stella came in. Her eyes lit up. Pretty soon she reappeared with a billy-can. That became our morning routine. I would make a pot of tea and take a cup up to Jean. Then Stella and I would sit together and have a cuppa and a talk and she would fill her billy and take it back over to her camp in the big bough shed.

The old low level bridge at Fitzroy Crossing. In the wet season the river was known to rise thirty feet over the bridge

Stella was very efficient and soon had us learning the ropes; how to make bread with the hop yeast and so on. We hadn't been there very long when we met our first centipede, a fiercesome-looking thing about eight inches long with its hundred legs all going at once. Stella showed me what to do. The centipede was intent on disappearing under the wood-box near the stove. The kettle on the stove was boiling. Stella picked it up and doused the contents over the centipede. And that was that! Not very nice for the centipede but their bite can make you extremely sick and we had no time to be sick. From the start we accepted that we were on duty twenty-four hours a day.

Stella was very good but Joe was lazy and slow. It was important to keep the tank of the kerosene fridge full because our supply of medicines was stored in it and if the flame went out we could lose the lot. The wick also had to be kept trimmed or it would smoke and lose the cold. This particular morning Joe just didn't get around to checking the tank. He would 'lookim bye'n bye' he told Jean sulkily. Jean got mad at him and told him off. It was a bit of a relief when Stella and Joe decided to leave. Almost as though by bush telegraph, Topsy and Freddie arrived. They suited us much better. Topsy was perhaps not as efficient as Stella but she was easy-going and friendly, always smiling, and Freddie turned out to be much more helpful than Joe and was very good in the garden and at his other tasks as well.

And one of the patients, an Aborigine woman from Leopold Downs who was said to be a very good bread cook, took over making the bread and it was lovely. Of course, we all shared the bread, patients and all. The flour would get a bit weevilly at times but you learned to live with it. At the week-ends we doled out sugar and tea to anybody who wanted to go walkabout up the river and there would be a lot of smiling faces and happy voices as they set off in little groups with their dogs and billy-cans to look for bush-tucker.

Jean and I soon found that it was easiest to alternate our duties weekly. When she was nursing and seeing to medical matters, I would be keeping an eye on the cooking and the household side of things. And then the following week we would swap over. But if someone came in with an injury that needed stitching, well, that was Jean's field. She had worked a lot in theatre. But somehow I always seemed to fall for the teeth. Aboriginals have good strong teeth which are well embedded in the jaw and quite a job to get out, though on the whole they didn't have too many tooth problems. The second year we were there, a dentist came round with his wife and a mechanic. He had the old-fashioned pedal drill, but it was more the Europeans that came in for treatment while he was there, than the Aborigines.

The nearest doctor was in Derby and we had contact with him by wireless. He made routine monthly visits by plane but any other time we only contacted him if we actually needed him. One doctor's visit, we had a ham cooking in the copper outside in the yard for a party we were organizing for the children for Christmas. The doctor's visit was a bit prolonged and by the time we remembered the precious ham and looked at it, well, it was no longer precious. It was in shreds! But we still had to use it because although the party was for the children, all the adults would come too, of course. So we resorted to rescuing what remained of the ham out of the copper with the garden fork.

We had plenty of callers from the properties round about who would drop in for cups of tea when they came into town. Of course, they always brought us some fresh meat. The Aborigines were more pleased to see a pile of quivering flesh than we were. They were very partial to the ox-tail. Also, travellers passing through would call in. We'd make them cups of tea or coffee and they would sit for an hour or two and talk and want to tell you about their travels – or their troubles. Sometimes your attention might wander a bit while listening because you had your mind on others things.

The worst night of my entire life – not just Fitzroy Crossing but my entire life – was when we had a little European boy brought in late one night. He'd been very sick with tonsillitis and his people were missionaries from a fundamentalist mission a few miles out. The mother had neglected to follow doctor's instructions to give him his *sulphaguanadae* prescription – one of the sulphur drugs. We heard this truck come tearing down the road to the hospital at midnight and they came rushing in with the child in their arms. He could hardly breathe. We quickly got Freddie up to get the fire going and to stoke the stove up. We needed plenty of kettles and pots of boiling water to make a steam tent. We rigged one up out of cotton rugs and connected oxygen into it. We had to be very careful about the oxygen because of the fire but we had to get steam into the tent. In between my prayers for the child's life, all I could think was, 'If this little fellow stops breathing we will have to try to do a tracheotomy and if we end up killing him his mother will never forgive us!' But by the grace of God he survived till morning, was evacuated to Derby, about one hundred and twenty miles south, and recovered.

On one occasion we received word from down south that Lady Slim, the wife of the Governor General, was coming on an official visit. We got goodness-knows how many instructions about using correct silverware and table-cloths and so on. But our common sense told us she wouldn't expect us to have the sorts of things that they would have at Government House. However, by instructions, when the day came, we wore our best uniforms and our veils. We never wore veils normally, of course, out in the bush like that. When the official car from the aerodrome pulled in, Lady Slim jumped out, and shook hands with us. Then she looked at our veils and said, 'Are they for me?' and laughed. We said, 'Yes! They are!' and then we all laughed. So after that we could relax and enjoy having our important visitor and pleased to show her what the Inland Mission was doing in our part of the Kimberleys. We showed her around and then came afternoon tea. Of course, people from the stations had rallied round and loaned us china and tea-spoons and a tea service. The only thing that went amiss was that, serving the tea, I realized I was straining the hot water from this borrowed silver pot into the cups instead of the tea! But Lady Slim didn't seem to notice it, or if she did, she pretended not to.

OUTBACK ICECREAM

Pint milk (Sunshine, Carnation, or goats')
¾ cup sugar
1 teaspoon gelatine
level dessertspoon plain flour
pinch salt
2 ½ tablespoons Sunshine Milk creamed.
vanilla essence

-----------Method-----------

Heat milk. (Do not boil)
Blend sugar, gelatine, plain flour, salt with little of milk.
Add to warm milk on stove.
Add vanilla.
When cool put in freezer tray.
When mixture has set an inch around edges remove.
Beat in basin until mixture doubles.
Refreeze

The Reverend Fred McKay who was the Superintendent of AIM expected the staff to refrain from drinking alcohol, but neither Jean nor I drank, and in any case we wouldn't have because we were always on duty. You never knew when you would be called upon for some emergency. But one time in the very hot weather we did try to make some lovely ginger-beer. It was a great success. Then someone brought us in a supply of lemons, so in our innocence, we thought we would try making lemon-beer instead of ginger-beer. Unbeknown to us, lemon-beer, with sugar and raisins, is far more potent than anything the pub sold! It blew bottle-tops and bottles all over our store-room. Much to the locals' great amusement!

One night two German fellows from the Bureau of Mineral Research came to dinner. They brought a bottle of wine but we said we were sorry but we couldn't drink because we were on duty. They seemed a bit bemused about this but just as dinner ended the owner of Fossil Downs station was brought in with a severe injury to his arm which needed immediate suturing for Jean to attend to, which proved our point about not drinking.

One night I went to a bush dance that was going to be held on a station about thirty miles out, sitting in between the policeman and his wife in their vehicle. I'd had a bad arm and bouncing around on the rough road made my arm swell and become infected. The next thing I knew there was a plane coming out to get me and I was being evacuated to Derby hospital with a pulmonary embolism and septicaemia. Afterwards I was supposed to rest for six weeks but I came back to Fitzroy Crossing. About two weeks later the same doctor was there on his routine visit. We had a busy day with a lot of people to see. Towards the end there was one Aboriginal woman who needed minor surgery. The doctor said, 'Now, I'll have to have some anaesthetic for this.' So then and there, for the first and last time, I had to give an open ether anaesthetic, which involves placing a wire frame over the patient's face and dripping ether very slowly until they lose consciousness. I'd only ever seen it done once at Prince Alfred and hadn't done it since. In the middle of things he said to me, 'You're supposed to be resting!' but there was nothing for it but to keep going because we had to get him off the ground by nightfall on to his way to his next call.

We didn't have many deaths while we were there. One was of an old man. We laid him out formally and locked the body in a spare shower-room at the back until the police came and took it away. Another was of a tiny new-born baby who died from what we thought was tetanus. He seemed to have the symptoms, the stiff neck and so on. It was possibly something to do with his mother's placenta. When someone died in the camp there would be such a lament. The wailing would go on all night. The worst of it was that the women would hit their heads with stones to produce 'sorry cuts'. Then of course we would have the job of doctoring them up!

One New Year's Day we went out with friends to a place called Giekie Gorge[4], about nine miles up the river. It was a beautiful spot but you wouldn't dare swim because you could see the crocodiles' eyes in the gorge. The locals said they were only freshwater crocs and wouldn't hurt you, but all the same! We had a lovely day but, Oh! When we got back!

[4] Geikie Gorge, Tunnel Creek and Windjanna Gorge cut through uplifted ranges that were part of an ancient barrier reef which developed during the Devonian period about 350 million years ago

This old nanny-goat had got into the hospital grounds and systematically eaten all our pawpaws! She was still in the yard and I was so furious I could have killed her! I grabbed a hammer and chased her round and round the hospital and got her cornered against the fence. She just looked at me with big innocent goat-eyes. Do you think I could hit her? After that we got some mesh wire and some star-picket droppers and put a fence around our precious pawpaws and vegetables. Goats are very important in the bush. They mean meat and milk to many bush people but give them an inch and they'll take a mile. Not to mention lovely ripe pawpaws!

Every year the Aborigines went on walkabout. It was their annual holiday. They knew when they were due back. But one year Topsy and Freddie were due back but didn't show up when we really needed them. Instead, they sent in a lovely big barramundi 'for the Sisters.' We were very appreciative but would rather have had them back themselves. But what could you say! Smoothing the way with a barramundi was almost an accepted practice. Another time I was temporarily at Kununurra helping with setting up the first hospital there. A European woman came in from one of the stations and she had this terrible tooth-ache. The doctor had come from Wyndham but he had forgotten to bring his dental instruments. She begged me, 'Oh, please! Please, will you take this tooth out! It's driving me out of my mind!' So I did a mandibular block! For the first and only time! Unlike Aboriginals', the tooth came out relatively easily. The woman was very grateful and once again, next day, we received a big barramundi.

Surprisingly, we had very few accidents from the picnic races that were held every year. Often a horse would tear off the track and disappear into the scrub and you would hold your breath expecting to see a rider being carried out unconscious or decapitated by a low branch. But it seemed never to happen. After the races there was a dance at night which was held at the hospital – but not too late. No band; the music was provided by the locals from records. But it was a good evening.

Another highlight was the famous Round Australia Redex Trial of 1954. The cars came hurtling over the crossing and past the hospital, each trailing a long plume of dust. One would no sooner race past than another would come tearing along. It was a huge excitement. The world seemed to be coming to Fitzroy Crossing. The Aborigines sat along the road and waved but if anyone waved back it was the navigator, the drivers were too intent; crouching over their steering wheels, vroom-vrooming through the gear-changes on our pot-holed road. When it was all over things seemed a bit quiet for a while.

We didn't have many church services but on one occasion a visiting padre and his wife came and took a communion service in the corrugated-iron shed. I had made some ice-cream for the lunch afterwards which was a bit of an effort in a kerosene fridge. You never knew when that fridge was going to play up. For ice-cream you used Sunshine powdered milk beaten up with sugar and vanilla and put into the two freezer trays. You had to wait until about an inch around the edge of the mixture had frozen in each tray, then you tipped it into a large bowl and beat it, by hand of course – no electric beaters – until it 'doubled its quantity.' Or so the recipe promised. At the time we had a young Aboriginal mother in with a new baby that wasn't feeding well and the long and short was that I forgot about the ice-cream. Each of the two trays was frozen solid. I thought, 'Oh! Well! Can't be helped!'

and beat the daylights out of it to try to get it to 'double'. Well, of course it wouldn't. But 'Waste not. Want not!' At lunch, after the roast beef and vegetables, I produced this sad-looking 'ice-cream'. This padre thought it was hilarious. He wouldn't let up about it. He went on and on. Suddenly I heard myself saying, 'Oh! Will you shut up about the bloody ice-cream! I don't want to hear another word about it!' To say he looked shocked is putting it mildly. I was a bit shocked myself but after two years of being on call twenty-four hours a day, seven days a week, you tend to get a bit short tempered at times. It used to annoy the daylights out of me that a lot of the Aboriginal women that came in had shocking head wounds from fighting one another with their nulla nullas. I would get very short with them. Though that is how we got our wonderful bread-cook from Leopold Downs. Her head was perpetually in a bandage!

We had lots of dust storms, and then, come the Wet, rain and more rain. The river came down with a roar and deposited piles of debris on the banks. Then, at the beginning of 1963, I was at Kununurra AIM, and was asked to go back down to Fitzroy Crossing to hold the fort for three weeks in between nurses coming and going. When the time finally came to leave, the river had risen and we had to be taken to the aerodrome in a boat. I had never seen the river so high. The plane somehow got in and managed to take off. And it wasn't a flying-boat, either!

19

Clargie Saltmere

ॐॐॐ

Introduction

Clargie Saltmere has such presence, such an aura of dignity and wisdom, that when I was introduced to him by Ray Fryer in 2002 at the Camooweal Race Course, where Clargie lived as groundsman, with his wife Ruby, I was awed. I knew of Clargie's reputation as a 'top man' with cattle and horses. I knew he had been head stockman on well-known properties across north-west Queensland and for twenty-three years head stockman on Rocklands, an historic station six miles north of Camooweal. Clargie's reputation in the far north-west is such that cattlemen, both black and white, are proud to say they have known and worked with him in their time.

I was so inhibited by the reputation of this notable old man that I was shy of asking him if he would tell me about his time in the cattle industry, feeling that being asked by a white woman 'from down south' to tell his life story could be misconstrued as an intrusion, not only upon his privacy, but upon his stature within his community. Regretfully I let the moment pass.

A couple of years later I was delighted to find Clargie Saltmere's story in the Gammage and Simpson Collection, The Australian Drovers' Project, in the archive of the National Library in Canberra. Professor Bill Gammage of the Australian University and ex-drover and bush poet Bruce Simpson have travelled all over the outback collecting material on the history of the droving industry and had interviewed Clargie at Camooweal. It was fitting that Clargie should have been interviewed by Bill and Bruce. The interview would have been on a man-to-man basis and Clargie more comfortable swapping yarns with fellow-drover Bruce. Sometimes, in the man's world of the far north-west, it is diplomatic for 'a mere woman' to know her place in the scheme of things. I'm OK with that. All that matters is that the stories are told and the techniques, the characters and history of the droving industry are recorded for posterity, while there is yet time.

Born Under The Stars

Clargie Saltmere

'Those days you wouldn't get a job if you didn't know cattle.'

Yeah, well, I was born at Lake Nash, under the stars; 5th August, 1925. And reared around there. Clargie is not a nickname; it's my proper name. Me old mother gave me that name and that was it. And then me old people went down to Headingly, and the old stepfather got a job off-siding on the horse teams. And as I grew up, I went along as a horse-tailer's off-sider. I used to hold the horses on camp while they're hobbled up, or, y' know, yoked up in the morning. As soon as the horses came to the camp, I would have had me breakfast and just held the horses. I was about eight year old.

Sometimes, you'd have about sixteen horses in the team and it was my job to bring the spare horses along. That old teamster, he was carrying just around the stations, carting the wood to the bores. Those days, the bores had all steam engines on them, so you were carting wood to keep the steam engine going. Your team horses, your leaders in a team are important. You don't have reins on them. You call them round. They're all named, eh! And you just sing out the leader's name; tell him what to do, and he'll steer 'em whichever way you want to. See, they used to say, 'Yo! Gee back!' Well, that's, 'Come over!' and, 'Gee off!' That's for the leader to go the other way.You have the reins tied back but you don't use them; you walk. He walked miles that old fellow; on the side.

That teamster, he was old Jimmie O'Briens, eh! Well, he was stationed on the property, on Headingly. He had one eye. So, anyway, they were asleep there and this old fellow, old Jim, was sleeping and he had a glass eye. And he was asleep but his glass eye was still open and I said to myself, 'This old bastard's watching me'. So, when they woke up I said to old George, old George Speatley, 'You know what, George?' 'No.' he said. I said, 'That Old Jimmie fellow never went to sleep. He's been watching me all night with one eye!' And he laughed like hell. 'No', he said, 'That's his glass eye'. He said, 'He's only got one eye' Yeah! But I reckoned he was watching me!

Then I was boundary riding on Headingly, up the top end, with old Billy Fell. And pumping up there, three bores, and go around the fence now and again with old George Speatley and this old Jimmy O'Brien. There was nothing to do. We had all the wood carted – he does it all in the winter, and then they used to fire-plough the track. There was two bores. The other bore at Comet was just a windmill. I used to have to go around them three bores to see if they're pumping all right. I'd go in a triangle and come around. They used to pump day and night with those steam engines. The two old fellows used to take it in turn. I used to just come around and have dinner there and spend a few hours pumping for 'em while they have a sleep. If the bore broke down, well, then I'd have to ride in. There was no motor-car then. That's what I was there for. I'd have to ride forty mile to the station to get help to fix the bore, y' know; to tell the manager the bore's broke down.

When I first started, for four or five years, I had no boots at all, when I was with that horse team mob. Just barefoot and shorts and no hat. You know, them days, you didn't get much money. Well, you didn't get any money, them days. You'd only just get a clothes order and take it to the copper in town, or Urandangi, or wherever you was, and they'll give you a set of clothes.

So then, as I grew up, I went into the stock-camp at Headingly. They had a fair few cattle those days, all shorthorns. The head stockman was a bloke named Ted Jones. He was a good man. You'd have to be good in them days because otherwise you wouldn't get a job, eh! You'd have to know a bit about cattle. I was in the camp on Headingly for a fair while. I seen two managers out and nearly three head stock-mans.

One old stockman, he died on the job up at Bob's Lagoon. He was camped there, see. Well, him and old Sam Fuller went to town, to Urandangi. So they came home that night and old Sam dropped him off and went home. The old fellow, he went to bed and never woke up. Old Sam was horse breaking, eh. He was good but he was rough.

Station horse team - Headingly Station.

I stayed there on Headingly till about '45. I came to Barkly (Downs) and I was there for, oh, a good while. When I first come there, the head stockman, he was Geordie McLennon, and after that it was Alec Duncan, from down round Mitchell. I stayed there with those fellows for a few years. After Barkly I went with Nat McNamara (a drover) for a couple of trips. He took a couple of mobs from out here, from Rockie (Rockhampton Downs station). I got married in '49, eh. And Nat ended up marrying my daughter Shirley.

I run the camp at Barkly for six years, then old Ivor Payne took over. I run the camp for Ivor for six years. And broke in horses there. So I left there and I came back to Camooweal and then I done a bit of mail run for old Les Peake. Peake had a lot of trucks; supplied most of the stations, carting rations and loadings and fuel and stuff. Them days, they were all forty-four drums of fuels. Then I went back droving with Alan Doyle.

Then I got with the Rockland mob with old Robey, and I run the camp on Rocklands there. I seen, what… four managers out there[1]; old Robey, Ray Jensen and old Kevin Ryan. [I] Stuck to the job, yeah. I was twenty-three years running the camp there. We had the

[1] Outlasted four different managers

good managers. You couldn't get a better man than old Robey. I got on with Kevin Ryan. I got on good with him. He didn't stay long [on Rocklands]. He would have stayed longer but his missus didn't want to stay in the bush no more. She wanted to go back in town because she was a Mount Isa girl. The boss's wife, she was not a person most ringers got to know. You don't see much of her, [a manager's wife] y' know. She was always in the house. Well, she always had old Aboriginal gins to do everything for 'em, eh! They done all the washing, the old lubras, and stuff. And you'd hardly see 'em out [managers' wives].

Camooweal was pretty rough in them times. They had two pubs in those days; the Top pub and the Bottom pub. Yeah, they were wild days. And usually the drovers played up a bit when they delivered. You had the Hatton brothers. They were wild men. Yeah. And old Laurie Troy. And old Wason Byers. They reckon he grabbed old Mick Cousens at the Ranken once and sat him on the stove. Got him and grabbed him and put him on the hot stove. Held him there till it burned through the overcoat and the trousers and then let him go. They were old military coats, them days, too. He was tough, that old bugger. Yeah, it wasn't hard to get a fight. Someone would say something wrong and they'll be into it. And Dajarra was the rail head; y' know, the main rail head, eh! Everything went to Dajarra from far away as Western Australia. [i.e. all the cattle]

The branding in those days was all bronco yard. All posts and bloody wire, that's all. Now broncoing is being used in competitions around the country. I do a bit of catching.[2] Yeah! Around here, anyway. There's nothing much to it. You get on your bronco horse[3] and, well, you better have your rope well positioned, y'know, so you can throw it out till you get a calf. That's all to it. Then you pull it up to the ramp. Well, when you've got two bronco horses, you just pull it up half-way to the ramp and wait till the other fellow finishes and he goes back and you just keep going around in rotation then.

And you've got a team of men on the ground. You have two on each leg rope, two on the hind leg rope and two on the front leg rope. One fellow puts it on and other bloke pulls it and holds it. And then, when you pull the calf down, well, the other fellow, the hind leg fellow, grabs the hind leg while they brand it. And the other fellow holds the head while they brand it and earmark.

And you got the fellows on the brand; one fellow on the numbers. They used to put a number on the cheek, y'know. And the other fellow brands. So there was six men involved on the ground. And these branding irons were all kept hot in a fire in the yard. There was a forty-four drum with holes cut, and a space for the brand to fit in. They had to be really hot, yeah, otherwise on some of them old shorthorns, you get the old hairy fellows there, you've got to have a brand pretty hot to burn through the hair. And there's one man on the knife for the male calves, castrating. He's there all the time to cut. Maybe the head stockman cutting 'em and tallying 'em, see; so he'd know how many he ran in a day. Maybe five hundred one day.

---

[2] Clargie partnered fellow-octogenarian Charlie Rayment as 'catcher' in the Camooweal Senior Bronco Branding Championships of 2005.

[3] bronco horse; a horse of heavier build trained to pull the calf to be branded into position. A heavier harness, usually a draught collar, is used for the purpose.

Yeah, well, and the balls, you'd just chuck them on the coal and have a bit of a feed if you wanted it. They're good. Even some used to take 'em home and fry 'em. But, you know, while they're working there, some of 'em might get the small ones and chuck 'em on the coal. They were good, yeah.

You start pretty early. And your cattle are yarded the night before. Yeah! They got to be in the yard. You start before sunrise and get straight into them. You'd have to do sixty; a calf a minute. Or sometime you'd have to do a bit more than a calf a minute. When you've got three bronco horses you can do more than a calf a minute, see. When you've got a good team on the ground. After every fifty calves, you change over and get another team on the ground.

And mothering-up, if you haven't got time that day to let 'em out, you take 'em out next morning. Mothering-up is very important. You might have to take a couple of hour mothering 'em till most of the calves find their mother. Then you feed 'em around for a couple of hours, then you take 'em down to water and then you hold 'em on the water, mother 'em up. But a lot of the cows, see, they get hungry, they have that bit of a pick and a drink of water and they have a look at their calf and then they want to go back and feed again. So the little calves they end up going back to the yard looking for their mother, where they've seen their mother last. That's where the cows generally go back to. If you don't mother-up those calves the dingoes will get 'em or they'll get weary and die. Well, those days, you wouldn't get a job unless you looked after cattle properly.

You only had a few white men in the bloody camp – only the cook, and the head stockman and his mate, eh. They always had a couple of white fellows. If the head stockman wasn't there, his mate takes over the boys; looks after them. Them days they called them 'blackfellas.' There was no such thing as an Aboriginal,[4] eh. You know, even my colour, we were just 'Yellafellas'[5], eh! But, you know, we done all right in that sort of job. We got respect. Most of the drovers were out of 'em, eh! And most of the stock camp out of 'em.[6]

Rocklands station, outside Camooweal, from the water-colour by Sir Daryl Lindsay.

But they wouldn't allow you around the pub, y' know, walking around the pub verandah. If you were caught on the pub verandah the old copper would put the boot behind you. He wouldn't allow any Blackfellas or Yellafellas

[4] The terms Aborigine and Aboriginal were introduced as official terminology in the early 'sixties.

[5] Persons of mixed race

[6] Clargie is stating the accepted truth that stockmen of Aboriginal and Mixed Race origin were integral to the development of the cattle industry in the Northern Territory, North Western Australia and outback Queensland, seeming to have a natural aptitude for the arduous and often dangerous work.

mooching around. That was Under the Act. Yeah! I was Under the Act until I was twenty-one, eh. Old Charlie Payne got me out of that.

I've broken a lot of horses. Every time they wanted a horse broke into the camp they used to give it to me. And training your camp horses, if you got a colt and reckoned, 'Oh, this fellow might make a camp horse', well, you'd just work on him and if he don't grow to the standard, well, you reckon, 'Oh, I don't think he'll be good enough for a camp horse. No!' And you give him to one of the boys that works on the face of the camp.

It's a bit of a difference when you're drafting bullocks. You've got to take them steady and it's up to you whether to have your horse steady or fast. The camp horse, he can do the both jobs. And you don't use that camp horse for nothing else. That's his job. You just use him for cutting out and then when you finished cutting out, you just let him go and grab your other horse. If you want to go on a bit further somewhere; even if you want to yard up; if you got to go, you just change to another horse[7].

Them days in the stock camp it was pretty rough living, you know. The only vegies you got is potato, pumpkin and onion. Maybe there was a bit of cabbage from the garden if you've got a gardener on the property. A lot of stations did have gardeners in them days. That was only the winter season. And after, when the summer come, well, you couldn't grow nothing. So you'd have to go back to the potato and onions[8].

Some of them old camp cooks in the stock camps was pretty good. All camp ovens and the old fire of gidgea coal. That old Jim Bramson, he was an old codger, a gnarly old cook. He wouldn't take any cheek from no-one. But he was a good old cook and I got on good with him because, y'know, I never went against him at all. If you go in with 'em, well, you had no trouble. A lot of those old gnarly cooks, I got on good with. You've got a happy camp when you've got a good cook. So you put up with their bits of temper. You got to, y'know, especially if he's a good old cook. And, old Bramson, he didn't like you sitting on his ovens, and these jackaroos used to. Y'know, head office fellows used to send them out. So, anyway, old Jim reckoned, 'I'll fix some of these fellows up.' So just before smoko time he went and hottened the oven lids. 'Yeah!' he said, as they came back. He didn't go crook or anything; he just let 'em and when they

Clargie Saltmere and Charlie Rayment, both octogenarians, were Senior Champions in 2005, in the Camooweal Drovers' Camp.

[7] The camp horse was regarded as so excellent at the highly specialized task of cutting out that it was not used for any other purpose

[8] The 'potato' was very often the dried sort, in small cubes that were reconstituted in water before cooking.

sat on the oven, 'Oh!' And he went away smiling. Yeah! Them old cooks they liked their own space around the fire.

And another old fellow, old Bill Sloggs, was cooking for the camp down at Headingly. And there was a mob of the fellows sitting around the fire, right around, you see, and old Bill he wanted to put a log on the fire. This McInerey fellow was in his way and, oh! there was three or four of 'em, so Old Bill he just threw that bloody log in the fire and there was ashes and sparks went everywhere on top of these fellows and on top of this McInerey. Old Bill, he sort of couldn't get to the fire and that's the only way he reckoned it'd break 'em up. This McInery was covered in ashes and he got up and he wanted to fight. Him and the old cook had a few hits and I broke 'em up. 'Hey!' I said, 'Come on!' I said, 'It's not his fault! It's you fellows' fault, sitting around his fire!' See, I always make a fire away a bit. You get a fire-tin or something for the men, away a bit. Yeah! It was hard to get a good cook, them days. Some of 'em only wanted a job for a while and they took off again. They'd stay out in the bush for a while and then they'd want to go to town.

We never had any trouble holding our cattle, before the drovers took them. They never played up or rushed. They were handled from a little baby calf right up, eh. That's the secret. You've got to handle 'em properly. We never had any trouble with bullocks at all or cows. And there's been a big change in the type of cattle that are turned off stations today.

One time you've got your bullocks, store bullocks, fattened them up and they might be three, four or five year old before you sent him away. Yeah! Well, these days they send almost bloody calves away now up here to, whatsaname? Indonesia! Baby beef, they call it. Well, them days, you'd have cattle buyers coming around every year and have a look at your cattle, eh! Some of those buyers were good. They could look at a mob of fats in the paddock or in the yards and tell you pretty close to what they go [in weight].

I never had any bad time with cattle. If you feed 'em properly and give 'em a good drink, well, they'll sleep all night. If you work your cattle right, you don't have bad times. And if you've got a good manager behind you, well, you stuck to him. But today, that's all gone. They just shove 'em in the road-train.

And all this Aboriginal Land Rights. I reckon, if they went back to where they were in the early days, they lived better. These fellows here, y'know, they had workers here in the office here and they got houses built for 'em. I never had a house built for me at all. Only for the racecourse up there I wouldn't have anywhere to live.

But I never get involved with this Land Rights. See, if I got involved here they'd be saying, 'Oh, you want to get back to Lake Nash where you were born!' You know, I lived in the bush all me life. And out in the stock camp you only had a swag to live in. Sleep on the ground under the stars. That's all we had. I don't have anything to do with any Aboriginal Rights. Me son is tangled up with 'em and, you know, he's always fighting for the Aboriginals. I never worried about it. I just said, 'Look! It took me seventy-five years to get to where I am and that's where I'm going to stop!

20

Brian Beveridge

ॐॐॐ

Introduction

Charters Towers, 130kms inland from Townsville, through undulating open forest, is the beginning of the real west. Head up over the Mingela Range, and you are into cattle and mining country, and the Outback. In The Towers you can wait to cross the main street and see nothing but dust-coated, four-wheel-drives go past, many with swags and a blue heeler, or two on the back. The driver will be wearing a well-run-in Akubra pulled low over his – or her – eyes.

But the gracious streets of this lovely old town have splendidly Victorian public buildings, grand hotels and imposing banks, many heritage listed. The historic Stock Exchange has been restored to its former magnificence. The town's stylish architecture dates from the heady days of the gold era when, from 1871 until 1911, Charters Towers was a booming mining centre with a population of thirty thousand, the second largest town in Queensland. It was known affectionately to its proud residents as The World.

A visit to the Towers today would seem a step back in time but for the youthful presence of the many boarding school students in their distinctive uniforms – the fresh, invigorating climate is the draw-card – and the feeling that this is a town where people love to be, and where exciting things are happening.

The mayor of this beautiful inland city is Brian Beveridge; six foot two of enthusiasm, energy and charm. Brian prefers to be called Councillor; i.e. one of the blokes. If something needs to be done, Brian is the man to roll up his sleeves and get on and do it. He says his father's motto was, 'Push! Pull! Or get out of the bloody way!' Brian has been not 'getting out of the bloody way' all his life. He leads from the front. From early boyhood he could hunt, shoot, ride and work like a man. He has cut cane, lumped wheat, made a successful career in the police force. He is currently president of Great Inland Way Tourism, Director of the Local Great Eastern Councils Group, Member of the Mount Isa / Townsville Economic

Development Group and of the North Queensland Development Group, Member of the Regional Roads Group and Chairman of the Counter Disaster Group.

For relaxation Brian likes to go 'chasing sapphires', gold-panning, shooting or fishing; anything that takes him out bush with his sons. 'Most important of all', he says, 'I've always got to have a few cattle.' Brian has been Mayor of Charters Towers for thirteen years, and looks set to beat the record for time in office. He says, 'It's a joy to work with Towers' people for the benefit of the town. They're prepared to get stuck in and have a go. The country friendliness never fails.'

The Mayor of the Towers

Brian Beveridge

'Push! Pull! Or Get Out of the Bloody Way'

'Push! 'Pull! Or get out of the bloody way!' was a saying of my father's. He'd talk about the Depression years, when if you weren't pulling your weight it was, 'Take your coat and leave your pick!' as the standard way you got sacked. Dad was a good hard worker and his claim to fame was that he had never been sacked in his life. He was a timber worker. When the war broke out he was busting a gut to enlist but the timber industry was 'protected' and he was 'manpowered'[1]. Dad was a responsible sort of bloke and could turn his hand to anything. I was born in August 1940, a war model.

My forebears were among the first free settlers in Victoria. They came from Scotland; 'idge' means 'island' in Gaelic. They were the 'Beaver Islanders'. And way back in the fifteenth century there were two of these Beveridges, brothers, that were convicted of brewing adulterated liquor, and they did time in the dungeons for it. And the name was corrupted in the records to 'Beverage' which is how the word 'beverage' came into the language. The town of Beveridge in Victoria is named after the first-settler Beveridges. Ned Kelly was born there.

After the war the demand for timber dropped off and we were on this property called Hiawatha, outside Goomeri, in the range country in the South Burnett; cattle and grain, and breaking draught-horses. It was a bit isolated but women went with their men in those days.

[1] During World War Two some industries were declared to be 'essential'. Workers in these could not change from one employer to another without official authorization, nor could they enlist in any of the armed services. This was known as being 'manpowered'.

Mum would send me up the paddock with a billy of tea and an enamel plate that'd have a piece of cake, or scones, with a tea-towel tied around it, and the corners tied at the top, for Dad's smoko. The tea was cold by the time I got there, of course. He would throw me up on the neck one of these draught horses, and I would hang on to the hames. And, oh! hell! It was a hundred feet to the ground! A bit later he would sit me in the seat and put the reins in my hands, and I'd be right. I'd have been five or six. But you worked like a man. You had to. All bush kids did.

I was too little to harness these big draughts. They were massive. Father would harness them and put them into the implement – called a board – that was dragged over the paddocks. It was like the side of a lavatory; weather-boards, and it would break the clods. And mowers; two horses to a mower. Making hay, you'd mow or you'd rake.

Mowing in those days you knocked the legs off the odd hare or a rabbit or cat, now and then. Or a quail. Depending on the weather, the hay could dry in a day or so. Then when it was raked, we'd stook it with a pitch-fork. There was a special way you threw it on to the wagon, and then to pack your haystacks in, you took it off in the same sequence, and lastly, formed the cone on top to shed the rain.

Those flats along Benara Creek were snake country. We got a lot of common browns and red-bellied blacks. When you stooked the hay a little bit green, the whole paddock was bare and during the night, in the warmer weather, the snakes would come up out of the cracks in the ground and curl up under the stooks. So it wasn't unusual to be throwing a forkful of hay up and have a snake drop on you. You moved real quick!

One time, sinking post-holes – I was probably about six or seven, because that crow-bar was bloody heavy – and it was hard sinking, and the blisters'd come up and were starting to burst, and m'hands were starting to bleed, and were sliding up and down the bar, and I said, 'Geez, Dad, some gloves'd be good! He said, 'Gloves! Ah! You weak bastard! You'll be sitting down to pee next!' I didn't complain about anything to him ever again!

To me engines were a big deal. It was my job to ride up into the hills at the back of the property, where Dad had a well, with a two-inch semi-rotary pump with a bloody-great handle on it. I'd pump two one-thousand gallon tanks for the troughs by hand, and then fish the dead jackasses out of them!

And if there was a tree there that had a hive in it, what you'd do, was build a bit of a smoky fire to put the bees off a bit. Then you'd fall the tree and cut the section out with an axe, and put the comb in a sugar-bag. Then you beat the hell out of it, to break up the comb, and you'd hang it from a branch over a tub. After a couple of days when it was finished dripping, you'd put the sugar-bag with the wax into the copper, with a bloody-great rock on it to hold it down, and heat the copper up, and boil it up. Next day the wax would be sitting on top of the water. You'd lift the wax off, and melt it to make candles. You used a piece of pipe for your mould, and when the wax was set, you'd run it over a flame and the candle would slide out.

Brian passed 'Schollie', the State Scholarship at the end of primary schooling, and went on to Gatton College, the Agricultural College outside Brisbane.

That copper was used for everything, not just boiling the clothes on washing day. The Christmas pudding was boiled in it, and when you killed a chook, you heated the copper to loosen the feathers in boiling water before you plucked it. Mum made her own soap in the copper. After killing-day, she'd boil the fat and caustic soda and a bit of borax until it was a clear honey-colour. She'd put about a cupful of kerosene in to make it soft and a few gum-leaf tips tied up in a rag to give it a nice smell.

Sometimes rats were bad. Then Dad would have a half-drum of water, and you'd tie a bottle over it with a board up to the bottle, and you'd hang your bait from the rafter over it. The rats come looking for the bait and they get on to the bottle and just slip off into the water and drown. You'd catch hundreds of them! In a rat plague you couldn't keep the drum empty! There is nothing made, ever, that is more efficient for catching rats than that!

When Father was working in the timber I'd go with him. For snigging they used dozers that were left behind after the war. In wet weather Dad would put chains on the truck to get traction. Hoop pine comes in patches, generally in swathes just down from the ridge. To load, he would get the truck against a log ramp with a winch, and he would run the rope over the log, and as the rope shortened, it would roll the log on to the truck.

I learned all my timber work from Dad. When we were falling a tree, Dad would walk around it and see which way it was leaning. Then he would scarfe it to the direction he wanted it to fall, by leaving most wood on the side it had to fall to, and that would skew the tree around as it fell. Dad could fall a tree so accurately he could have driven a peg with it. And falling pine, if the pine you were falling was smaller than the trees you were in, you had to be accurate, or it would hang up in the other trees, and you'd lose half a day getting the bloody thing down. So, I was an outdoors kid, growing up in the bush, and I just picked this stuff up naturally, from the time I could walk. It was the way of life.

The camps we had in the scrub always faced east, to get the first warmth of the sun in the morning. The hut would have a few sheets of iron for the roof, and walls made of hessian. You slapped a mixture of cement-dust and water on with a lime-brush. It dried hard, and that gave you a reasonable camp fairly cheap. For cooking, you had a galley out the front; three sheets of iron around the fire, and a couple of sheets over the top to keep the rain out. Your beds were chaff-bags pulled over two saplings up on forky-stumps dug into the ground, and your blankets were 'waggas' - corn-sacks lined with newspapers and stitched together.

Everything you needed to do in the bush Dad knew how to do it. So Dad was my hero. Mother came from Echucha on the Murray. She went to the convent, and then started as a chamber-maid in a big hotel. In those days hotels were hierarchical. You graduated to the various dining-rooms, and then to the silver-service, learning the trade as you went. Everything had to be done just right.

Gatton Agricultural College in the 1950's.

As dairy farmers, the family's financial position revolved around how the bank manager received Dad when he went to town. If the manager put his head down and walked past, Father knew he was in trouble. If the manager said, 'How y'going, Jim?' it was 'No worries!' Your cream cheque always went to the bank to pay the mortgage. And anything else, you lived on. You didn't eat anything you could sell.

Any pocket money I got came from what I could shoot, but it always depended on how much needed doing round the farm first, and whether Father would release me. A packet of .22 bullets was only a couple of bob, but you couldn't afford even that most of the time. Wallaby skins were worth sixpence, if they didn't have a bullet hole in the hide, so you'd stalk them for hours to get close enough for a head-shot, so's not to down-grade the skin. Whiptails liked those sweet valleys right up the top of the hills. Their skins were worth a lot because they used to make toy koalas out of them. And if you came across a dingo, you were made! The bounty for dingoes was a quid each, which was real good money. You'd walk until dark, and then find your way home in the dark. And when you got the skins home you'd salt them. The salt used to mix with the juice and suck the moisture out and then, as it dried, the skin would suck the salt back in and that would protect it. If you didn't have salt you could just peg them out flat with bits of number-eight wire for pegs, but then the weevils used to like those. They wouldn't touch the salty ones.

There were always snakes in that range country. I'd kill any I came across. And I've had a few try to go for me. Then I'd have nightmares. I'd kill one and another one would arrive. Then they'd be coming at me from everywhere. Then you'd get up this tree and they'd come up after you. Then you'd get on to the end of the branch and the buggers would still be coming after you! And the moment you dropped off the branch, you woke up! That was a recurring nightmare for years. And goannas! They'd pinch the chooks' eggs and try to get up a tree. If you shot him in the back legs he'd hang on with his front ones, so I'd shoot him in the front so he'd drop off the tree. Their skins were worth good money. They've got a very pretty pattern, and were used for making handbags. Every couple of months I'd roll up all my skins in hessian, and send them off to M.E. Humphries & Co, in Brisbane. Then you'd get back a cheque for maybe £10 and, oh! God! You were a millionaire!

I could split posts from the age of ten; cross-cut saw, axe and wedges. Never cut a toe off! No boots, of course. On winter mornings, bringing the cows in barefoot, the ground would be so frozen that you'd stand in a fresh hot cow-pat to thaw your toes out a bit. I like cattle. You know where you are with them. With your head stuck into the side of a cow, milking with the water running down off her when it's raining, you get that way you almost learn to think like a cow. Like a good camp-drafter, you learn to out-think them. Dad and I would muster together from the time I was that little I had to lead the horse up to a stump to get into the saddle. We'd get up on the top of the range and looking down the ridges you could see where your cattle were. They were Herefords; baldies. Dad would go one way and I'd go the other and we'd meet at the bottom of the range and box them and drive them along together.

I started school on Correspondence, but I'd already taught myself to read by the time I was five. I could just about get a picture of an entire page in my mind, and write it out, punctuation and all. I loved it. I devoured just about everything I could get my hands on. The big brown envelopes from the Correspondence School came every second Tuesday with the mailman, for me and my sister, Aileen – she was four years younger – and my little brother Kev.

Then there came a point when Father decided I was old enough to ride my pony to the road on my own, to go to school in Goomeri. The 'school bus' was the cream truck with a couple of planks bolted on up front, to sit on. I'd ride the pony the eight mile to the mail-box on the road and put him in the paddock, and hop on the cream truck. Then you'd sit on these planks to go another thirty miles into Goomeri. In the afternoon I'd come back on the truck, catch my pony and saddle him and ride the eight miles back home again.

I did 'Schollie' – the State Scholarship – and got 75% which put me up in the top percentage. Then I went away to Gatton College.[2] For Gatton, you were graded, A, B, C and D. The D's were the ones that failed Scholarship, but they took them just the same, to give them a bit of a chance of an education. But an A got you eleven school subjects plus four practical subjects. Half your time you were rostered for various jobs on the farm. Gatton had a butter factory, a cheese factory, a slaughter-yard, a farm section, a dairy section and a poultry section. It was a working farm. They provided vegetables and meat and dairy

[2] Gatton Agricultural College was established in 1897. In 1942 the college was taken over by the Americans as an army hospital. The temporary wards were subsequently used as boarding accommodation for country students. In 1962 secondary school teaching at the college was phased out. Gatton became the campus of the University of Queensland's School of Agricultural Science.

products for gaols. You were working! But I was a reasonable athelete and made the State finals for high-jump, and played most team sports. Dad said, 'You couldn't have worked too hard during the week, if you had enough energy to play football at the week-end.'

When I finished Gatton College Father said, 'Well, that's your education! This farm is not a bloody bank!' So for eighteen months, I rode my push-bike into Kilkivan to a clerk's job in the Shire Office for £8 / 7/ 6d a week. Part of my job was to count the dingo scalps, no matter how smelly they might be, then burn them in the incinerator and credit the people a pound a time. But I always had this dream of getting a property of my own, and I was never going to buy one at that rate. The big money was in seasonal work, and by then I was my full height, 6'2". I thought to myself, 'Bugger this!' and decided I'd shoot through. I bought a 500cc Matchless, and I rode it across to Dalby, and got a job lumping wheat for the Darling Downs Wheat Board.

There was no bulk loading in those days. It was all bags at wheat dumps at the rail-sidings. The bags came off the truck and had to be manhandled on to a slide, to build the stack, thirty, maybe forty, feet high. There was an elevator driven by a motor. You grabbed each bag by the ear, and got it into the crook of your arm, as it came off the elevator. There was a knack to it. You got your balance and tossed it ten or fifteen feet. Usually you worked with a mate. A bag of wheat holds three bushels, 180 lbs, and the worst part about it, was that you would wear your shoulder through. What the old hands did was pee on their hands, and rub the pee into their shoulders, and that toughened the skin. I soon learned.

Brian learned 'all he knew about timber' from his father, who had been in the timber industry most of his life.

You roofed the stacks by putting four-by-three timbers and iron across, then you dropped hessian down the sides and laced it down with bag-needles, to protect them from the weather. A ganger showed you the hang of it, and if you didn't pick it up, well, it was, 'Hoo-roo! See you later.' That was the nature of things in those days. These wheat-stacks were all over the Downs. We're talking '58 so I would have been eighteen. There was good money in it; about double the average wage.

I was working with Louie and Frank de Marchie, a couple of migrant boys. They were from Northern Italy, blue-eyed and ginger headed, like me. They said they had a cane-cutting gang up north and would take me on. And they didn't like to work with someone who's not pulling his weight, so you worked like hell. It takes you most of your first season to get the rhythm of it. We cut for different mills; Babinda, Mirriwinni, Woopen Creek, Fishery Falls and up round Edmunton.

It was a difficult cut that year in Babinda – three hundred and sixty inches of rain for the year. You were cutting in a foot of water, killing eels with your cane knives. There were always snakes. Just on dark you'd walk along the edges of the rows to begin your burn for the morning and there'd always be dead snakes afterwards.

The cane was burnt in blocks – so many rows which the gang could cut in a couple of days before the sugar content started to drop, as it does after burning. We'd push the cane over in the row, and clean the ground of trash on the upwind side, so the fire wouldn't get away and burn out the neighbour's place. The fires were an awesome sight; flames leaping thirty or forty feet into the air, and sparks and burning trash going hundreds of feet up. The bits of burning trash were called floaters, and could start spot-fires where you didn't want them. We always had someone downwind watching for those. There'd be flames roaring and gas in the hot stalks crackling and sizzling.

Burning made cutting so much faster with all of the rubbish gone. You could get on with cutting just the bare stalks. It also got rid of vermin[3] and the 'hairy mary' hairs on the cane leaves, which embedded themselves in your skin and itched like hell. The only cane we cut green was for planting the new crops.

At the end of a day's cutting you couldn't tell Europeans from Islanders.[4] We were all black and sticky from the juice. You got under the shower fully clothed, and dropped your clothes on the floor and stamped up and down on them, while you soaped up. That got most of the soot and dirt out, and you threw them over a fence to drip dry. In wet weather you'd be putting on wet clothes next morning. It didn't matter much. You'd be wet before you got to the paddock anyway, which is where the Ipswich flannels came in. They were work-shirts made of grey blanket-material. You could be wet, but you didn't get cold, but it was like like wearing a shirt made of hairy caterpillars.

The average cane-gang was four to eight men. Each farm had its own cane-cutters' quarters, a long corrugated-iron building of separate rooms, and a kitchen with a wood stove. There'd be the odd carpet snake in the rafters. Out at the front was where you pulled a chair after tea and had a smoke. Lighting was kerosene lanterns. We took it in turns to do the cooking. One bloke would knock off a bit earlier, and go back to get the stove alight, and get a bit of tucker on the go. And they used to eat anything! Any meat at all to mix with their spaghetti; pelicans; ibis! They'd have a fridge full of them! In some areas the birds nearly disappeared. As far as they were concerned they were just protein; poultry was anything with feathers.

Once the cane was cut it was taken away to the mill on cane-trains. There were portable

[3] Weill's Disease; *leptospirosis*; a bacterial infection which could prove fatal among workers in the sugar-cane industry in the early years of the twentieth century in North Queensland. It was spread by rat urine in the cane. It was believed that burning the cane before cutting could lessen the danger. This became the major demand of an industrial dispute which resulted in the introduction of burning in 1934.

[4] South Sea Islanders, termed *kanakas*, brought in to Australia as cheap labour for work on sugar plantations from 1863 onwards. Many were 'black-birded' or lured on board ships illegally. By the late 1880s, regulations had been introduced to control the trade and in 1908 many were returned to their homelands. Some opted to remain and became valued citizens of North Queensland.

steel lines, each section about fifteen foot long, and about three foot wide, with flat steel sleepers. Each section locked onto the next. We'd have to lay these lines to get the trucks of cane to where the steam locos from the mill could pick them up.

We'd be up before daylight and we'd wait for just enough light, usually in pouring rain. And, surprisingly, it gets bloody cold just on daylight in Babinda in the Wet. Loading was done first thing in the morning. You'd walk the row grabbing the bundles of cane and throwing them onto the wagon, so they lay flat across, and could be chained down. The farmer hauled them away by tractor, and the steam loco from the mill picked them up at the permanent mill line – up to a half a mile of trucks – and took them back to the mill, and brought empties back. The last job of the day was moving the portable rails to the new cut ready for the next day, either manhandling them across, or by extending the line. The farmer laid the junction with the mill line, and delivered the wagons to the start of your new section.

But we didn't work week-ends. No, fear! That wasn't on! It was a Union show. So I'd go to Cairns on my new Aerial Red Hunter, and we'd play up like two-bob race-horses; get on the booze; chase girls; go to dances at the old Trocadero, have a good time.

Then I got a scrub-falling contract out from Murgon; so much an acre. Scrub-falling is an art. First you'd work up the slope with a brush hook, and get rid of all the lawyer-vines. Then you work back up with an axe – no chain-saws then – and cut all your trees about three-quarters of the way through. Then at the top of the slope you select a big tree. When you cut this fellow through, he would fall and take the next one out, and then the next one and the next one, until whole hillside would go, one after another, in waves like a domino effect.

But all this time I was under pressure from Dad to join the police force. He reckoned I was getting a bit on the wild side, running all over the country. He said I'd be ending up in gaol. I was making good money, but putting money in a dairy-farm kid's hands was like putting Dracula in charge of the blood bank. In seasonal work there's a bit of drinking goes on. Father didn't drink. And mother, being a good Catholic, thought drink was the root of all evil. So I put my application in for the Queensland Police Force. I was just turned twenty. I was sworn in on the 19th December, 1960.

We did our lectures and drill at the old Police Barracks on Petrie Terrace in Brisbane. Then I was posted, first to Roma Street and then to the Mounteds. They always gave the new man the worst bloody horse, so I got bloody old Hawk. He was about nineteen hands. You could brace your boots against the knee-pads, and bust your gut hauling on the reins, but nothing pulled him up. This was all on bloody tram-tracks, and they were shod horses, so on ceremonial escorts for the Opening of Parliament, and that sort of thing, I would make sure I had a bloke on either side that would wedge him in if he started playing up. At the Ekka[5] we were always billed to do displays, figure-of-eights and that sort of thing.

[5] The colloquial name for the Royal Brisbane Show, originally the Exhibition of the National Agricultural and Industrial Association of Queensland, first held in 1876. The Ekka is a major family entertainment event in the calendar for most Queenslanders. Only once has been cancelled, in 1919, during the epidemic of Spanish 'flu.

There was no pulling this bloody old Hawk up, so in the middle of the ring, everyone else had to be aware of where he was, or he would iron 'em out! Whack!

And then they gave me Falcon. Police horses were mostly ex-race horses that had been donated. Falcon was an ex-trotter, and was used to being hit with the hooks in training. On these ceremonial parades, we had to trot down George Street to Parliament House. The ceremonial uniform was pretty impressive; navy blue with the white pith helmet with the bloody spiky thing on the top, and the white gloves with the dangly things. And you had a lance with a pennant, in a little boot on the side of your stirrup. And as you came to the area where you Presented for Inspection, you'd waltz your horses sideways in pairs. From Straight Ahead, you wheeled into Double Line Formation and did this waltz. And this bloody Falcon would get up on his hind legs to do this waltz. At this point, most blokes who had ridden him would ditch the lance. But it was just a matter of balancing with him. And then, in the line-up for official photos, the horses of the entire squad would be Eyes Right and this bloody Falcon, you could bet on it, just as the Governor went past he would be Eyes Left! The coot just had to be different.

I got the job of taking the sting out of the Inspector's horse. He was a pretty horse, always on corn, and shiny and fat and round. But could the bastard pig-root! The Inspector couldn't ride a bloody stick-horse to the shit-house, so it was my job to give this fellow a few laps around the paddock so that the Inspector could look good and not get chucked off in front of the crowd.

After this I got a permanent spot on the city drink van; the Black Maria – a big Ford ute with a cage on the back, with a canvas cover. Any brawl in the city area, and we were the first cab off the rank. The driver wouldn't be first into the brawl, nor the sergeant. Being the rear gunner it was me. And you'd give as good as you got. I'd done boxing at Gatton, but that doesn't help when you're getting king-hit from behind. You'd often finish a shift with a black eye.

Cracked a bone in m'hand one night chasing a fellow up a lane near Petrie Bight. I ran him down over a hundred and fifty yards and he's looking over his shoulder and sees me right on his tail, so he jumps up on this six-foot weatherboard fence, and I'm right behind him. We're both hanging on one-handed and swinging with the other. He gets his second wind, and gets in a couple of swipes, and I see a few stars go up. I think, 'I'd better put my best foot forward here!' Next time he swings, I duck and let him have it. Dropped him to the ground. That finished proceedings. My hand didn't hurt till later! But you'd go to work expecting brawls. That was your job! Keeping order in the roughest part of Brisbane.

We also copped the 'deros' – the derelicts. They would have usually spewed or messed themselves so they were always a bit ripe. You couldn't get the smell out of the vehicle. It was my job to search them at the watch house – no surgical gloves then! Some of those old deros would get pretty low – constant drinking, very little food, no bathing or change of clothes and living on a park bench, or under newspaper, or a bush on the riverbank. Most were infested with lice. You would charge them with vagrancy – rather than being drunk, and they would have to front the Beak next morning. The magistrate would give them a month or two in the Big House – fresh clothes, hair cut, regular baths, clean bed, good regular meals and no booze – a chance to dry out. They would come out looking men again.

Then I was in Traffic and on Motor Bikes all over Brisbane, or doing wide-load escorts down to Wallangara on the border, during the night. In winter you'd be coming back at daylight, and it'd be white frost for miles. Talk about cold! But it was extra money.

I had married a girl I'd met in Cairns, and I still wanted some sort of a property so we bought forty acres at the head of the valley out at Brookfield. It was right up on the range and looked down on Mount Cootha. So I had a big house, a big family – five boys then – and a big mortgage. I grew pawpaws and tomatoes, and we reared our own cattle and pigs, and we slaughtered them and butchered all our own meat. I used to make my own sausages with a hand-mincer. I'd take the hides into Granlunds' Tannery at Newmarket, and make kids' school-bags out of the leather.

As well as the cattle and pawpaws we had Queensland nuts[6]. The bush rats would come out of the National Park for them. Those rats had teeth that could gnaw through a Queensland nut shell! Then there'd be carpet snakes that would come after the bush rats. One of my boys, Frank, used to love damned carpet snakes. He'd catch them and bring them back to the house, and he'd stretch them out, and get a couple of his brothers at either end to hold them while he measured them. He might say, 'Nuh! That's not as big as the last one I got!' and he'd cart him back to the National Park and let him go. But carpet snakes are dim. If you occupy their attention and they don't see what you're up to, you can grab them behind the neck. Not much threatens them in the bush because of their size so they don't need to be fast or vicious. But if they came around the house I would cart them away. They didn't hurt you but they'd give you a heart-attack in the middle of the night if you stood on one in the dark.

I used to save my holidays for two years because I wanted to get the mortgage paid off quick, so on the first day of my holiday I'd get the Courier Mail and look through the jobs and decide where I was going to line up. We needed the money and I've always liked the physical side of things so most of the time I held down two jobs. One holiday I was a brickie's labourer. Another time I started as a labourer on a sewerage job at Corinda and finished up two months later as leading hand. I did landscaping at week-ends. I couldn't tell anyone I was a copper on leave because some of the fellows they had working for them in those places were scallywags on the run. So as far as they were concerned I was just a pawpaw farmer and things were a bit quiet on the farm.

I was in the Information Centre as Senior Constable for seven and a half years. Information handled the traffic from all over Queensland; four different radio channels,

[6] Macadamia nuts, previously known as Queensland nuts, noted for their extraordinarily hard shell.

all the Triple O calls. It could get busy. You could have a dozen cars going all directions; domestics going on here, a brawl somewhere else, a break-entry, a high-speed chase, a bank hold-up. At the end of the shift you'd walk out of there and have to sit somewhere in a quiet corner to get yourself together again.

But time came for a change, and I applied for nineteen positions; Camooweal, Muttaburra; Aramac; Thursday Island, Palm Island, the lot! And I got Charters Towers. I came up here on promotion. The police station had fourteen on strength. At that time, '77, Charters Towers was a falling-down sort of a place that needed a bit of a paint-job. It wasn't doing too good at all. But then, in '86, the gold mines came back, using big machinery to work large low-grade deposits, and the town started to come back to life. My boys all liked the place and they did well at school. They were all big fellows, pretty physical, and always on for adventure.

We'd go chasing sapphires down to Central Queensland, outside Anakie, at Tomahawk Creek, where you'd get the yellows; very expensive ones, and up at Lava Plains, the other side of Greenvale. And down past Cunnamulla, at Yowah, after opals. And to Gumlu, south of Ayr, for garnets. And if you go up the Clarke River where they pump the gravel out from the tin mines, you'd get amethysts and zircons. It takes half a day to get your eyes accustomed to picking them out, because all gravel looks the same at first. At most of these places you just set up camp and stroll over and have a look at what everyone else is doing. It's like anything else. You learn on the job. You pick it up as you go. And we did a lot of shooting. I've still got crook hearing from it.

And gold-panning. Kilkivan, where I grew up, had gold before Gympie! An old couple in their eighties taught me how to use a dish and a cradle. You'd find just a trail, a little tail of fine yellow in the dish. You'd usually get ironstone in the dish with it and you see the black and then the gold tail follows it. When you see that colour, it's a buzz!

I've been interested in cattle all my life, and I've always had to have my few cattle. Ever since I came north with the boys I've had a few out at Mosman Creek. Then we ran out of feed so I moved them down to Nunkumbil, at the top of the desert country. That was hard country. You'd breed a few and you'd lose a few. It was the heartleaf. If cattle eat it, they get the staggers and they go down. I was down at Numkumbil one time and I thought, 'Something's getting into these bloody cattle! I'm starting to lose them!' And a group of these fine big steers on a ridge got a bit of a gallop on, and next thing they went down, and never even put a kick-mark in the dust where they hit! It was as though they'd been shot. That's how heartleaf affects them. There is a big stretch of it right through that country, all the way up to Mount Garnet. So I got out of Numkumbil and moved closer in.

Post Fitzgerald Report was a bad time in the Queensland Police Force. Morale went through the floor. When the state was regionalized anybody with a university degree could transfer from some other Department. So every day I was getting more big brown envelopes, with some new operational procedure. The problem was these university types weren't police people. I knew damned well what the people of the Towers wanted. They wanted to be safe and secure where they lived and where they worked. Simple. So when the mayor's position was coming up there was a constant stream of people into my office urging me, 'Why don't you have a go at it!' So in 1994 I put my hand up. I didn't campaign. I just said I'd do it. I had two ex-mayors, a deputy mayor and a councillor against me, and I got in. So here we are. I'm on my fourth term, and I'll have been in office fourteen years by the time I'm through. I think that's the record. Tiger Titley did thirteen, and I think he died in harness.

My great-great-uncle was on the Council here in the late 1800s. He was a major shareholder in the Black Jack mine. He came from Victoria by coastal steamer with his team to Port Denison – Bowen – and walked them over the range with freight to Ravenswood. But Ravenswood was on the decline, so he came on to the Towers, and built a house on the corner of Mary and Rutherford Streets, with horse-yards down the back. The house is still there. The film *The Irishman* was his story. In the end he got pushed out by motor-transport, so he went up the Tablelands into the timber industry.

The highlight of the office is working with people for the benefit of the town. In the Force you never got used to delivering death messages to people, especially where the death had been sudden and violent; when bodies have come out of creeks or vehicles, or you're investigating suicides and cot deaths. You see the look on people's faces as they go through all the emotions and there's not a damned thing you can do to help them. Then you'd have to witness the post mortem. You never really got used to it.

But in local government, well, there is just so much to do. It's been a long ten years, but now this term is the best one. The difficult years are behind. Tourism is flourishing. We've got our history on record for the future. We got runner-up in the Nationals of the Tidy Towns, and we got the State Award in 2000. We stage the Outback Festival, the Goldfield Ashes, the Music Festival and the races. All the schools are flourishing. Now we're working on developing industry to provide jobs for the future. People are proud of the place.

Towers people are impressive. They are largely self-made and when they take something on they know what they're doing. And they're prepared to work; to get stuck in and have a go. They are self-motivated and have the nounce to go with a challenge. It's a joy to work with them. Charters Towers is really a big country town and that country friendliness never fails. I'm right at home here. I guess they will plant me here one day.

21

Phoebe Atkinson

ॐॐॐ

Introduction

Throughout the north, Phoebe Atkinson, of Camel Creek station, north of Charters Towers, was 'Phoebe' to all; her liberal hospitality as renowned as her care of her employees. Though nobody could more enjoy an occasional holiday among the bright lights, Phoebe Atkinson was a woman who never wanted to live or work anywhere but on the five hundred and sixty square miles of cattle country that she and her husband Reay took over in the nineteen thirties, and transformed into a viable station. But as much as she loved the land and the cattle, Phoebe Atkinson did not confine her interests to them. She was a great reader, wrote freelance articles and was well known for her appreciation of good taste in dress, furniture, and home decoration.

It was widely believed that the most competent cattleman could not have accomplished more than Phoebe Atkinson did, after she was left a widow with an under-developed property, the upbringing and education of five children and a heavy burden of probate duties. But the praise she received for her achievements from those who knew and dealt with her at that time, was echoed by such as Jack Kelly, surveyor of the cattle industry of the north for the Commonwealth Bureau of Agricultural Economics, and by Dr. Herbert Coombs, Governor of the Reserve Bank and by many others.

Phoebe Atkinson's youngest daughter, Helen Clark, took me to meet her remarkable mother at the Good Shepherd Retirement Home in Townsville. Situated on the banks of the beautiful Ross River, enfolded on two sides by the lush splendour of Townsville's Palmetum Gardens, a more beautiful place to spend the late afternoon of life would be hard to find. On a quiet side verandah we began recording the story of an outstanding life. Ninety-year-old Phoebe Atkinson soon proved herself more than equal to the task. I found myself yielding Chair of Proceedings to this redoubtable Senior Citizen, recognizing a lady who had taken command of many a situation in a long and challenging life; from being lost as a child in the vast Mungana caves, to travelling alone for five days to get to boarding school, to making a success of taking over and running the family cattle property after her husband's death, a saga of a life lived not only with indomitable courage, down-to-earth common sense and hard work, but with elegance and charm; a story to make the reader feel re-energized by the innate potential of the human spirit for high achievement and fulfillment.

ॐ ॐ ॐ

Bred by a Bloody Woman!

Phoebe Atkinson – Pastoralist

'Gentlemen! They were perfect! And bred by a bloody woman!'

When I was growing up in Mungana, where my Dad, Arthur Wilson, had a butcher's shop, there were only horse-drawn vehicles, no motorcars. If we had to go into Chillagoe we would go in a horse-drawn trap. We kids used to walk everywhere barefoot although there were a lot of bindi-eyes. The Mungana area was full of caves. That area had a very dry heat but it was beautifully cool inside the caves. Some of the adults used to go caving every weekend. Once, some of us children became separated from the grown-ups. We could have been lost for ever, but we had the sense to follow a little stream along and eventually found our way out. After that we weren't allowed in the caves alone. It was too dangerous. It was said that the Mungana Caves were far more extensive than the well known Jenolan Caves.[1]

One special cave that we children found, we called the Stage. It was like a theatre. There was a date written in pencil on the wall, 1907; this was about 1927. It was like a properly made theatre and at the front was a stage that was about thirty feet wide and the top was as if a curtain had been pulled back and tied. It was all rock by that time, but the pattern was still there, a pattern of lace-like roses, flowing down. At the sides of the theatre were rooms, four along each side; the floors were perfectly smooth and the walls were a reddish colour. It was really incredible. They say there are no straight lines in nature but there were straight lines in that theatre. It seemed as though it must have been made by people many centuries before. I am nearly ninety now and it is just as clear to me now as it was then – every detail.

When I was about two I was very sick. I became partly paralyzed and couldn't walk. Mum was heavily pregnant with my sister Marjorie at the time. She was only about eighteen, so

---

[1] Chillagoe – Mungana Caves National Park is 215 kilometres west of Cairns on the northern edge of the Atherton Tableland. Both Chillagoe and Mungana were once tin-mining centres but Chillagoe, the larger, had a smelter. Set among dry, open tropical forest, the limestone caves systems of the area were laid down 400 million years ago and have been weathered, dissolved and reformed by water to create caverns of spectacular beauty.

my Nana, Jessie McCulloch, took me home to bring me up herself. I loved being with her and after about two years I could walk again. Nana had remarried a retired school-teacher, Ted Kiernan. He introduced me to books and I developed a love of literature.

Up until I was about six, Nana ran a hotel and a butcher's shop in Einasleigh. She also owned a bough-shed butcher's shop at The Oaks goldfield at what is now Kidston. Dad's father, H.C. Wilson, manager of nearby Carpentaria Downs, used to sell cattle to her. At peak production The Oaks goldfield had a population of about four or five thousand people. Before he was married Dad ran Nana's bough-shed butcher's shop. He slaughtered up to twenty beasts a week. The Oaks field was all nuggets and the miners used to settle their bills with nuggets so Dad had a cage made for his sister Emily, who was fifteen, to sit in and weigh out the gold in safety.

When I was eight, Nana took sick with cancer. By that time we were living in Brisbane, and so Nana, her son Sandy McCulloch, and I boarded the train for Cairns. Upon arrival, Nana was so ill she went straight into hospital. The next day Sandy took me in the train up to Mungana, arriving that night. I was tired, covered in coal-grit and very upset. No welcome or anything. Mum just pulled this chamber-pot out from under a bed and said, 'Use that. Then get into bed.' There was someone else already in the bed. I didn't know that it was my younger sister Marjorie. I never felt so wretched in my life. I was crying into my pillow and I could hear Mum and Dad out in the kitchen talking. I heard Dad say, 'You should go in and comfort the child.' Mum said, 'She has got to learn to fit in.' I never did get on very well with my mother.

Later we moved to Conjuboy, between Carpentaria Downs and Valley of Lagoons. It was a block that Dad and his brother Vaughn drew in a land ballot in 1916. When the tin mining operations were winding down at Mungana, Dad sold his butcher's shop and went droving to pay out his brother's share. Dad had five teams of drovers and was Boss Drover of one of them. The original house at Conjuboy was very primitive; a harness shed, thirty feet by thirty, with rails where all the pack-saddles were put and a big wagonette at one end. We all slept upstairs. Mum and Dad's room was in the middle, Marj and I, D'arcy and Beryl, and later on, Marsey and Henry, slept on the front verandah, and Dad's drovers, about eight of them, when they were all there, slept on another verandah.[2] There was no water laid on. Water had to be carried from a permanent

[2] In later years a brick homestead was built, and today, due to the pioneering efforts of Arthur Wilson and his family, Conjuboy is a well-established cattle property.

spring that came from under a basalt wall and flowed past the house. Dad dug a hole in the spring and Marj and I used to have to dip kerosene-tin buckets in and carry them about fifty yards up to the house. A gallon of water weighs ten pounds and those buckets held four gallons and there were two of them to carry at a time so that was eighty pounds weight. The wire handles used to cut into our hands so we'd wrap pieces of rag around them for protection. There was a tank at the house that had to be kept filled for washing and cooking.

All the clothes were washed by hand in big tubs. The linen and towels were boiled up in a copper. On one occasion Mum told us to take off all our clothes and wash them as well. So we all stripped off, Mum too, then jumped into the spring for a bath, and up rode a visitor! We couldn't get out as we didn't even have a towel!

During one drought Dad dug a trough at another spring further out. But in that black soil country the cattle used to bog. They were so poor that once they bogged it was hopeless. It was Marj's and my job to ride up there and pull them out. We'd ride bareback because saddles would have got muddy. One time the whole spring was full of bogged cattle but we dragged them all out. Poor things! They could hardly walk. They would just stagger off. But the mud! We were covered! So we took off our clothes and rode home starkers! We were both on grey horses. Mum was a great one to watch to see if you were wasting time when you should have been working, so she was at the railing, watching out for us. She sang out, 'Where have you been! What kept you?' But as we got closer the tirade got less and less! These two naked kids covered in black mud on these grey horses! Even she was stopped in her tracks to see us. I'd have been thirteen and Marj eleven.

In 1930 and '31 I went away to boarding school at Blackheath College in Charters Towers. Marj had to wait for her turn later on. Mum had to have someone at home to do all the work! It used to take me five days to get to school. Dad used to take me forty miles to Spring Creek station in the buckboard drawn by two horses. I slept there overnight and then on to Carpentaria Downs. Slept there. Then to Einasleigh and slept there. The rail-motor went from Einasleigh to Alma Den. That railway in those days was not very straight. There were no tunnels through the hills; the line went round them. And the bridges! You would swoop down into them. How the damned thing didn't fall off the rails I don't know! Then there was a steam train down to Cairns. Then down to Townsville, sleeping overnight along the way and getting to Townsville at nine o'clock that night. Then there was that old mixed-goods train up to Charters Towers! They'd hitch a second engine on at Reid River to push it up over the Mingela range and it was the slowest train God ever put rail under! We'd get there about five o'clock in the morning, tired and covered in travel-grit and dust and I would have to go straight to school that day.

At Blackheath I was in Archibald House – an 'Archie Girl.' Miss Bullow was the principal. But all we had was cold showers. At Thornburgh the boys had warm showers, and they boasted about it. At Blackheath you only got a warm bath in the upstairs bathrooms when you had your periods. I never went home for the holidays, except for Christmas. It was too far. But I got on well with some of the teachers and they used to take me home with them.

When I left school I had to take over all the cooking for the family and Dad's droving plants as well. I had to make all the bread; nine loaves at a time; small loaves that they could fit in the pack-saddles. There were five plants, four drovers and a boss for each plant. They'd take cattle down to the meat-works from all the Atkinson places and other neighboring properties; Spring Creek, Valley of Lagoons, Lyndhurst and Forest Home. At a quarter to four in the morning I would hear Mum's voice, 'Phoebe! Marjie! Get Up!' My first job was to get the men's breakfast on the go. The washing-up seemed to go on and on. Big cast-iron pots and heavy old pans. I never saw my mother with her hands in the washing-up water in all my life. Marj's first job in the morning was to get the cows in and do the milking and separating. I'd make butter every third day.

I met my future husband, Reay Atkinson, at Conjuboy on New Year's Day, 1936. All I knew about him was that he was the youngest son of the Greenvale Atkinsons and that his father had died in 1934. In no time flat he came courting. I thought he was all right! Too bloody right I did! He was good-looking; a very handsome man! He looked good to me, I tell you! But he could have looked cross-eyed! Anything to get away from that washing-up!

He and I used to sit in the front of his vehicle and talk; not tripe either. We would talk seriously. His brothers were married and he was on his own so he must have been lonely. He was very shy. He was mustering at Wyandotte at the time and would ride eleven miles across to Conjuboy at the drop of a hat to see me. He proposed one Sunday, on his day off, when he and the other men usually did their washing. One of his mates offered to do his washing for him so he could come over to see me. When he said, 'Do you think you would marry me?' I couldn't wait to tell Mum! Then later on he proposed again properly under one of the palms on the Strand in Townsville. We'd gone down but I must have had a friend or a relation with me; Mum would never have let me go on my own. You would never go alone with a man without a chaperone! He gave me an engagement ring. So then I had two valuable things of my own, an engagement ring and a gold-bar brooch with a nugget from The Oaks goldfield.

We were married at St Peter's Church in Townsville on 26th October, 1936. The dress was lace, buttoned all the way down the back, with a long lace veil loaned to me by Reay's mother. I had a huge bouquet almost to the floor. I had only the one bridesmaid, my sister Marj. She had to wear a silk headpiece like a turban because her hair had been shaved and was still short. She'd been bitten by a redback spider and what Mum used to put on everything was iodine, and you should never put iodine on bites! You should put ammonia! But Mum didn't know. Marj broke out in abscesses from the top of her head all the way down one side of her body. She very nearly died. She had to be taken out to Einasleigh and then to Mareeba hospital. Those redbacks were in every crevice at Conjuboy.

Reay and I went to Sydney for our honeymoon. He had grown up in Sydney and gone to school at Cranbrook, then King's School. I loved Sydney. We took films of one another, smoking cigarettes in our pyjamas and jumping up and down on the bed. Reay was beautifully built. He wasn't very tall; only about five foot ten, but, oh! He was good looking! He was seven years older than I was and a very handsome man. And it was the first time I had ever been to a nightclub! It was all very exciting. I felt like singing all the time.

Then we had to come back to reality and to Camel Creek, so named because it was the haunt for many years of an old camel abandoned by an Afghan driver in the early days. Camel Creek was a block cut off Greenvale. It was five hundred and sixty square miles and, with a mixed herd of cattle and a plant of working horses, was Reay's inheritance from his father's estate. Camel Creek was virtually virgin country, open, broken ridges, with some good creek flats and stands of ironbark, poplar, box and bluegum. The only improvements were at the homestead: a partly built set of cattle yards, a galvanized iron hut, an almost finished, stark, unpainted two-room cottage with a verandah front and back, with a 500 gallon tank, a separate kitchen partly-built, a small outside bathroom and two pit lavatories. Our furniture was meagre – a small wood stove in the kitchen and a battery-operated radio that Reay had taken in lieu of a bad debt. We also had a gramophone cabinet of polished timber, the sort with the handle on the side, and a cuckoo clock; both wedding presents. We camped on the floor in our swags for the first twelve months then Reay bought a good bed for £5 at a sale. No cows or goats for milk but there was a hen that laid two eggs a week.

Out on the run there were two badly silted dams with walls that had broken several times. They'd been built with horse and bullock teams; one in 1917 and the other in 1920. Fencing was non-existent for any practical purposes. Apart from some mud springs at the extreme northern end of the run and the Burdekin River at the southwestern corner there was no natural permanent water. The only other water available for stock was waterholes in the creeks that lasted only a few months after the Wet. Once they dried up, water had to be bailed from under the sand. The carrying capacity was rated at fifteen hundred to two thousand head in the wet season. The herd consisted of about two thousand mixed cattle but to even matters up there was a £7,000 overdraft at the bank. The estate of H. J. Atkinson drew a heavy probate and death duties and this was Reay's share of the unpaid balance.

Camel Creek homestead

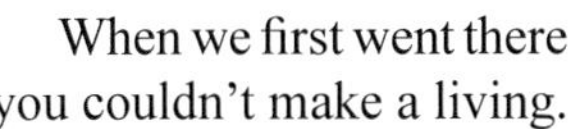

When we first went there you couldn't make a living. The main problem was water. Reay decided dams would be the quickest and cheapest solution. One day we were going down the Mt. Spec road via Ewan and we saw an Alice Chalmers crawler tractor snigging logs. Reay said, 'That's the answer! If that tractor can snig logs it can manage a scoop!' The tractor was purchased from Townsville and brought up to Camel Creek. There were no books to learn from but the dams were built. Some failed, but the majority held. Reay learned to rebuild time and again if necessary and also the need for constant maintenance. He did not like to use watercourses to make dams. He would use a natural hollow and build a wall across it. He never disturbed the surface of the ground. By using hollows and ridges he learned that a small catchment area with a large holding capacity worked best, especially during storms. A by-wash[3] would be put in some distance from the wall to reduce the possibility of the water scouring it away. The dam might take ages to fill but once the water was there it stayed and became a natural waterhole.

But as we got more established and the kids started coming I said to Reay, 'We'll have to enlarge this place. It's no end of trouble fitting everything in. And there are always people coming.' Reay said, 'But we can't afford it! We have to put more dams in.' I said, 'Well, I'll tell you what. I'll go back into the kitchen and save the cook's wages. The money can go to the extensions.' So I did that for three years though I took time off to have two more kids.

We had eleven-foot verandahs put down each side of the house and extended out the front. And inside I got the builder to put in two big open archways to let the light and the breeze through. I said to Reay, 'Look, no one ever comes in the front way. They all come in at the back.' So where the front steps were we got an open brick fireplace put in because in the winter it could get very cold. It made a very friendly, open sort of house. In the winter time – May through to September – you would walk in and the fire would be burning with big logs and it was very welcoming and pleasant. With some wedding-present money, I bought a twelve-foot-long silky oak table from McKimmon's in Townsville for £10 and twelve chairs for £1/15/- each; five chairs for each side and a carver chair at each end. These went into the upstairs dining room. Reay would sit at the head of the table and carve and I would sit at the bottom and pour the tea and so forth.

The kitchen was a separate building at the back. We got a big JR Number Nineteen Range, a cast-iron stove, the best stove I ever cooked in; a massive stove. It had a big firebox that you could fit a lot of wood in. There was a huge oven on either side. It would fit a whole rib roast, boned-out and rolled, as it came off the beast. I would do two big roasts at a time; one for the meal that night and one for cold meat next day. At different stages during the mustering there were something like ten musterers to cook for. The men ate in the dining room that adjoined the kitchen, usually with the family, all together, but if cattle buyers or someone like that were there, the visitors and the family would eat in the upstairs dining room. By this time we had a thirty-two volt lighting plant and batteries for power, which was in turn coupled to a wind charger to help charge the batteries. We also had a couple of kerosene refrigerators which were later replaced by a larger electric unit built to our own design. That made life a lot easier.

During the first couple of years, I went down to Sydney to have some time off. While I was there I visited Reay's aunts who were very proper, so I dressed accordingly. Reay had given me furs, so I wore those too. On the way I saw a shop that sold knives. Remembering that we needed a good castrating knife back home, I went in and asked the bloke behind the counter for the best castrating knife he had, one I could fit neatly in my hand. His jaw dropped and his eyes opened wide. I don't think he had ever heard such a request from a

[3] By-wash; a wide drain at the side of the dam wall, lower than the actual wall itself, to enable rising water to flow downstream without scouring the wall of the dam.

young, well-dressed woman. But when I explained where I came from and why I needed it, he was all right and I got my knife.

During World War Two, when the Japanese invasion seemed imminent, all the northern property owners were told to shoot their cattle and poison their dams. We could not comply even if we wanted to. We couldn't get bullets for love nor money and we were certainly not going to poison our dams because we depended on them. However, we were ready to leave if we had to. Camel Creek and the neighbouring properties were involved in the training of a special bush cavalry unit. A Light Horse captain from World War One trained them. If roads and bridges needed to be blown up, the men were to move ahead of the enemy doing it. Reay hid any petrol we had, otherwise it was commandeered for the war effort.

The Mount Fox road down to Ingham, my God! It was barely a road! Coming up it in the Wet, when you got to the foot of the range you had to put chains on your wheels and you didn't take them off until you got home. There were several bad pinches; Wade's Pinch, named after an old teamster, was the worst. The road was very narrow and very slippery. If you'd gone over the edge, well, that would have been that. Two vehicles couldn't pass. If you were going down and someone was coming up, well, you'd have to back into a bit of a lay-by to let the other person come past. Timber trucks from the Mount Fox sawmill also used the road during the week. We didn't like meeting one of those! It used to take us all day to get down to Ingham. In the Wet we didn't even try, unless it was really necessary.

At the house I had a very good woman, my housekeeper, Mrs King, who helped with the children. Oh! God! She was a blessing! She was with me seven years. Her three boys, Cyril, Tunny and Kevin worked at Camel Creek. Also her three grandchildren, David, Dossie, Johnnie and her mother, Mrs White, were there with her as well. At this time just when we had our family, the three boys and two girls, and the property was getting established, Reay got sick. In the end he was so bad he had to be flown out by aerial ambulance to Cairns. He returned home but later had to be taken down to Ingham Hospital. But his cancer was too advanced to operate on. I went with him to Brisbane where he had radium treatment for six weeks but in the end it had got into his spine and brain. The doctor told me, 'He's not going to live. Take him home.' So we flew north and when we got to Townsville I knew Reay was too sick to go home to Camel Creek. I booked a room at the Queen's Hotel. He was too sick to know what was going on. He hadn't made a will and I didn't want the property to fall into the hands of the Queensland Trustees. They wouldn't to do any repairs or replacements, and in a thousand ways they used to let a place go broke and then sell it. I didn't want that to happen to Camel Creek so I put myself totally in charge. I got Colonel North from the Solicitors, Roberts, Leu and North and Dr Breinel to witness the will. Reay was so weak he could only sign with a cross. At this time our eldest son, Toby, was eleven, Lindy was eight, Keith was six, Donald was nearly three and Helen was only seventeen months old. Reay died in late 1949 and was buried at Ingham. I was thirty-two at the time.

After Reay's funeral I knew I would be able to face up to the future, because during the four years that Reay had been sick, I had got used to looking after things. But oh! Those death and probate duties! That was hell! At that time there were twenty six-people on the place to be fed. We had sixty chooks and the man that was sent to value the place lived in town and he'd never been on a property before. He insisted that with sixty chooks I must be selling the eggs for profit and valued them too! But those eggs all got used for feeding the men – they'd all want a couple of eggs each with their breakfast – and also for making cakes and biscuits for smokos. Another thing was that Reay had, at one time bought some pine chairs, and as they got broken over the years he put them out in the back of the shed. And this Probate man said those chairs could be mended and he even valued those! Those valuers should have been strangled! The lot of them! When Reay died the place was heavily in debt to about £40,000 and the death and probate duties brought the debt to around £70,000.

The man I'd left in charge while I was away heard rumours that I was going to replace him. He sacked the stock camp, turned the work-horses bush, and walked out, leaving all the gates open. The domestic staff packed up and left for town with him. Luckily my sister, Beryl, was with me so I wasn't alone. Disaster piled. I found the head-stockman's house riddled with white ants and on the verge of collapse. You either laugh or you cry. When we found the butcher's shop was falling down too, my sister and I collapsed into helpless giggles.

I had to do a bangtail muster for death and probate duties. The herd, about eight thousand head, all Shorthorn Devon, was a mess because Reay had been sick for so long and things had been neglected. The men, who were very loyal to me, came back and Dad came over from Conjuboy. Together we went through the cattle. As each mob came through the yards we drafted off the cows that weren't suitable for breeding – any big-titted cows that meant they had lost a calf, or wouldn't have been able to feed a calf, or cows with bad temperament, we culled. We wanted a quiet herd. Anything that was wrong was speyed. In that way we cleaned the herd up.

We had a preponderance of heifers and a shortage of bulls so I swapped Dad a hundred heifers for fifty bulls, mainly Herefords with a touch of Brahman to make the British breeds tougher. I kept those bulls five years and took them out and sold them again because I wanted to put a touch of baldy-face – the white face – into them. Buyers, particularly southern buyers, are always scared of getting cattle with dairy-cross in them, which makes them weigh light. But with the broken-baldies they knew they were getting all British breeds and I could always sell and get a good price. I really enjoyed the breeding aspect of things.

Then in 1951 the worst drought in a hundred years hit the country. It was a nightmare that seemed unending. Dams dried up, and the men worked for months without a break, helping to save as much of the herd as they could. They would get home late at night, walking beside horses too tired to be ridden. Elephant grass was planted for feed, and they were given molasses as well. I think we were one of the first to use molasses on a large scale as drought feed. At first the sugar mills in Ingham would not sell it to us, but there was still a regulation in place that allowed cane farmers four drums a month to feed their work horses. They no longer

used it, and so many of them started collecting their ration and passing it on to us. We had a three ton Maple Leaf truck and would collect nine drums, three drums to a ton, two or three times a week. It was poured into troughs at water points. We also mixed it with water and sprayed it onto the dry grass, but the herd numbers still dropped to under four thousand and we lost almost the entire calf drop that year. The probate and death duties fell due at the same time. That was bottom. I thought, 'From now on things have got to get better!'

When the end of the drought came and we got some rain, I was making up the wages. I used always to bring each man into the office separately and go through his wages with him. The first man was Owen Bosworth. When I came to, '…and your overtime,' he said, 'Forget the overtime, Missus! You and the kids need it more than I do.' And every one of those men said the same thing. By the third or fourth man I could hardly write the cheque for the tears streaming down my face. Those old hands, some of whom had been with us from the beginning, were invaluable. And others, too; Annie King, Harry Jennings and my father. Toby had a special permit to drive at thirteen, and got his driver's licence at fifteen. He regularly took the truck down the range to Ingham for loading, and kept up the maintenance on the machinery.

The next year, to reduce the overdraft and to give the country a chance to recover, I sold an extra thousand head to the meat-works. The buyer was not used to dealing with a woman and it took me three weeks to get a price. I got £35 a head; a hell of a good price in those days. The buyer said, a bit sarcastically, 'And I suppose you want us to pay for the droving too?' I knew they were short of cattle, so right away, I said, 'Yes! Of course!' He'd put himself in! But he agreed, and took delivery at our boundary.

The best compliment I have ever been paid in my life I heard indirectly. The Angliss Meat Company had properties up in the Peninsula and every year one of their top men used to go up to the Gulf to see that the quality was being kept up. And later they would get all the managers down to have a meeting to discuss the breeding programme. After one of these meetings one of them told me that this top man had said to them, 'I was at Upper Stone, west of Ingham, and I saw a mob of cattle being brought down through Mount Fox. Gentlemen! There were nine hundred of them and they were perfect! Dark red, peas in a pod, with just a touch of broken baldy.' And he said, 'I inquired where they had come from and was told Camel Creek' Then he said, 'Gentlemen! I must tell you! I've never seen a better mob. And bred by a bloody woman!'

My sister Beryl and her two children, Carol and Allan, were with us when my cousin, came up from Sydney in 1952 with her three youngest children, Diana, David and Stanley. Her older two girls came up for holidays. We always seemed to have a host of kids. Life was not all work. We had time off to let off steam and enjoy ourselves occasionally; tennis parties, Christmas parties, or just get-togethers. Neighbours would come over and friends from town. For the opening of the new tennis court, forty or so were expected, but twice as many turned up. A bloke with a Tiger Moth aircraft was there giving joy rides. I was up with him, and down below, coming along the road, were all these cars! I told him, 'Quick! Put me down in a hurry!' It was a great weekend!

One time I had a letter from my father at Conjuboy that an economist from Canberra, Jack Kelly, was on his way. He was travelling right across the north of Australia to see how places that had been started up and were making a go of things were doing it. My father had told him, 'If you want to see a place that is still building, go and see my daughter at Camel Creek.' So this day, I'd given the men their five o'clock breakfast and cleaned up, and what I always did next was to make the dessert for that night, so I was making a fruit pie. It was still early and I hadn't got the kids up yet. Dad had told me this Jack Kelly liked his rum. So when he lobbed in at the house I said 'My Dad tells me you like a rum first thing. Would you like a cup of tea first or would you prefer a rum first and then a cup of tea?' He said, 'Oh! A rum!' So we both sat down and had a rum. Then I went on making this pudding while we talked. I asked him, 'Exactly what are you doing?' He said, 'Well, we have a set of thirty-two questions I'd like you to answer when you have time.' Well, I'd always done the books for the place, so while I was rolling the pastry for the lid of this pie I answered every question he asked. And when he went back down to Canberra he told them, 'She was the only station owner that could answer these questions without referring to the books and what's more, make an apple pie at the same time!' So I was invited to Canberra and I had a lovely time down there.

A ten shilling note of the 1950's with a signature of H.C. Coombs, Governor of the Reserve Bank of Australia, who invited Phoebe Atkinson to Canberra to discuss the cattle industry of the north.

I had an interview with Dr Herbert 'Nugget' Coombs, Governor of the Reserve Bank. His name used to be on the bank notes. It had been arranged that I was to see him at eleven o'clock. The woman behind the desk outside his office was a real dragon type. I told her I was there to see Dr Coombs. But he was sacred! Nobody got to see him! But when she looked in her book she found that, yes, Mrs Atkinson did have an appointment! So I went in and I sat across the desk from him. He looked at me and I looked at him. It was the longest ten seconds! But I wasn't after a loan so I wasn't nervous. He said, 'And what can I do for you, Mrs Atkinson?' I said, 'Dr Coombs, it is not what you can do for me. It is what I can do for you. Jack Kelly told me...' Ah! Jack Kelly! And then the penny dropped![4]

So in the end we were very relaxed and I was able to tell him what he wanted to know. I told him the north needed better roads; that it took three weeks to walk the cattle to the meat-works in Townsville. A good drover does ten miles a day but bad weather and heat sometimes make that impossible. He said, 'Can't you send them by vehicle?' I told him. 'The roads are shocking. There are bad creek crossings and practically no bridges. Even the road from Ingham to Townsville is not good, with deep creeks and low, narrow bridges.' He didn't say much at all. He just asked questions and listened. We also discussed the need for beef research in the tropics. He could see I knew what I was talking about. He was very easy to talk to; a very pleasant man. And afterwards, Jack Kelly told me that Dr Coombs had said to him, 'I have learned more from that woman in an hour and a half than I have learned in six and a half years!' Because I had spoken from the producers' point of view. It wasn't long after that that they started to put the Beef Roads through the north.[5] And the Toorak beef research station was set up near Julia Creek and another at Swans Lagoon near Millaroo.

Not long after Phoebe Atkinson's meeting with Dr Coombs, the construction of the Beef Roads began.

The mailman came every Monday with the mailbag and I always gave him tea. He had

[4] Perth-born Dr Herbert Cole Coombs (24 February 1906- 29th October 1997), Australian economist, commonly known as 'Nugget' Coombs, was appointed by the Chifley government to the position of Governor of the Commonwealth Bank in 1949. It was regarded as the most important post in the regulation of the Australian economy. He presided over the long period of post-war boom under the Menzies government and was appointed Governor of the Reserve Bank in 1960. Other great interests of his life included the welfare of the Aboriginal people and issues of the environment.

[5] The Beef Road schemes were among the most important rural projects of the 1960s. The term 'Beef Road' was coined to distinguish roads for which the Commonwealth Government had supplied the funds, as distinct from the State Main Roads Department. In 1949 the State Government began to provide funds aimed at promoting the operation of road trains for moving livestock. The network of roads was originally planned to be gravel only, at a cost of $44 million, to be completed by 1970 but eventually more money was provided by the Commonwealth to allow bitumen surfacing. Some roads, such as that from Georgetown to Mount Surprise were completely new; others involved major diversions from the original track. It was during this period that droving as a means of moving cattle between breeding and fattening areas and to railheads to export meat-works on the coast, began to disappear. It can be assumed that the official invitation to Phoebe Atkinson to travel to Canberra and speak with Dr Coombs played a significant part in official thinking on the subject.

a big truck and sometimes he would bring up station stores as well. Then he would go on to Valley of Lagoons and spend the night there and go on to other stations, pick up our outgoing mail on the return trip.

The Correspondence School for the children was excellent. The papers were well set out and if you followed the directions it was no trouble at all. One of the side verandahs became the schoolroom and the other became the sleep-out. I bought proper school desks and blackboards. All the Department of Education supplied were the Correspondence papers for each week. They paid the post both ways. Each kid had their own set of papers in a big brown envelope with two exercise books, one for arithmetic and one for writing. When the week's work was finished it was sent back for appraisal and correction. The teachers would write the copy in and the children had to copy it. One time Toby had to write 'Bennie has a black horse' to be copied so many times down the page. He wrote it beautifully but instead of putting the 'o' in 'horse' he put an 'a'; 'Bennie has a black harse.' Oh! We laughed! But we had to send it. And I hope the teachers down there got a laugh out of it because we did. Any children on the property, as well as my own, came to school too, and two from Mount Fox used to come across and stay the week.

We grew our own vegetables. It was cheaper to have a gardener than it would have been to send down to town for the vegetables we had to have with all the people on the place. We grew practically everything; tomatoes, peas, beans, peas, cauliflower, cabbage, carrots, beetroot, and oh, yes, sweet potatoes. But not English potatoes. I had beautiful

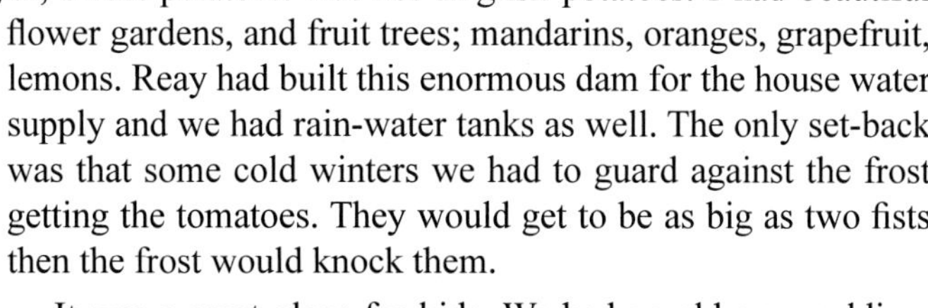

flower gardens, and fruit trees; mandarins, oranges, grapefruit, lemons. Reay had built this enormous dam for the house water supply and we had rain-water tanks as well. The only set-back was that some cold winters we had to guard against the frost getting the tomatoes. They would get to be as big as two fists then the frost would knock them.

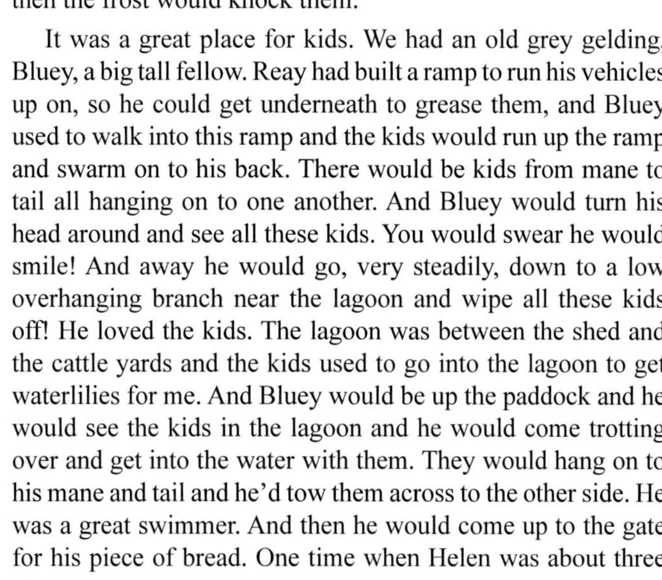

It was a great place for kids. We had an old grey gelding, Bluey, a big tall fellow. Reay had built a ramp to run his vehicles up on, so he could get underneath to grease them, and Bluey used to walk into this ramp and the kids would run up the ramp and swarm on to his back. There would be kids from mane to tail all hanging on to one another. And Bluey would turn his head around and see all these kids. You would swear he would smile! And away he would go, very steadily, down to a low overhanging branch near the lagoon and wipe all these kids off! He loved the kids. The lagoon was between the shed and the cattle yards and the kids used to go into the lagoon to get waterlilies for me. And Bluey would be up the paddock and he would see the kids in the lagoon and he would come trotting over and get into the water with them. They would hang on to his mane and tail and he'd tow them across to the other side. He was a great swimmer. And then he would come up to the gate for his piece of bread. One time when Helen was about three years old we spotted the way she used to get on his back. He would put his head down and she would grab hold of his mane and walk up his front leg and use his mane to swing over on to his back. He was so gentle, so quiet; just one of the kids.

I used to read to the kids every night. In winter we would light the fire early. They would all sit on the big couch in front of the fireplace and I'd read; Rudyard Kipling, *The Swiss Family Robinson*, *Treasure Island*, the *Just So Stories*, *Winnie-the-Pooh* or *Lassie Come Home* and *Black Beauty*. I loved doing the voices. The kids were always in bed pretty early. We all had early nights.

Once, when my kids were at Blackheath and Thornburgh in Charters Towers; I was in Townsville at the Queens, waiting to pick them up for the holidays. I saw these two little boys in Thornburgh uniform, about the same age as my two, and they seemed worried. I said, 'What's wrong? You're out of school early.' They said they had to catch an aircraft up to New Guinea because they came from Samarai but didn't know what had happened about their tickets. When I checked at the airline office there was a mix-up with their booking. I knew most of the Qantas pilots as they were mates of Reay's and had been good to me when he died. I was able to arrange with one of them, Captain Bird, who was doing a charter, to take these kids with him. He was able to connect with a seaplane flight to Samarai. Later I wrote to their mother, Mrs Perry, and suggested they come to Camel Creek with my children for the mid-year holidays in future. That was in 1952 and so Chad, Kingsley and later their sister Leonora, spent many holidays with us over the next seven years.

At the end of the holidays word always got around that I would be taking the kids back to school, so often I had the neighbours' kids as well. I would take them all down to Townsville on the back of the Maple Leaf truck. We'd get to the Queens and when all these kids started to off-load, the hall porter, Herb, would say, 'Chrise! It's worse than a bloody Pioneer Bus!' I would guide this tribe into the foyer and Miss Bryant would be behind the desk. She would say, 'How many do you have this time, Mrs Atkinson?' I would say, 'I don't know! You count 'em!' because there were different prices for the different ages. And time after time I would end up with half a kid!

Looking back, they were wonderful years! Hard work, yes! But happy, happy, years.

Appendix 1

Bobbie Buchanan Remembered

Lyz Buchanan-Risby

Bobbie Buchanan was the great-granddaughter of Nat Buchanan, explorer, cattleman and outback pioneer. Bobbie was born in Alice Springs and lived as a child in Wyndham and Old Halls Creek. The family later moved to the site of present-day Halls Creek where Bobbie's father, Gordon Buchanan, was responsible for the establishment of the new township. Roberta Avenue in Halls Creek was named after Bobbie.

Bobbie's mother, Norma Buchanan, was matron for many years at the Wyndham Hospital and during the air raids of World War Two, Bobbie would be taken quickly to hide in the bush by an Aboriginal lady named Lucy so that Norma could remain on duty at the hospital in case of casualties.

Gordon Buchanan was relocated to Elliott in the Northern Territory, as Pastoral Inspector, and Bobbie spent many years at Elliott before moving to Adelaide to train as a nurse. She then returned to Wyndham to work in the hospital. It was there that she met her future husband, local bank manager, Don Risby. Bobbie went on to write books documenting the history of the Top End of Australia. Her first was *In the Tracks of Old Bluey* (CQU Press,1997) the life of her famous great-grandfather, Nat Buchanan. The book is now in its fifth reprint.

In 1998 she ghost-wrote two further books for CQU Press, *Battlers of the Barkly*, the life of Alf Chambers, and *Lipstick, Swag and Sweatrag* for Beth Beckett, wife of an outback padre. She went on to write *Not So Silent Sam* about Sam Calder, noted northern pastoralist, politician and ex-World War Two fighter-pilot, (CQU Press 2000), and *Keep the Branding Iron Hot*, the story of Pat Underwood, noted cattleman of the Kimberley area. (CQU Press,

2002).

Bobbie worked as an historian for Agtours throughout the Top End, and this and her writing made a significant contribution to keeping alive the history and culture of the region.

Bobbie's last wish before her untimely death on the 6th October, 2005, was that her ashes be returned to Wyndham. They were lovingly placed by her daughter, Lyz, and son Jim, on the magnificent summit of Mt Bastion in 2006, near Wyndham. Family members, friends, including ninety-year-old Pat Underwood, cattlemen and fellow writers travelled from all over Australia to be there to honour Bobbie's memory and to scatter the bright yellow flowers of the north's kapok trees at the spot. Kelly Dixon, of '*Put Him in the Long Yard*' fame, wrote '*Song for Bobbie*' especially for the occasion. In June 2007, a group of North Queensland cattlemen under the leadership of Ray Fryer of the Camooweal Drovers' Camp, made a return journey to place a memorial plaque on Bobbie Buchanan's mountain-top final resting place.

'Then, will my spirit fly, forever free
To span the Northern Wilderness I love;
To seek each place where I might long to be
And gaze upon my memories from above.' *Bob Morrow; Halls Creek*

Appendix 2

The Drover's Letter Home

This charming fragment of a letter written in 1938 by his late father as a young man was sent to the Camooweal Drover's Camp organizers by Damian McGreevy of Brisbane. Frances Bernard McGreevy, known as "Flan" was born in Ipswich in 1918 and is believed to have worked on Soudan Outstation on Alexandra Downs in the Northern Territory and Thorntonia and Riversleigh in North West Queensland. He also served in the army in New Guinea during the war. The letter is a succinct account of the distances travelled by drovers of the 1930s and of the routes they followed and as such is a valuable little fragment of documentary evidence of the period.

The remainder of the letter is missing, but this fragment conveys a sense of a cheerful-natured young man, new to the droving game but making a go of things, and justifiably proud of the distances he had travelled and places he had seen. His youthful enthusiasm would have been an asset to any camp.

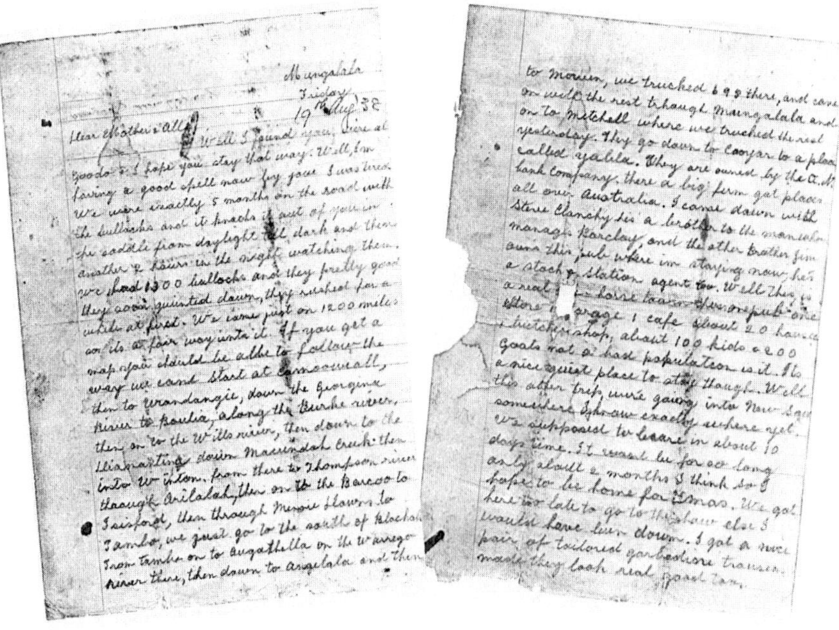

Mungalala
Friday
19th Aug '38

Dear Mother & All,
Well I found you. [illegible] at
good & I hope you stay that way. Well, I'm
having a good spell now for [illegible] I was [illegible]
We were exactly 5 months on the road with
the bullocks and it knocks it out of you in
the saddle from daylight till dark and then
another 2 hours in the night watching them.
We had 1300 bullocks and they pretty good
they soon quieted down, they rushed for a
while at first. We came just on 1200 miles
[illegible] at fair way into it. If you get a
map you should be able to follow the
way we came. Start at Camooweall,
then to Urandangie, down the Georgina
River to Boulia, along the Burke river,
then on to the Wills river, then down to the
[illegible] down Macunda Creek then
into Winton. from there to Thompson river
through Arilalah, then on to the Barcoo to
Isisford, then through Maroo Downs to
Tambo, we just go to the south of Blackall
From Tambo on to Augathella on the Warrego
river there, then down to Angelala and then

to Morven, we trucked 693 there, and came
on with the rest through Mungalala and
on to Mitchell where we trucked the rest
yesterday. They go down to Cooyar to a place
called Yalila. They are owned by the A.M.
Land Company, there a big firm got places
all over Australia. I came down with
Steve Clancy his a brother to the man who
manages Barclay, and the other brother Jim
owns this pub where im staying now he's
a stock & station agent too. Well this is
a real [illegible] horse town there's one pub one
store [illegible] garage 1 cafe about 20 houses
butcher's shop, about 100 kids & 200
Goats not a bad population is it. Its
a nice quiet place to stay though. Well
this other trip we're going into New Guinea
somewhere I don't know exactly where yet.
We're supposed to leave in about 10
days time. It won't be for so long
only about 2 months I think so I
hope to be home for Xmas. We got
here too late to go to the show else I
would have been down. I got a nice
pair of tailored gabardine trousers
made they look real good [illegible].

Dear Mother and all,

Well I found you were all goodo and I hope you stay that way. Well, I'm having a good spell now. By jove I was tired. We were exactly 5 months on the road with the bullocks and it knocks it out of you, in the saddle from daylight to dark and then another 2 hours in the night watching them. We had 1300 bullocks and they pretty good.

They soon quietened down, they rushed for a while at first. We came just on 1200 miles so it's a fair way isn't it. If you get a map you should be able to follow the way we came. Start at Camooweal, then to Urandangie, down the Georgina River to Boulia, along the Bourke River, then on to the Wills River, then down to the Diamantina down Mackunda Creek then into Winton, from there to Thompson River through Arrilalah, then onto the Barcoo to Isisford, then through Minnie Downs to Tambo, we just go to the south of Blackall. From Tambo onto Augathella on the Warrego River there, then down to Angellala and then to Morven, we trucked 698 there, and came on with the rest through Mungallala and onto Mitchell where we trucked the rest yesterday. They are owned by A.N.bank company. They are a big firm, got places all over Australia. I came down with Steve Clanchy, he's a brother to the manager of Barclay, and the other brother, Jim owns this pub where I'm staying now, he's a stock and station agent too. Well this is a real one- horse town, there's one pub, one store, one garage, 1 cafe about 20 house, 1 butcher shop, about 100 kids and 200 goats, not a bad population is it. It's a nice quiet place to stay though. Well this other trip, we're going into New South somewhere. I don't know exactly where yet.

We supposed to leave in about 10 days time. It won't be for so long, only about 2 months I think so. I hope to be home for Xmas. We got here too late to go to the show else I would have been down. I got a nice pair of tailored gaberdine trousers made them, look real good too.

You can tell Dad I'll be down to ride "Knickerbockerbuckeroo", after I've been out here for another year or two. It's a great place for work out there if any of them louts down there want a job but I suppose they're too useless for it. The cattlemen got a rise the other day the wages are £3/13/00 now. Has Goodna changed at all, is the McSellands still there. Mitchell is a nice little place, so is Winton, but the other places aren't much.'

The 'Tell Dad I'll be down to ride Knickerbockerbuckeroo' is a joking reference to his increasingly improved riding skills, with perhaps just a hint of pride that, so far, he is 'doing OK'. 'Knickerbockerbuckeroo' was a notorious buck-jumper of the period, the star-turn of country shows. Many a hopeful country lad, unable to resist the spruiker's, 'Five quid if you can stick to him!' found himself flying through the air ignominiously, in the mode of the hopeful rider of the equally legendary 'Mandrake', who 'stayed two seconds, one up; one coming down.' The 'show' referred to in the letter is doubtless the 'Ekka', the Royal Brisbane Exhibition, for which the writer had had a hopeful pair of 'real good' gaberdine trousers made.

Mitchell can rejoice that the young drover found it a 'nice little place' but of 'the other places' all he can be said is that he takes obvious pleasure that in passing through them, '*as the stock are slowly stringing*', he was now receiving the princely sum of £3/13/0d a week; about $7 in today's money.

GLOSSARY

1080; 'Ten-eighty' a dingo bait, spread aerially.

attend a muster; to be present at a muster involving cattle from neighbouring properties in order to reclaim stray beasts from ones own.

Beef Road; one of a system of roads funded by the Australian Commonwealth Government in the 1960s to promote transport of cattle between breeding and fattening areas and to railheads for transport to coastal meat-works.

bluestone; medicated powder to prevent development of proud flesh in healing wounds.

by-wash; a wide drain built at one end of a dam wall, lower that the actual wall itself, to enable rising water to flow downstream so that it does not erode the face of the dam wall.

coachers; a mob of quiet cattle accustomed to being handled, into which musterers can drive or shoulder individual wild cattle in order to quieten them.

Coolgardie safe; food-storage safe of perforated metal cooled by water-evaporation from a covering of wet sacking.

DPI; Department of Primary Industries

face of the camp; the outer edge of the perimeter of the mob of cattle being held by stockmen during cutting-out of selected beasts, for instance, all the cows and calves or all the fat bullocks. The face-of-the-camp man takes the beast that has been cut-out by the camp horse and pushes it across to the secondary mob being held a short distance away by other stockmen.

fats; cattle of sufficient weight and condition to be marketable.

gazetted distance; the distance drovers are legally required to move a mob of cattle per day.

gone out with the blades; obsolete; A reference to shearing sheep with hand-blades prior to the introduction of machinery.

green pickings; re-growth after rain especially of grass previously burnt off

heads; verb; (of a river) has its source

killer; beast selected to be slaughered for home consumption.

Kanaka; A term derived from the Melanesian word for 'man', used in former times of South Sea Islanders in the North Queensland sugar industry.

landing; connecting walkway between detached kitchen and homestead.

Manpowered; During World War Two when Australia was facing the threat of invasion all employment was regulated by government control. Workers could not change jobs without official permission nor enlist in the armed services. This was known as being 'manpowered'.

muddy; muddies; large salt-water crabs found in mangroves.

munjeri; cranky, foul tempered

Murries; Aborigines

nulla nulla; wooden club, often the thickened root-section of a gidyea, or similar, tree.

pig-root; to buck with stiffened legs; also 'rooting'.

pump-jack; a motor-driven device fixed to the top of a bore or well to continue pumping when the wind has dropped and is not turning the mill.

ringers; stockmen; said to be derived from the need to get a mob of cattle to 'ring' or circle in upon themselves in order to bring them under control.

rooted; pig-rooted; bucked.

round yard; small circular yard for breaking-in and training horses.

septic toilet; water-flushing toilet with an underground tank in which sewage is decomposed by anaerobic bacteria.

shoot through; Leave suddenly; depart.

six o'clock sundown; drovers' time; the the accepted time at sunset on a droving trip from which two hourly night watches of the cattle were timed.

skin, cracking; craving for alcohol

stores; beasts with insufficient weight and condition to be marketable.

stranger; a beast strayed on to a property from a neighbouring property or on a droving trip, one that has joined the mob while passing through a property.

stringing; a natural pattern into which a mob of cattle falls as they feed along quietly when on the move, the stronger more dominant beasts towards the front, the quieter, perhaps weaker or sore-footed ones towards the tail. The 'string' can be as much as a mile.

throw; procedure used when no yards are available. The beast is seized by the tail, thrown off-balance, usually from horse-back, and brought to the ground. Its hind legs are bull-strapped to immobilize it while it is ear-marked and 'tipped' or partially dehorned before being pushed into a mob of coachers.

Tilley; portable incandescent lamp.

trap; a light, two-wheeled, horse-drawn vehicle.

wagga; An improvised blanket of the Depression years made by lining a corn-sack with newspaper.

Yellafella; colloquial usage for person of mixed race; accepted as not intentionally offensive, in North West Queensland and the Northern Territory.

BIBLIOGRAPHY

Adams, David (ed); *The Letters of Rachael Henning*, Angus and Robertson, 1963

Allen, Geoff, *The Gun Ringer – From Queensland to the Kimberley*, Central Queensland University Press Press, 1998.

Black, Jane; *The Pioneers of North Queensland,* Charters Towers Printing, 1887

Buchanan, Bobbie; *Keep the Branding Iron Hot*; Central Queensland University Press, Rockhampton, 2002

Clarke, Harry; (1) *Joseph Hann and Family; Settlement in North Queensland* 2) *Expedition of Exploration to the Endeavour River Cape York Peninsula, 1872; Reconstructed from their diaries and two notebooks.*

Durack, Mary; *Kings in Grass Castles*; Constable and Company, London, 1957

Furlong, Monica; *Flight of the Kingfisher, A Journey Among the Kukatja Aborigines,* Harper Collins, 1996

Gibson-Wilde, Dorothy; *Gateway to a Golden Land, Studies in North Queensland History*, James Cook University Press, 1984.

Houldsworth, Marion; *The Morning Side of the Hill – A Townsville Childhood; 1939 – 1945;* James Cook University Press, Townsville,1995

Houldsworth, Marion; *Barefoot Through the Bindies; Growing Up in North Queensland in the Early 1900s.* Central Queensland University Press, Rockhampton, 2002

Houldsworth, Marion; *From the Gulf to God Knows Where, Living in Australia's Outback; Volume One;* Central Queensland University Press; 2006

Idriess, Ion; *One Wet Season*, Halstead Press, Sydney, 1955

McKnight, David; *Lardil, Keepers of the Dreamtime*, Chronicle Books, San Francisco, 1995

Miller, Ada; *The Border and Beyond – Camooweal since 1884*

Perkins, Di; *Outback Insights; A Social History of North West Queensland,* 1925 -1950; Mount Isa Historical Society; Merino Press; 1996

Reynolds, Henry (ed); *Race Relations in North Queensland*; James Cook University Press Press; Townsville; 1992

Roberts, Annette; *Sister Eileen, A Life with the Lid Off*, Access Press, W.A. 2002

Sabadina, H. et al; *A Walk with Our Pioneers;* Charters Towers and Dalrymple History Association; 2000

Smith, Anne & Dalton, B.J; *The Bowly Papers, Letters, Reminiscences and Photographs*, James Cook University of North Queensland, 1995.

Squires, Kirsteen; *Newcastle Waters, Its History*; Tennant Creek Printing.

Unpublished transcripts of the Australian Drovers' Project of the National Library of Australia, Canberra, collected by Bill Gammage and Bruce Simpson; Reg Hart, Wayne McCulloch, Clargie Saltmere, Tommy Saville and with reference to an unpublished transcript of an interview of Edna Zigenbine by Judith Hosier of the Australian Stockman's Hall of Fame, Longreach.

INDEX

Books by

Marion Houldsworth

The Morning Side of the Hill

Barefoot Through The Bindies

Red Dust Rising

From Gulf to God Knows Where

Maybe It'll Rain Tomorrow

The Immigrant Boy